MEETING THE DEVIL

Meeting the Devil

A book of memoir from the

London Review
OF BOOKS

WILLIAM HEINEMANN: LONDON

Published by William Heinemann 2013

2 4 6 8 10 9 7 5 3 1

First published in Great Britain in 2013 by
William Heinemann
Random House, 20 Vauxhall Bridge Road,
London SW1V 2SA

www.randomhouse.co.uk

Addresses for companies within The Random House Group Limited can be found at:
www.randomhouse.co.uk/offices.htm

The Random House Group Limited Reg. No. 954009

A CIP catalogue record for this book
is available from the British Library

ISBN 9780434022670

The Random House Group Limited supports the Forest Stewardship Council®
(FSC®), the leading international forest-certification organisation. Our books carrying
the FSC label are printed on FSC®-certified paper. FSC is the only forest-certification
scheme supported by the leading environmental organisations,
including Greenpeace. Our paper procurement policy can be found at
www.randomhouse.co.uk/environment

Typeset in Quadraat by Palimpsest Book Production Limited,
Falkirk, Stirlingshire

Printed and bound in Great Britain by
Clays Ltd, St Ives plc

Contents

Preface
Alan Bennett

THIS IS A rich and delightful book, which I probably shouldn't say since I figure in it. But the variety and oddity of the contributions make it an adult version of the annuals one was happy to find in one's stocking as a child.

I have met some of these reminiscing writers and reading their memoirs makes me wish I had known them better. Or not. Susan Sontag I came across a couple of times and found her arrogant, condescending and utterly without humour, an impression I am glad to have confirmed here by Terry Castle. This doesn't mean Sontag wasn't a richly comic character (in this not unlike another sharp-edged personality, Harold Pinter) as evidenced by Castle's account of Sontag restaging street fighting in Sarajevo in the more amenable circumstances of a Palo Alto mall. Beckoning the embarrassed Castle to follow she dashed among the bemused shoppers, ducking from doorway to doorway in an impromptu demonstration of how to dodge sniper fire. You couldn't, as they say, make it up.

Richard Wollheim's memoir almost makes me wish I had been born a Jew if only because of his rich and melodramatic family life and the number of his relations and indeed servants. I am not talking about *douceur de vivre*, only that childhoods populated by a shifting population of nannies and whatnot are a blessing to a writer. And somehow Jews seem to keep their relatives in play much longer than we ever did.

An elegant and sophisticated figure Wollheim was fastidious to a degree though I did not know until reading his memoir that this extended to avoiding (or even smelling) newsprint. He is engagingly frank about himself, dating the dawn of moral responsibility to the first time he was allowed to wipe his own bottom and speculating as a child on how painful it would be to catch his infant scrotum in the clasp of his mother's handbag. He does not say so but I take this unwinking self-scrutiny to be one of the fruits of analysis. Wollheim's memoir incidentally takes us at one bound back into the world of Diaghilev, who was a friend and associate of his impresario father. I wish though he had written more about life and less about thought as his aesthetics and philosophy are to me impenetrable.

We also learn how Bill Johnson lost his leg, Alan Taylor his wits and Jeremy Harding his bearings. So it is not all fun. Still, bleak though some of them may be, most of the memoirs, interviews and reminiscences in this book are comforting and enjoyable with by far the most moving (and enraging) piece Joe Kenyon's 'Working Underground', an account of his early years at the coalface in South Yorkshire. I'd like Baroness Thatcher's coffin prised open and the text slipped inside with a note: 'This is what she never understood.'

But what bullies people are: Sontag a bully, Empson, Wynne Godley's analyst and even my own Miss Shepherd – all adverts for the triumph of the will and knowing what you want.

Not everyone, though, and it's a comfort to learn how at sea Edward Said often felt (perhaps because he was tormented at school by Omar Sharif) and Keith Thomas's confession about the contents of his cellar makes me feel better about our attic. Uncertain too is Tony Harrison in the Hunslet cemetery 'V' has made famous though Jenny Diski putting down roots in the rather classier necropolis at Highgate has fewer qualms.

As the masthead of the *News of the World* used to say (though Henry James said it first) 'All human life is here.'

27 August 2013

Meeting the Devil
Hilary Mantel

THREE OR FOUR nights after surgery – when, in the words of the staff, I have 'mobilised' – I come out of the bathroom and spot a circus strongman squatting on my bed. He sees me too; from beneath his shaggy brow he rolls a liquid eye. Brown-skinned, naked except for the tattered hide of some endangered species, he is bouncing on his heels and smoking furiously without taking the cigarette from his lips: puff, bounce, puff, bounce. What rubbish, I think, actually shouting at myself, but silently. This is a no-smoking hospital. It is impossible this man would be allowed in, to behave as he does. Therefore he's not real, and if he's not real I can take his space. As I get into bed beside him, the strongman vanishes. I pick up my diary and record him: was there, isn't any more.

This happened in early July. I had surgery on the first of the month, and was scheduled to stay in hospital for about nine days. The last thing the surgeon said to me, on the afternoon of the procedure: 'For you, this is a big thing, but remember, to us it is routine.' But when I woke up, many hours later, he was standing at the end of the trolley in the recovery room, grey and shrunken as if a decade had passed. He had expected to be home for dinner. And now look!

Hospital talk is short and exclamatory. Oops! Careful! Nice and slow! Oh dear! Did that hurt? But the night after the surgery, I felt no pain. Flighted by morphine, I thought that my bed had grown as wide as the world, and throughout the short hours of darkness I made up stories. I seemed to solve, that night, problems that had bedevilled me for years. Take just one example: the unwritten story called 'The Assassination of Margaret Thatcher'. I had seen it all, years ago: the date and place, the gunman, the bedroom behind him, the window, the light, the angle of the shot. But my problem had always been, how did the ArmaLite get in the wardrobe?

Now I saw that it just grew there. It was planted by fantasy. If a whole story is a fantasy, why must logic operate within it? The word 'planted' started another story, called 'Chlorophyll'. By morning, I had the best part of a collection. But when I sat up and tried to write them down, my handwriting fell off the lines. I kept trying to fish it up again, untangle the loops and whorls and get them back to the right of the margin, and when I think of my efforts then, I think of them in the present tense, because pain is a present-tense business. Illness involves such busywork! Remembering to breathe. Studying how to do it. Plotting to get your feet on the floor, inching a pillow to a bearable position. First move your left foot. Then your other foot, whatever they call it . . . any other foot you've got. Let us say you're swaying on your feet and sweating, you think you might fall down or throw up – you have to rivet your attention to the next ten seconds. After the crisis is over, time still behaves oddly. It takes a while for the hour to stretch out in its usual luxurious fashion, like unravelling wool. Until you are cool, settled and your vital signs good, time snaps and sings like an elastic band.

When I write my diaries I talk to myself with an inward voice. For the next week I am conscious that my brain is working oddly. Imagine you were creating all your experience by writing it into being, but were forced to write with the wrong hand; you would make up for the slow awkwardness by condensing phrases, like a poet. In the same way, my life compresses into metaphor. When I sit up and see the wound in my abdomen, I am pleased to see that it has a spiral binding, like a manuscript. On the whole I would rather be an item of stationery than be me. It is as if my thoughts are happening not inside my head but outside me in the room. A film with a soundtrack is running to my right. It keeps me busy with queries based on false premises. 'Is it safe if I drink this orange juice?' But I blink and the orange juice isn't there. Therefore I study reality carefully, the bits of it within reach. For a while I think I have grown a new line on one of my hands, a line unknown to palmistry. I think perhaps I have a new fate. But it proves to be a medical artefact, a puckering of the skin produced by one of the tubes sewn into my wrist. We call those 'lines', too. The iambic pentameter of the saline stand, the alexandrine of the blood drain, the epidural's sweet sonnet form.

Within a few days, the staff are tampering with my spiral binding when the whole wound splits open. Blood clots bubble up from inside me. Over the next hours, days, nurses speak to each other in swift acronyms, or else form sentences you might have heard in Haworth: 'Her lungs are filling up.' But I have undentable faith in my own body. When I am told I need a blood transfusion, I plead: 'Let's give it 24 hours and see.' I have never been accepted as a blood donor, and I don't like the idea of a debt. When the blood comes, the stranger's precious blood, it leaks everywhere from the cannula on my neck, which needs to be taken out and resewn. The night sister looks meaningfully at the vampire's kiss and says: 'Another two of those wounds would do it.' Finish me off, she means. She is real but I accept her words are not. A hallucination has to be gross before I can pick it out.

My internal monologue is performed by many people – nurses and bank managers to the fore. There is a breathless void inside me, and it needs to be filled. I should put money in it, I think. Like a cash machine in reverse, notes slotting between my ribs. Certain items are taken away – the drain that takes blood from my side, a bridle that feeds me oxygen – but they are never taken far enough away, they easily come back. I clamp a smile on my face and drift. I have a switch I can press for 'patient-controlled analgesia'. But the staff seem uneasy about giving up control over my pain. Some say I am pressing the button too often, some say too seldom. I want to please them so I try and make my pain to their requirements.

Illness strips you back to an authentic self, but not one you need to meet. Too much is claimed for authenticity. Painfully we learn to live in the world, and to be false. Then all our defences are knocked down in one sweep. In sickness we can't avoid knowing about our body and what it does, its animal aspect, its demands. We see things that never should be seen; our inside is outside, the body's sewer pipes and vaults exposed to view, as if in a woodcut of our own martyrdom. The whole of life – the business of moving an inch – requires calculation. The suffering body must shape itself around the iron dawn routine, which exists for the very sick as well as the convalescent: the injection in the abdomen, pain relief, blood tests, then the long haul out of bed, the shaking progress to the bathroom, the awesome challenge of washcloth and soap.

This is a small private hospital, clean and unfancy, set in the sprawling campus of a vast public hospital of which I have experience, and have reason to distrust and detest. I feel guilty, God knows, about all sorts of things, but not about buying myself a private room. The staff looking after me are the same people who would be working at the larger institution, but they are less rushed and so more considerate. It's usual in talking about the health service to say that the system needs all sorts of reforms but the workers are wonderful. I think that the workers are as apt to fail as the system is. Some people, on a hospital ward or anywhere else, always do what they say they'll do, and others just don't; to them, promises are just negotiating ploys, and the time on the clock is secondary to some schedule of their own. Some can imagine being in pain, and some don't want to. A single extra minute to settle a patient comfortably can mean the difference between a neutral experience and an experience of slowly building misery. Some take the human body to be made of flesh, some of jointed metal. A polite radiographer bends my arm back over the side of a trolley so that it feels as if he's trying to break it. And I too think of my body as consisting of some substance that I can split apart from myself, and hand over to the professionals, while I take an informed interest in what they do to it. Far from being isolating, my experience is collaborative. The staff are there to reassure me, and I am there to reassure them; in this way we shield each other from an experience of darkness. One day soon after the surgery I vomit green gunk. 'Don't worry!' I exclaim as I retch. 'It will be fine! It's just like *The Exorcist*,' I say, before anyone else can.

And so I spin away, back into the 1970s; I am easily parted from the present day. I remember the cinema queues and the evangelicals working their way along the jeering lines, trying to dissuade us from going in. I wish I had been dissuaded. 'What were those flickering skulls about?' I asked as we filed out. (Apart from those, I thought the film quite true to life.) No one else I knew saw the skulls, not then, though by now it seems everybody did. If you have a million years to spare, you can follow the internet discussions on what 'quasi-subliminal' images may or may not have been embedded by the film-makers, but when I was young I would always reliably see what was almost not there; when I was a student, earning a little money by being an experimental subject for trainee psychologists, I did many dull routines involving word association and memory tricks, but what I remember best is the flicker of screens with letters I could just read, and being asked, disapprovingly: 'How do you *do* that?' This was not a professional question, but an aggrieved, human one; people suspect you are sneaking some mean advantage. No doubt I have lost this ability now, if ability is what you call it. It's something you'd think age would wither. But given my record with the vaporous, I am not

as surprised as some would be when in the hospital I blink and life
flits sideways. The second world, the whirl of activity on my right-
hand side, wakes up just after the first world, so that for a moment,
as I push back the bedcovers, I am united, I speak with one voice. A
second later, reality has fallen into halves. In my notebook, hour by
hour, I record the hallucinations and my own scathing comments on
them. But the footnotes are no more sensible than the main text,
since while criticising and revising I am still hallucinating. What is
this preposterous stuff, I demand of myself, about getting the nave
of the church measured? 'As if,' I write, 'this were not a hospital, but
a Jane Austen novel with a wedding at the summit?'

A voice from the secondary world rebukes me for thinking so little
of my real father, whom I never saw after I was 11. 'Why, he sold
tickets to make brickets from granite. He collected clothes and kit
for historical re-enactments.' I do not mention my two worlds to the
staff, as they have enough to do and it seems tactless. Most of my
preoccupations are literary or religious, so they seem an elitist pursuit,
and for many of my nurses, English is not their first language, or
Christianity their religion. 'The existing vicar,' a voice tells me, 'will
go to a smaller parish somewhere.' At once the existing vicar bobs
into view, followed by an anguished Muslim father, who pleads to
know: 'What are the chances of her losing her honour?' The vicar
explains loftily that he and his clerical colleagues do not exist to
answer that sort of question. 'They do not believe that honour lies in
fearful nasties.' Sorry, I write, I misheard: that should read 'fearful
chastity'. A hooded youth approaches me on the street, holding up a
plucked chicken. 'You give me this bird,' he complains, 'and this bird
were gay.'

There is no obvious reason for voices and visions. My temperature
is near normal and my pain relief is the usual moderate regime. Later
the hallies, as I think of them, become less threatening, but more
childish and conspiratorial. I close my eyes and they begin to pack

my belongings into a pillowcase, whispering and grinning. One sharp-faced dwarfish hally pulls at my right arm, and I drive her off with an elbow in her eye. After this they are more wary of me, intimidated. I see them slinking around the doorframe, trying to insinuate themselves. The staff are concerned that I don't cough, then that I cough too much. In soothing nurse-talk they smooth symptoms away. 'I have a raging thirst,' I say. 'Ah, you are a lit-tul bit thirsty,' says the nurse. I wonder if they laugh at the patients, who come in so brave and ignorant. None of us thinks that the complication rate applies to us.

The visitor's idea of hospital is different from the patient's idea. Visitors imagine themselves trapped in that ward, in that bed, in their present state of assertive well being. They imagine being bored, but boredom occurs when your consciousness ranges about looking for somewhere to settle. It's a superfluity of unused attention. But the patient's concentration is distilled, moment by moment: breathing, not being sick, not coughing or else coughing in the right way, producing bodily secretions in the vessels provided and not on the floor. The visitor sees the hospital as needles and knives, metal teeth, metal bars; sees the foggy meeting between the damp summer air outside and the overheated exhalations of the sickroom. But the patient sees no such contrast. She cannot imagine the street, the motorway. To her the hospital is this squashed pillow, this water glass: this bell pull, and the nice judgment required to know when to use it. For the visitor everything points outwards, to the release at the end of the visiting hour, and to the patient everything points inwards, and the furthest extension of her consciousness is not the rattle of car keys, the road home, the first drink of the evening, but the beep and plip-plop of monitors and drips, the flashing of figures on screens; these are how you register your existence, these are the way you matter.

For the month of July, my world is the size of the room that, as an undergraduate, I shared with a medical student, who kept a box of bones under her bed and a skull on our shelf. I think of the long wards of the hospitals I visited as a child, fiercely disinfected but with walls too high to be cleaned properly: those walls receding, vanishing into grey mist, like clouds over a cathedral. Wheezing and fluttering, or slumped into stupor, my great-aunts and uncles died in wards like those. Wrapping and muffling themselves, gazing at the long windows streaming rain, visitors would tell the patient: 'You're in the best place.' And as the last visitor was ushered out on the dot, doors were closed, curtains pulled, and the inner drama of the ward was free to begin again: the drama enacted without spectators, within each curtained arena a private play, and written within the confines of the body a still more secret drama. Death stays when the visitors have gone, and the nurses turn a blind eye; he leans back on his portable throne, he crosses his legs, he says: 'Entertain me.'

A few days after the surgery I take a turn for the worse. No human dignity is left; in a red dawn, I stagger across the room, held by a tiny Filipina nurse, my heart hammering, unspeakable fluids pouring from me. Hours later, when my heart has subsided and I am propped up and reading the *Observer*, I think this moment is still happening, still being enacted; I live in two simultaneous realities, one serene and one ghastly beyond bearing. When my dressings are stripped off I bob up my head to look at my abdomen. My flesh is swollen, green with bruising, and the shocking, gaping wound shows a fresh pink inside; I look like a watermelon with a great slice hacked out. I say to myself, it's just another border post on the frontier between medicine and greengrocery; growths and tumours seem always to be described as 'the size of a plum' or 'the size of a grapefruit'. Later a nurse calls it 'a wound you could put your fist into'. I think, a wound the size of a double-decker bus. A wound the size of Wales. It doesn't seem possible that a person can have a wound like that and live, let alone walk about and crack jokes.

On 12 July I am attached to a small, heavy black box, which will vacuum out the cavity and gradually close its walls. A clear tube leads from beneath my dressings into the box, and the box is plugged into the wall. It snorts like an elderly pug, and bloody substances whisk along the tube. Through August, as the weather warms up, it will smell like a wastebin in a butchery, and flies will take an interest in it. I can unplug myself for a few minutes, but reconnecting is painful. There is a shoulder strap, for use by the robust, those on their way to mending, but when I get out of bed I carry the box before me in both hands. Its ferocious gasping will soon start to suck the dressings inside the wound, and sometimes in the night it will whistle and cheep, to continue until a keeper comes with knowledge of its workings.

Until now I have been giddily optimistic, but the arrival of the black box sobers me. It takes an hour each time to dress my wound. During one session, a subdued screaming comes from another room; I hope it is from another room. I have an aversion to expressing pain, an aversion which in a hospital is maladaptive. You should squeal, flinch, object and ask for relief. But I have a rooted belief that if you admit you are hurting, someone will come along and hurt you worse. As our parents used to say, 'I'll give you something to cry for.' My brain seethes with ideas, so when my wounds are dressed I go limp as an old sheet and start novels in my head; one can always start them. My favourite story is set in the Raj and its heroine is called Milly Thoroughgood; she is somewhere between Zuleika Dobson and Becky Sharp. The beauty of a novel in the head is that you can run to stereotype: the blushing young clerk with a conscience and secret lusts, the charming military blackguard with the wrecked liver. The novel is composed in elaborate Jamesian circumlocutions, and I breathe along with the punctuation. Sometimes I smile at Milly's scathing comments to her beaux. The nurses think I'm gallant, a tractable patient; they don't know I'm in another country. My least favourite nurse huffs and puffs while he is doing the dressing, and sometimes kicks the bed, as if startled to find it there. My abstraction allows the staff to talk across me: 'Kim said that David should apologise to Jules, but I said he should apologise to Samira, and she said he should apologise to Suzanne, and Suzanne said she wasn't going to apologise to anyone, ever. But I think they should all apologise to me.'

Controlled movements still pose a problem. On Bastille Day I wake myself up by throwing a glass of water in my own face. With the black box to accommodate, every excursion needs care and precision, so I start to make a heap of my possessions on my bed on the window side, and here I hoard my books, an extra towel and a clean sheet, and tussle with anyone who offers to tidy them up. There are three things I need, apart from pain control. One is a reading light, pointing at me and not across the room; I read all the time, whether I'm in or out of my wits. The second is a fan, pointing at me also. The third is a closed door, to shut out the noise of groaning and retching, and also the cheerful rattle of cutlery and the smell of other people's dinners. It's a happy half-hour when I can secure all these three things together. It doesn't happen often and when it does I feel blessed. Hospital dramas are small, desperate, self-centred: 'I had my pill, then I fell over.' 'They said they would . . . but instead they . . .' 'The tea came three hours late and was coffee.' I have no problem with asking for something six times, because eventually I will get it. And what is time, to me, in here? The trick is to keep smiling and not refer back to the other failures. Each moment one is made new.

I reread Evelyn Waugh's *Sword of Honour* trilogy, and three Ivy Compton-Burnett novels, though later I can't remember which ones. I read a new biography of Catherine of Aragon in proof. I read *On Being Ill*, by Virginia Woolf. What schoolgirl piffle, I think. It's like one of those compositions by young ladies mocked in *Tom Sawyer*. I can't understand what she means when she complains about the 'poverty of the language' we have to describe illness. For the sufferer, she says, there is 'nothing ready made'. Then what of the whole vocabulary of singing aches, of spasms, of strictures and cramps; the gouging pain, the drilling pain, the pricking and pinching, the throbbing, burning, stinging, smarting, flaying? All good words. All old words. No one's pain is so special that the devil's dictionary of anguish has not anticipated it. There is even a scale you can use to refine it: 'Tell me,' the doctor says, 'on a scale of one to ten, how much this hurts': one being a love bite, I suppose, and ten the fiery pit of hell. Pain may pass beyond language, but it doesn't start beyond it. The torture chamber is where people 'speak'. No doubt language fails in that shuttered room called melancholia, where the floor is plush and the windowless walls are draped in black velvet: where any sound you make carries only feebly to the outside world, and can be taken for some accidental, natural sound, a creak or a sigh from doorframe or drawer. But then, mental suffering is so genteel; at least, until the dribbling sets in. Virginia only has decorous illnesses. She has faints and palpitations, fevers and headaches, though I am mindful that at one stage they tried to fix her by pulling out her teeth. But she is seemly; she does not seep, or require a dressings trolley, she does not wake at dawn to find herself smeared with contact jelly from last night's ECG. Virginia never oozes. Her secretions are ladylike: tears, not bile. She may as well not have had bowels, for all the evidence of them in her book.

When the date I should have gone home has long passed, I see that it was probably an error to have read the Catherine of Aragon biography, because the twists and turns of Reformation theology have been added to my already ecclesiastical concerns. I write: 'I feel as if someone has given me a set of Endurances, the opposite of Indulgences.' The nurses are worried that I never eat. They give me a warm croissant and it takes me five minutes to work my way through one bite. If I can't think of anything else I ask for a fruit salad, but I begin to feel I am being bullied by kiwi fruit, its jealous green eye falling on me as I poke it about with a spoon. One night I say, aghast: 'I won't *die*, will I?' But the next moment I am writing and laying plans and asking for an omelette. It is a yellow sprawl, like a window cleaner's chammy slapped on a plate; that is what an omelette looks like, but I have forgotten. I wonder if it's a joke they're playing. I list in my head all the window cleaners I have ever known. After prolonged study of my fork I apply a tine to the edge of the object. Fifteen minutes pass and I'm not much further on. If beaten eggs prove too much of a challenge, they say, I can have jelly instead. I want to say tartly that, unlike Virginia Woolf, I still have my own teeth.

I wonder, though, if there is a little saint you can apply to, if you're a person with holes in them? I can hardly expect the Trinity to care about my perforations, and I see the value of intercession by some lesser breed. Sebastian, shot full of arrows? It seems like overkill. There is a term for what is happening to St Teresa in Bernini's sculpture; it is 'transverberation'. But she was pierced suddenly by the fiery lance of God's love, whereas I was pierced by prearrangement, in a hospital just off the M25. After that initial cut, nothing went on time or to plan, and it was no one's fault. Most of July was gone before I was told I could leave the hospital, and after its clean, clear spaces, my own house seemed dimity, fringed, a patchwork of colour, full of overcrowded and complex angles. There was too much of everything and it smelled of the past – it was as if, without me to order it around, it had reverted to the character suitable for a building put up in the 1860s. I still had the black box tied to me, and for that first weekend of freedom, though the hallies were back in their holes, I needed to study, moment by moment, how to get up and lie down, how to sleep always on my back. Two days later I was back in hospital, driven along a moonlit road, 11 o'clock, a perfect summer night that I would never have seen if I had been less precarious. When we arrived at the little building the main door was locked and so, clutching a vomit bowl made in the shape of a cardboard hat, I sat on a bench, breathing in icy dew. The hospital campus has one beautiful building, a curve of shining white. As you sight it you say: 'What is that lovely thing?' It is the mortuary.

But re-entering the life I had so recently left, if not the very room then one just like it, my dreams were of birth, not death. Perhaps it was because of the weight of dressings on my abdomen that I dreamed I was carrying a child. It was born offstage as it were: at a fortnight old it talked like a philosopher. Only it would not acknowledge me as its mother. But then it offered to address me as 'Queen Mary', and everybody seemed happy with that solution. The line between hallucinations, dreams and waking nightmares had blurred, and for a time I wondered if it would ever stand firm again. Once again my concentration was on details: pens, notebook, reading glasses, watch, breathe in, breathe out, pick up that fork and show those eggs who's boss. I was discharged, returned once more, and when I went home finally, still with the wound and the vacuum machine, day to day life was complicated and onerous. I had pictured a mild and productive convalescence. Instead I found the illness had used up all my resources. I imagined every day would be better, but then things would go wrong in totally unexpected ways. For a good part of the time I felt so cowed and humiliated that I would have liked to sit in a corner with a sheet over my head, but this was not practical. I kept trying to rearrange my life so that illness was only a feature of it, and not the whole, but illness insists on its pre-eminence. Now the black box has gone, and it takes ten minutes to dress my healing wound, but I am woken in the night by the itching and burning of the process of repair. Sometimes I incorporate the sensations into nightmares and imagine, for instance, that the bed is on fire. One night in my dreams I meet the devil. He is 32, 34, that sort of age, presentable, with curly hair, and he wears a lambswool V-neck with a T-shirt underneath. We exchange heated words, and he raises a swarm of biting flies; I wake, clawing at my skin.

Just before my discharge I scribbled: 'When I go home I could write up my hospital diary. Or, you know, I could not. I could defiantly leave it unprocessed, and that way the marks of experience might fade.' The truth is that, needing more surgery, I am not sure what kind of story I am in. Perhaps a shaggy dog story, or a mangled joke with the punchline delivered first. The poet Jo Shapcott used a nice phrase recently about confessional writing: 'chasing your own ambulance', she called it. I am guilty of that. In my defence I can say that I am fascinated by the line between writing and physical survival. In the days after the procedure I was sometimes so exhausted by movement that I would wait patiently for someone to come in and give me a paper cup of pills that was almost, not quite, out of my reach. But somehow, I would always contrive to get my pen in my hand, however far it had rolled; my mood was even, despite uprushes of shame, and the only thing that would really have upset me was running out of paper. The black ink, looping across the page, flowing easily and more like water than like blood, reassured me that I was alive and could act in the world. When Virginia Woolf's doctors forbade her to write, she obeyed them. Which makes me ask, what kind of wuss was Woolf? For a time, into September, my religious preoccupations continued, as if the operation had been on my brain and not my guts, as if the so-called 'God spot' had been stirred up by a scalpel. Even now I am content that the unconscious should continue to empty itself into waking life, like some constantly flushing lavatory. 'Are we somebodies?' the voice on my right asks. 'Yes, we are somebodies,' comes the reply. 'The church counts us all. But very few of us are saved.'

4 November 2010

James Bulger
Andrew O'Hagan

THE ABDUCTION AND murder of James Bulger, a two-year-old boy from Liverpool, has caused unprecedented grief and anger. Hours before the two ten-year-old boys accused of the crime arrived at South Sefton Magistrates' Court, a large, baying crowd had formed outside. As a pair of blue vans drew up, the crowd surged forward, bawling and screaming. A number of men tried to reach the vehicles, to get at the youths inside, and scuffles spilled onto the road. Some leapt over crash-barriers and burst through police cordons, lobbing rocks and banging on the sides of the vans. Many in the crowd – sick with condemnation – howled and spat and wept. Kenneth Clarke has promised measures to deal with 'nasty, persistent juvenile little offenders'. Those two little offenders – if they were the offenders, the childish child-murderers from Walton – were caught on camera twice. First, on the security camera at the shopping precinct in Bootle where they lifted James, and again by the camera of a security firm on Breeze Hill, as they dragged James past – the child clearly in some distress.

Watching those boys on camera brought into my head a flurry of pictures from my own boyhood. At that age, we were brimming with nastiness. I grew up on a scheme in the last of Scotland's New Town developments. There were lots of children, lots of dogs and lots of building sites. Torture among our kind was fairly commonplace. I remember two furious old teachers driving me and my six-year-old girlfriend Heather Watt home early one morning. In recent weeks, we had been walking the mile to school in the company of a boy, smaller and younger than ourselves, a fragile boy with ginger hair called David. I think we thought of him as 'our boy'. We bossed him. Occasionally, when he didn't walk straight or carry our bags or speak when we wanted him to, we'd slap him or hit his hands with a ruler. We had to pass through fields to get to school, with diggers going and 'workies' taking little notice of us, though from time to time they'd bring over empty lemonade bottles which we could exchange for money or sweets at the chip shop. We must have looked innocent enough, holding hands, Heather and I, walking the younger boy to school.

Over time, we started to hit the boy hard. Our way to the school was dotted with new trees, freshly planted and bound to supporting stalks with rubber belts. We got into the habit of removing belts every day: we began to punish David with them whenever we thought he'd 'been bad'. Just a few hits at first on top of his shorts, not so's you'd notice. It got worse, though, and on the last morning, when we were caught by the two old lady teachers, we were beating his bare legs with the coiled-up straps. Though we'd set out on time that morning we were late, having spent the best part of half an hour on top of an out-of-the-way railway bridge practically skinning the screaming boy's legs.

That incident caused a scandal in our square. My mother was employed as a cleaner in another local primary school with David's mother and – although I remember crying and being confused and not quite knowing what we'd done wrong – I could see that we'd caused a lot of embarrassment. Up until the age of ten, I'd both taken part in and witnessed many such incidents. My three elder brothers had reputations for being a bit mad; other boys said they'd 'do anything'. I watched them do any number of crazy things to other kids around the squares, and I watched the other kids do some crazy things in return. Early in the 1970s, on Halloween Night, a scarlet-faced man appeared at the door, shouting the odds and holding up a torn frock. My eldest brother and his pals had been ripping at the man's daughter's clothes 'for a laugh' and, as usual, it had got out of hand: they'd torn her dress to shreds and then taunted the girl, leaving her distraught. My mother and the rest of us sat in the kitchen biting our nails and covering our ears as my father, upstairs, gave Michael the beating of his life for that.

Another time, the whole family had to sit in front of a children's panel. That's what happens in Scotland if a child under 16 commits an offence: the social work department calls in the whole family in an effort to assess what the real problem is and decide whether the child should be in care – which in my brother's case would have meant a residential List 'D' school. In the event that didn't happen, but it took a long time for the community – especially our teachers – to forget what he did. With a friend, he'd burned down a wing of our local Catholic secondary school.

It's not that any of us were evil; even the more bookish and shy among us were given to a bit of destructive boredom and stupid imagining. Now and then it got out of hand. The boys I hung around with in my pre-teen years were always losing the head. During the good weather, the light nights, what started off as a game of rounders or crazy golf would end up as a game of clubbing the neighbour's cat to death. A night of camping on the playing-fields could usually be turned into an opportunity for the wrecking of vegetable gardens, or the killing of frogs and people's pet rabbits. Mindless stuff. Yet now and again people would get into things that you sensed were about to go over the edge, or were already over it. My memory tells me that that point was much more difficult to judge than I'd now like to think.

My friend Moggie began taking accordion lessons at the house of a rather anti-social woman who lived in the corner of our square. She started going out when she was supposed to be teaching him, leaving him to babysit her child, who was not yet a year old. Moggie would have been about seven or eight. One day I was in with him, bashing uselessly on her old piano, when he shouted me to the front of the living room.

'I'm biting the baby,' he said. 'D'you want to?'

The baby was lying on a white towelling nappy and Moggie was bent over her, biting her arms and then her legs and then the cheeks of her face. He said he did it all the time and that the baby liked it. He said it was like tickling. I didn't want to do it but said I'd stay and watch. Another game he played was to put on a record, hoist the baby onto her legs and shake her in time to the music. She obviously wasn't walking yet, but he would jostle her and jam her legs on the carpet. Her head would jerk about and she would cry. Some time later, the bite marks were discovered and Moggie was barred from the house, although everyone – including the baby's parents – said that she had been bitten by the dog. I got to stay, since the woman reckoned I was sensible. Another boy who came to that house used to swallow handfuls of the woman's pills (she always had a great variety lying around, so much so that her daughter was eventually rushed to hospital after eating a load). Moggie joined the navy and the pill-swallower was part of a mob of boys who killed someone at a local cashpoint ten years later. In the years that I hung around it, that house (and there were many others like it) had been the site of a large number of life-threatening games, solvent abuses and youthful experiments gone wrong.

Something happened when we all got together, even when we were that young. We were competitive, deluded and full of our own small powers. And, of course, we spoke our own language. We even had our own way of walking – which wasn't unlike that of the two boys on the video – dragging our feet, hands in our pockets, heads always lolling towards the shoulder. That culpable tilt gave the full measure of our arrogant, untelling ways. As only dependents can be, we were full of our own independence. The approval that really mattered was that of the wee Moggies and Bennas and Caesars we ran around with. There were times when I'm sure we could've led each other into just about anything.

Just William-type adventures – earning pocket money or looking for fun – would more often than not end in nastiness or threats to each other or danger to other people, especially to girls our own age and younger boys. There was badness in it, a form of delinquency that most of us left behind. The girls with whom I read books and coloured-in, with whom I regularly played offices, were the victims of verbal taunting, harassment and gang violence when I ran around with boys. We all carried sticks and were all of us baby arsonists who could never get enough matches. We stole them from our houses, stole money out of our mothers' purses with which to buy them and begged them from construction workers. I can remember pleading with my mother to buy me a Little-Big-Man action doll from Woolworth's and then burning it in a field with my pals. Most of our games, when I think of it, were predicated on someone else's humiliation or eventual pain. It made us feel strong and untouchable.

If all of this sounds uncommonly horrific, then I can only say that it did not seem so then; it was the main way that most of the boys I knew used up their spare time. There was no steady regression towards the juvenile barbarism famously characterised in Lord of the Flies. We lived two lives at once: while most of the stuff detailed above went on, we all made our First Communions, sang in the school choir, did our homework, became altar-boys and some went to matches or played brilliantly at football. We didn't stop to think, nor did our parents, that something dire might result from the darker of our extra-curricular activities. Except when that murky side took over, and your bad-bastardness became obvious to everyone.

Bullies who had no aptitude for classwork – who always got 'easily distracted' scribbled in red ink on report cards that never made it home – had unbelievable concentration when it came to torturing minors in the playground, or on the way home. For many of the pupils bullying was a serious game. It involved strategies, points scored for and against, and not a little detailed planning. It was scary, competitive and brought out the very worst in those who had anything to do with it. Kids who were targeted over a long period we thought deviant in some way, by which I mean that they were in some way out of it – maybe serious, bright, quiet, keeping themselves to themselves. When I was nine, there was a particular boy who lived two squares up. For years I'd listened to boys telling of how they'd love to do him in. I sort of liked him but, even so, I joined in the chase when we pursued him in and out of the scheme and across fields. This stood high in our repertoire of time-fillers. 'Where's Broon?' – the boy's name was Alan Brown – took its place in a list of nasty games that included snipes (skinning each other's knuckles with cards after each lost game), kiss-cuddle-and-torture (with girls), Blue Murder (the same, but sorer) and that kind of thing. If anyone came to the door when these games had gone too far, our mothers and fathers went ape. Belted and sent to bed, many of us would get up after dark and stare out the window, over the square, into each other's bedrooms. We grinned and flashed our torches, trying to pass messages. The message, I remember, was always quite clear: it meant see you tomorrow.

Even the youths who came from happy homes enjoyed the childish ritual of running away. When parents, sick with anxiety, came to the door or to school looking for their children, we'd never let on. We'd help 11-year-old absconders get together the bus fare to a bigger place, all of us filling a bag with stolen tins and chipping in coppers for some hero's running-away fund. Of course, they'd always be caught and brought back, but not before we'd enjoyed the parental worry and the police presence in the classroom while the drama lasted. In Jeff Torrington's novel *Swing Hammer Swing!* a similar pleasure is taken by the boy Jason after the book's hero, Thomas Clay, takes him to the Kelvingrove Art Gallery. We hear of it in an exchange between Clay and the boy's mother:

'Dammit, how long was he missing for?'

'I've told you – two min –'

'You're a liar! Ten minutes, Jason says.'

'What's a wee boy know about judging time?'

'You damned eejit – that man could've been one of those perverts. Places like that hoach with'm. Come clean – how long did he have'm?'

'Two minutes at the outside. Get a grip on yoursel. That guy'd been a perv, d'you think he'd've taken the boy to an attendant? C'mon, think about it. Another thing, the man didnae lure Jason from me – Jason followed him because he was wearing the same clobber as me . . .'

Although I was fairly certain that the boy hadn't come to any physical harm – taken to a WC and interfered with, I mean – I didn't dig this being forced into lying complicity with my dress alike. Jason, like most imaginative kids, hadn't been content to tell of the incident as was – he'd jived it up some, flung a few more squibs on the fire.

We all did that at times. We all took and assigned roles in cruel little dramas of our own devising. Our talk would be full of new and interesting ways to worry or harass our parents, especially our fathers, who we all hated. Stealing his fags or drink brought a great, often awesome, feeling of *quid pro quo*.

I found many girls to be the same in that respect: I had a 12-year-old table-tennis friend Alison, who told us she'd been crushing old lightbulbs in a bowl and sprinkling them into her father's porridge. We thought that was great. Some of us knew how to stop it, though, while others just kept it up. A couple of my boyhood friends assiduously built bridges between their mindless, childish venom – their bad-boyish misdemeanours – and adult crime.

Around the time of our cruelty to the boy David, the local news was full of the disappearance of another David – a three-year-old boy who'd last been seen playing on one of the town's many open construction sites. Guesses were that he'd either fallen into a pipe trench and been covered, or that he'd been abducted. He was never found. We thought about him, in class we prayed for him, and when we weren't out looking for something to get into, we tried to figure out what had happened to him.

Our mothers' warnings to stay clear of the dumps taught us that David's fate could easily have been our own. And in silent, instinctive ways I'm sure we understood something of David's other possible end, the one that wasn't an accident. We knew something of children's fearsome cruelty to children, and we lived with our own passion for misadventure. Though we knew it neither as cruelty nor as misadventure. No one believed that David was playing alone at the building site that day. We didn't know it then, but as many of us grew older we came to think it not inconceivable that David had come to grief at the hands of boys not a lot older than himself, playing in a make-shift sandpit. All of these things have returned with the news of James Bulger's murder. More than once this week, a single image has floated into my head: a grainy Strathclyde Police picture of a sandy-haired boy, with its caption 'Have You Seen David?'

11 March 1993

Desperately Seeking Susan

Terry Castle

A FEW WEEKS ago I found myself scanning photographs of
Susan Sontag into my screensaver file: a tiny head shot
clipped from Newsweek; two that had appeared in the New
York Times; another printed alongside Allan Gurganus's obituary in
the Advocate, a glossy American gay and lesbian mag usually devoted
to pulchritudinous gym bunnies, gay sitcom stars and treatments for
flesh-eating strep. It seemed the least I could do for the bedazzling,
now-dead she-eminence. The most beautiful photo I downloaded was
one that Peter Hujar took of her in the 1970s, around the time of
I, Et Cetera. She's wearing a thin grey turtleneck and lies on her back
– arms up, head resting on her clasped hands and her gaze fixed
impassively on something to the right of the frame. There's a slightly
pedantic quality to the whole thing which I like: very true to life. Every
few hours now she floats up onscreen in this digitised format, supine,
sleek and flat-chested.

No doubt hundreds (thousands?) of people knew Susan Sontag
better than I did. For ten years ours was an on-again, off-again, semi-
friendship, constricted by role-playing and shot through in the end
with mutual irritation. Over the years I laboured to hide my growing
disillusion, especially during my last ill-fated visit to New York, when

she regaled me – for the umpteenth time – about the siege of Sarajevo, the falling bombs, and how the pitiful Joan Baez had been too terrified to come out of her hotel room. Sontag flapped her arms and shook her big mannish hair – inevitably described in the press as a 'mane' – contemptuously. *That woman is a fake! She tried to fly back to California the next day! I was there for months. Through all of the bombardment, of course, Terry.* Then she ruminated. Had I ever met Baez? Was she a secret lesbian? I confessed that I'd once waited in line behind the folk singer at my cash machine (Baez lives near Stanford) and had taken the opportunity to inspect the hairs on the back of her neck. Sontag, who sensed a rival, considered this non-event for a moment, but after further enquiries, was reassured that I, her forty-something slave girl from San Francisco, still preferred *her* to Ms Diamonds and Rust.

At its best, our relationship was rather like the one between Dame Edna and her feeble sidekick Madge – or possibly Stalin and Malenkov. Sontag was the Supremo and I the obsequious gofer. Whenever she came to San Francisco, usually once or twice a year, I instantly became her female aide-de-camp: a one-woman posse, ready to drop anything at a phone call (including the classes I was supposed to be teaching at Stanford) and drive her around to various Tower record stores and dim sum restaurants. Most important, I became adept at clucking sympathetically at her constant kvetching: about the stupidity and philistinism of whatever local sap was paying for her lecture trip, how no one had yet appreciated the true worth of her novel *The Volcano Lover*, how you couldn't find a decent dry cleaner in downtown San Francisco etc, etc.

True – from my point of view – it had all begun extraordinarily well. Even now I have to confess that, early on, Sontag gave me a couple of the sweetest (not to mention most amusing) moments of my adult life. The first came one grey magical morning at Stanford in 1996, when after several hours of slogging away on student papers,

I opened a strange manila envelope that had come for me, with a New York return address. The contents – a brief fan letter about a piece I'd written on Charlotte Brontë and a flamboyantly inscribed paperback copy of her play, *Alice in Bed* ('from Susan') – made me dizzy with ecstasy. Having idolised Sontag literally for decades – I'd first read 'Notes on Camp' as an exceedingly arch nine-year-old – I felt as if Pallas Athene herself had suddenly materialised and offered me a cup of ambrosia. (*O great Susan! Most august Goddess of Female Intellect!*) I zoomed around, showing the note to various pals. To this day, when I replay it in my mind, I still get a weird toxic jolt of adolescent joy – like taking a big hit of Crazy Glue vapours out of a paper bag.

Things proceeded swiftly in our honeymoon phase. Sontag, it turned out, was coming to Stanford for a writer-in-residence stint that spring and the first morning after her arrival abruptly summoned me to take her out to breakfast. The alacrity with which I drove the forty miles down from San Francisco – trying not to get flustered but panting a bit at the wheel nonetheless – set the pattern of our days. We made the first of several madcap car trips around Palo Alto and the Stanford foothills. While I drove, often somewhat erratically, she would alternate between loud complaints – about her faculty club accommodation, the bad food at the Humanities Center, the 'dreariness' of my Stanford colleagues ('Terry, don't you *loathe* academics as much as I do? How can you *abide* it?') – and her Considered Views on Everything ('Yes, Terry, I *do* know all the lesser-known Handel operas. I told Andrew Porter he was right – they *are* the greatest of musical masterpieces'). I was rapt, like a hysterical spinster on her first visit to Bayreuth. *Schwärmerei* time for T-Ball.

The Sarajevo obsession revealed itself early on: in fact, inspired the great comic episode in this brief golden period. We were walking down University Avenue, Palo Alto's twee, boutique-crammed main drag, on our way to a bookshop. Sontag was wearing her trademark intellectual-diva outfit: voluminous black top and black silky slacks, accessorised with a number of exotic, billowy scarves. These she constantly adjusted or flung back imperiously over one shoulder, stopping now and then to puff on a cigarette or expel a series of phlegmy coughs. (The famous Sontag 'look' always put me in mind of the stage direction in *Blithe Spirit*: 'Enter Madame Arcati, wearing barbaric jewellery.') Somewhat incongruously, she had completed her ensemble with a pair of pristine, startlingly white tennis shoes. These made her feet seem comically huge, like Bugs Bunny's. I half-expected her to bounce several feet up and down in the air whenever she took a step, like one of those people who have shoes made of 'Flubber' in the old Fred McMurray movie.

She'd been telling me about the siege and how a Yugoslav woman she had taken shelter with had asked her for her autograph, even as bombs fell around them. She relished the woman's obvious intelligence ('Of course, Terry, she'd read *The Volcano Lover*, and like all Europeans, admired it tremendously') and her own sangfroid. Then she stopped abruptly and asked, grim-faced, if I'd ever had to evade sniper fire. I said, no, unfortunately not. Lickety-split she was off – dashing in a feverish crouch from one boutique doorway to the next, white tennis shoes a blur, all the way down the street to Restoration Hardware and the Baskin-Robbins store. Five or six perplexed Palo Altans stopped to watch as she bobbed zanily in and out, ducking her head, pointing at imaginary gunmen on rooftops and gesticulating wildly at me to follow. No one, clearly, knew who she was, though several of them looked as if they thought they should know who she was.

In those early days, I felt like an intellectual autodidact facing the greatest challenge of her career: the Autodidact of all Autodidacts. The quizzing was relentless. Had I read Robert Walser? (Ooooh errrg blush, ahem, little cough, um: *No, I'm ashamed to say . . .*) Had I read Thomas Bernhard? (*Yes! – Yes, I have! 'Wittgenstein's Nephew'! Yay! Yippee!*

Wow! Phew! – dodged the bullet that time!) It seemed, for a while at least, that I had yet to be contaminated by the shocking intellectual mediocrity surrounding me at Stanford U. This exemption from idiocy was due mainly, I think, to the fact that I could hold my own with her in the music-appreciation department. Trading CDs and recommendations – in a peculiar, masculine, trainspotting fashion – later became a part of our fragile bond. I scored a coup one time with some obscure Busoni arrangements she'd not heard of (though she assured me that 'she had, of course, known the pianist' – the late Paul Jacobs – 'very well'); but I almost came a cropper when I confessed I had never listened to Janáček's *The Excursions of Mr Broucek*. She gave me a surprised look, then explained, somewhat loftily, that I owed it to myself, as a 'cultivated person', to become acquainted with it. ('I adore Janáček's sound world.') A recording of the opera appeared soon after in the mail – so I knew I'd been forgiven – but after listening to it once I couldn't really get anywhere with it. (It tends to go on a bit – in the same somewhat exhausting Eastern European way I now associate with Sontag herself.) The discs are still on my shelf. Given their exalted provenance I can't bear to unload them at the used CD shop in my neighbourhood.

And she also flirted – in a coquettish, discombobulating, yet unmistakable fashion. She told me she had read my book, *The Apparitional Lesbian*, and 'agreed with me entirely' about Henry James and *The Bostonians*. She made me describe at length how I'd met my then girlfriend. ('She wrote you a letter! And you answered? Terry, I'm amazed! I get those letters all the time, but I would *never* answer one! Of course, Terry, I'm stunned!') Though I was far too cowed to ask her directly about her own love life, she would reveal the occasional titbit from her legendary past, then give me a playful, almost girlish look. ('Of course, Terry, everyone *said* Jeanne Moreau and I were lovers, but you know, we were just good friends.') My apotheosis as tease-target came the night of her big speech in Kresge Auditorium. She had begun by reprimanding those in the audience who failed to consider her one of the 'essential' modern novelists, then read a seemingly interminable section of what was to become In America. (Has any other major literary figure written such an excruciatingly turgid book?) At the end, as the audience gave way to enormous, relieved clapping – thank God that's over – she made a beeline towards me. Sideswiping the smiling president of Stanford and an eager throng of autograph-seekers, she elbowed her way towards me, enveloped me rakishly in her arms and said very loudly: 'Terry, we've got to stop meeting like this.' She seemed to think the line hilarious and chortled heartily. I felt at once exalted, dopey and mortified, like a plump teenage boy getting a hard-on in front of everybody.

Though otherwise respectful, Allan Gurganus (in the Advocate obit) takes Sontag to task for never having come out publicly as a lesbian: 'My only wish about Sontag is that she had bothered to weather what the rest of us daily endure. The disparity between her professed fearlessness and her actual self-protective closetedness strikes a questioning footnote that is the one blot on her otherwise brilliant career.'

I have to say I could never figure her out on this touchy subject – though we did talk about it. Her usual line (indignant and aggrieved) was that she didn't believe in 'labels' and that if anything she was bisexual. She raged about a married couple who were following her from city to city and would subsequently publish a tell-all biography of her in 2000. Horrifyingly enough, she'd learned, the despicable pair were planning to include photographs of her with various cele-brated female companions. Obviously, both needed to be consigned to Dante's Inferno, to roast in the flames in perpetuity with the Unbaptised Babies, Usurers and Makers of False Oaths. I struggled to keep a poker face during these rants, but couldn't help thinking that Dante should have devised a whole circle specifically for such malefactors: the Outers of Sontag.

At other times she was less vehement, and would assume a dreamy, George Sand-in-the-1840s look. 'I've loved men, Terry; I've loved women . . .' she would begin, with a deep sigh. What did the sex of the person matter, after all? Think of Sand herself with Chopin and Marie Dorval. Or Tsvetaeva, perhaps, with Mandelstam and Sophia Parnok. In Paris, all the elegant married ladies had mistresses. And yet in some way I felt the subject of female homosexuality – and whether she owed the world a statement on it – was an unresolved one for her. Later in our friendship, the topic seemed to become an awkward obsession, especially as I came closer to finishing up an anthology of lesbian-themed literature I'd been working on for several years. She frequently suggested things she thought I should include: most interestingly, perhaps, her favourite steamy love scene from Patricia Highsmith's 1952 lesbian romance novel *The Price of Salt*. As far as Sontag was concerned, Highsmith's dykey little potboiler – published originally under a pseudonym – was right up there with *Buddenbrooks* and *The Man without Qualities*. Something in the story – about a gifted (yet insecure) young woman who moves to Manhattan in the early 1950s to become a theatre designer and ends up falling rapturously in love with a glamorous, outré older woman – must have once struck a chord: Sontag seemed to dote on it.

And invariably she would probe for sapphic gossip – sometimes about opera singers and pop stars, sometimes about other writers. Was it true what everyone said about Joan Sutherland and Marilyn Horne during the rehearsals for *Norma*? What about June Anderson? And Jessye Norman? Or Lucia Popp, for that matter? ('Of course, Terry, the perfect Queen of the Night.') Did I think Iris Murdoch and Brigid Brophy had had an affair? What was Adrienne Rich's girlfriend like? When was somebody ever going to spill the beans on Eudora Welty and Elizabeth Bowen?

Was there some way, I wonder now, that she wanted me to absolve her? Was the fact that she never mentioned, on any of the occasions we talked, her equally prominent female companion – they lived in the same Manhattan building – a sign of *grande dame* sophistication or some sort of weird test of my character? (Actually I did hear her say her name once; when someone at an otherwise fairly staid farewell dinner gave Sontag a vulgar present at the end of her Stanford visit – a book of glossy photos of the campy 1950s pin-up, Bettie Page – she said: 'I'll have to show these to Annie.')

I was never quite sure *what* she wanted. And besides, whatever it was, after a while she stopped wanting it. I visited her several times in New York City and even got invited to the London Terrace penthouse to see the famous book collection. ('Of course, Terry, mine is the greatest library in private hands in the world.') I tried not to gape at the Brice Mardens stacked up against the wall and enthused appropriately when she showed me prized items, such as Beckford's own annotated copy of *Vathek*. We would go on little culture jaunts. Once she took me to the Strand bookstore (the clerk said, 'Hi, Susan' in enviably blasé tones); another time she invited me to a film festival she was curating at the Japan Society. But there were also little danger signals, ominous hints that she was tiring of me. One day in the Village, after having insisted on buying me a double-decker ice-cream cone, she suddenly vanished, even as I, tongue moronically extruded, was still licking away. I turned around in bewilderment and saw her black-clad form piling, without farewell, into a yellow cab.

And the last two times I saw her I managed to blow it – horrendously – both times. The first debacle occurred after one of the films at the Japan Society. I'd been hanging nervously around in the lobby, like a groupie, waiting for her: Sontag yanked me into a taxi with her and an art curator she knew named Klaus. (He was hip and bald and dressed in the sort of all-black outfit worn by the fictional German talk-show host, Dieter Sprocket, on the old *Saturday Night Live*.) With great excitement she explained she was taking me out for 'a real New York evening' – to a dinner party being hosted by Marina Abramovic, the performance artist, at her loft in Soho. Abramovic had recently been in the news for having lived for 12 days, stark naked, on an exposed wooden platform – fitted with shower and toilet – in the window of the Sean Kelly Gallery. She lived on whatever food spectators donated and never spoke during the entire 12 days. I guess it had all been pretty mesmerising: my friend Nancy happened to be there once when Abramovic took a shower; and one of Nancy's friends hit the jackpot – she got to watch the artist have a bowel movement.

Abramovic – plus hunky sculptor boyfriend – lived in a huge, virtually empty loft, the sole furnishings being a dining table and chairs in the very centre of the room and a spindly old stereo from the 1960s. The space was probably a hundred feet on either side – 'major real estate, of course', as Sontag proudly explained to me. (She loved using *Vanity Fair*-ish clichés.) She and Abramovic smothered one another in hugs and kisses. I meanwhile blanched in fright: I'd just caught sight of two of the other guests, who, alarmingly enough, turned out to be Lou Reed and Laurie Anderson. Reed (O great rock god of my twenties) stood morosely by himself, humming, doing little dance steps and playing air guitar. Periodically he glared at everyone – including me – with apparent hatred. Anderson – elfin spikes of hair perfectly gelled – was chatting up an Italian man from the Guggenheim, the man's trophy wife and the freakish-looking lead singer from the cult art-pop duo Fischerspooner. The last-mentioned had just come back from performing at the Pompidou Centre and wore booties and tights, a psychedelic shawl and a thing like a codpiece. He could have played Osric in a postmodern *Hamlet*. He was accompanied by a bruiser with a goatee – roadie or boyfriend, it wasn't clear – and emitted girlish little squeals when our first course, a foul-smelling durian fruit just shipped in from Malaysia, made its way to the table.

Everyone crowded into their seats: despite the vast size of the room, we were an *intime* gathering. Yet it wouldn't be quite right merely to say that everyone ignored me. As a non-artist and non-celebrity, I was so 'not there', it seemed – so cognitively unassimilable – I wasn't even registered enough to be ignored. I sat at one end of the table like a piece of anti-matter. I didn't exchange a word the whole night with Lou Reed, who sat kitty-corner across from me. He remained silent and surly. Everyone else gabbled happily on, however, about how they loved to trash hotels when they were younger and how incompetent everybody was at the Pompidou. 'At *my* show I had to explain things to them a *thousand* times. They just don't know how to *do* a major retrospective.'

True, Sontag tried briefly to call the group's attention to me (with the soul-destroying words, 'Terry is an English professor'); and Abramovic kindly gave me a little place card to write my name on. But otherwise I might as well not have been born. My one conversational gambit failed dismally: when I asked the man from the Guggenheim, to my right, what his books were about, he regarded me disdainfully and began, 'I am famous for —,' then caught himself. He decided to be more circumspect – he was the 'world's leading expert on Arte Povera' – but then turned his back on me for the next two hours. At one point I thought I saw Laurie Anderson, at the other end of the table, trying to get my attention: she was smiling sweetly in my direction, as if to undo my pathetic isolation. I smiled in gratitude in return and held up my little place card so she would at least know my name. Annoyed, she gestured back impatiently, with a sharp downward flick of her index finger: she wanted me to pass the wine bottle. I was reduced to a pair of disembodied hands – like the ones that come out of the walls and give people drinks in Cocteau's *Beauty and the Beast*.

Sontag gave up trying to include me and after a while seemed herself to recede curiously into the background. Maybe she was already starting to get sick again; she seemed oddly undone. Through much of the conversation (dominated by glammy Osric) she looked tired and bored, almost sleepy. She did not react when I finally decided to leave – on my own – just after coffee had been served. I thanked Marina Abramovic, who led me to the grungy metal staircase that went down to the street and back to the world of the Little People. Turning round one last time, I saw Sontag still slumped in her seat, as if she'd fallen into a trance, or somehow just caved in. She'd clearly forgotten all about me.

A fiasco, to be sure, but my final encounter with Sontag was possibly more disastrous: my Waterloo. I had come to New York with Blakey, and Sontag (to whom I wanted proudly to display her) said we could stop by her apartment one afternoon. When we arrived at the appointed time, clutching a large bouquet of orange roses, Sontag was nowhere to be seen. Her young male assistant, padding delicately around in his socks, showed us in, took the roses away, and whispered to us to wait in the living-room. We stood in puzzled silence. Half an hour later, somewhat blowsily, Sontag finally emerged from a back room. I introduced her to Blakey, and said rather nervously that I hoped we hadn't woken her up from a nap. It was as if I had accused her of never having read Proust, or of watching soap operas all day. Her face instantly darkened and she snapped at me violently. Why on earth did I think she'd been having a nap? Didn't I know she never had naps? Of course she wasn't having a nap! She would never have a nap! Never in a million years! What a stupid remark to make! How had I gotten so stupid? A *nap* – for God's sake!

She calmed down after a bit and became vaguely nice to Blakey – Blakey had just read her latest piece on photography in the *New Yorker* and was complimenting her effusively on it – but it was clear I couldn't repair the damage I'd done. Indeed I made it worse. Sontag asked B. if she had read *The Volcano Lover* and started in on a monologue (one I'd heard before) about her literary reputation. It had 'fallen' slightly over the past decade, she allowed – foolishly, people had yet to grasp the greatness of her fiction – but of course it would rise again dramatically, 'as soon as I am dead'. The same thing had happened, after all, to Virginia Woolf, and didn't we agree Woolf was a great genius? In a weak-minded attempt at levity, I said: 'Do you really think *Orlando* is a work of genius?' She then exploded. 'Of course not!' she shouted, hands flailing and face white with rage. 'Of course not! You don't judge a writer by her worst work! You judge her by her best work!' I reeled backwards as if I'd been struck; Blakey looked embarrassed. The assistant peeked out from another room to see what was going on. Sontag went on muttering for a while, then grimly said she 'had to go'. With awkward thanks, we bundled ourselves hurriedly into the elevator and out onto West 24th Street – Blakey agog, me all nervy and smarting. When I sent Sontag a copy of my lesbian anthology a few months later, a thousand pages long and complete with juicy Highsmith excerpt, I knew she would never acknowledge it; nor did she.

Enfin – la fin. I heard she was dead as Bev and I were driving back from my mother's after Christmas. Blakey called on the cellphone from Chicago to say she had just read about it online; it would be on the front page of the *New York Times* the next day. It was, but news of the Asian tsunami crowded it out. (The catty thing to say here would be that Sontag would have been annoyed at being upstaged; the honest thing to say is that she wouldn't have been.) The *Times* did another piece a few days later – a somewhat dreary set of passages from her books, entitled: 'No Hard Books, or Easy Deaths'. (An odd title: her death wasn't easy, but she was all about hard books.) And in the weeks since, the *New Yorker*, *New York Review of Books* and various other highbrow mags have kicked in with the predictable tributes.

But I've had the feeling the real reckoning has yet to begin. The reaction, to my mind, has been a bit perfunctory and stilted. A good part of her characteristic 'effect' – what one might call her *novelistic* charm – has not yet been put into words. Among other things, Sontag was a great comic character: Dickens or Flaubert or James would have had a field day with her. The carefully cultivated moral seriousness – *strenuousness* might be a better word – co-existed with a fantastical, Mrs Jellyby-like absurdity. Sontag's complicated and charismatic sexuality was part of this comic side of her life. The high-mindedness, the high-handedness, commingled with a love of gossip, drollery and seductive acting out – and, when she was in a benign and unthreatened mood, a fair amount of ironic self-knowledge.

I think she was fully conscious of – and took great pride and pleasure in – the erotic spell she exerted over other women. I would be curious to know how men found her in this regard; the few times I saw her with men around, they seemed to relate to her as a kind of intellectually supercharged eunuch. The famed 'Natalie Wood' looks of her early years notwithstanding, she seemed uninterested in being an object of heterosexual desire, and males responded accordingly. It was not the same with women – and least of all with her lesbian fans. Among the susceptible, she never lost her sexual majesty. She was quite fabulously butch – perhaps the Butchest One of All. She knew it and basked in it, like a big lady she-cat in the sun.

Perhaps at some point there will be, too, a better and less routine accounting of her extraordinary cultural significance. Granted, Great Man (or Great Woman) theories of history have been out of fashion for some time now. No single person, it's usually argued, has that much effect on how things eventually turn out. Yet it is hard for me to think about the history of modern feminism, say – especially as it evolved in the United States in the 1970s – without Sontag in the absolutely central, catalytic role. Simone de Beauvoir was floating around too, of course, but for intellectually ambitious American women of my generation, women born in the 1940s and 1950s, she seemed both culturally unfamiliar and emotionally removed. Sontag, on the contrary, was *there*: on one's own college campus, lecturing on Barthes or Canetti or Benjamin or Tsvetaeva or Leni Riefenstahl. (And who were they? One pretended to know, then scuttled around to find out.) She was our very own Great Man. If there was ever going to be a Smart Woman Team then Sontag would have to be both Captain and Most Valuable Player. She was the one already out there doing the job, even as we were labouring painfully to get up off the floor and match wits with her.

In my own case, Sontag's death brings with it mixed emotions. God, she could be insulting to people. At the end – as I enjoy blubbering to friends – she was *weally weally mean* to me! But her death also leaves me now with a profound sense of imploding fantasies – of huge convulsions in the underground psychic plates. Not once, unfortunately, on any of her California trips, did Sontag ever come to my house, though I often sat around scheming how to get her to accept such an invitation. If only she would come, I thought, I would be *truly happy*. It's hard to admit how long – and how abjectly, like a Victorian monomaniac – I carried this fantasy around. (It long antedated my actual meeting with her.) It is still quite palpable in the rooms in which I spend most of my time. Just about every book, every picture, every object in my living-room, for example – I now see all too plainly – has been placed there strategically in the hope of capturing *her* attention, of pleasing *her* mind and heart, of winning *her* love, esteem, intellectual respect etc, etc. It's all baited and set up: a room-sized Venus Fly-Trap, courtesy of T-Ball/ Narcissism Productions.

There are her books of course: the vintage paperbacks of *Against Interpretation*, *Styles of Radical Will*, *Under the Sign of Saturn*, the quite-wonderful-despite-what-everybody-says *The Volcano Lover*. There's *Aids and Its Metaphors*, *On Photography*, *Where the Stress Falls*. The now valedictory *Regarding the Pain of Others*. And then there are some of my own productions, to remind her, passive-aggressively, I guess, that she's not the only damned person who writes. (Caveat lector: Lilliputian on the rampage!) But then there's heaps of other stuff sitting around, I'm embarrassed to say, the sole purpose of which is – was – to impress her. A pile of 'tasteful' art books: Popova, *The History of Japanese Photography*, Cy Twombly, Nadar, Bronzino, Hannah Hoch, Jeff Wall, Piranesi, Sol LeWitt and Jasper Johns, the big Bellocq volume (with her introduction). My 1930s picture of Lucienne Boyer. My Valentine Hugo photo of Breton and Aragon. The crammed CD cabinet – with the six different versions of *Pelléas*. (Will I really listen to any of them all the way through again before I die?) My little 19th-century optical toy from Paris: you crank a tiny lever and see a clown head, painted on glass, change expressions as if by magic.

Yet now the longed-for visitor – or victim – is never going to arrive. Who will come in her place? At the moment it's hard to imagine anyone ever possessing the same symbolic weight, the same adamantine hardness, or having the same casual imperial hold over such a large chunk of my brain. I am starting to think in any case that she was part of a certain neural development that, purely physiologically speaking, can never be repeated. All those years ago one evolved a hallucination about what mental life could be and she was it. She's still in there, enfolded somehow in the deepest layers of the grey matter. Yes: Susan Sontag was sibylline and hokey and often a great bore. She was a troubled and brilliant American and never as good a friend as I wanted her to be. But now the lady's kicked it and I'm trying to keep *one* of the big lessons in view: judge her by her best work, not her worst.

17 March 2005

Breakdown
A.J.P. Taylor

I T IS SOME time since I wrote a diary here. It will be seen I have had plenty to write about. I should explain that there are two versions of a period of my life. One is the version of other people, a version which others try to impose upon me. The other is my own version, a version equally genuine and much more unusual.

According to others such as my doctors and the members of my family, I had a mental breakdown, was the victim of fantasies and never moved from the hospital bedroom except to have a bath and did not read even the newspaper. This version can be disregarded. According to my recollection, I had a life of adventure interrupted by periods of relaxation, and never encountered insoluble difficulties. Most of my life seems to have been passed in some part of the North of England and at different periods. My first stretch was in Roman Britain, when I lived in York and was afterwards stationed on the Wall. These experiences were very instructive to me as an historian.

The Romans did not remain long. Nor did I waste much time at the court of King Arthur. The outstanding figure of my attraction was the king, though I did not manage to encounter him often. This was the period when I spent most of my time on the Yorkshire moors. I got lost pretty often, though always rescued by other wanderers. Gradually I moved into a more civilised existence. The centre of my life was now Harrogate, a place I have never visited in my life. I had difficulties here obtaining regular copies of the *Manchester Guardian*, which did not surprise me at all. I also attended a very expensive luncheon party one Sunday in Harrogate given by my daughter Amelia, who is not in the habit of giving expensive luncheon parties.

I gradually resumed a family life. The principal figures in it were my mother and father, both of whom had, I thought, been dead for some time. My father had taken over a medieval monastery – was it Furness Abbey? – which he had transformed into a boarding house for holidaymakers. My father was as delightful as ever and as efficient. I spent an occasional night with him during the summer. Though friendly, he never displayed much interest in my activities whatever they might be.

I sometimes went shopping with my mother in Manchester, a thing I had done often enough in real life. I found Kendal Milne a great obstacle against getting from one end of Manchester to another. One afternoon I encountered a birthday party given by some shop assistants. I wanted to get through, not to take part in it. My father took me out to his monastery, an event which somewhat puzzled me because in the general puzzle of my existence I was aware that I lived in the 18th century when motor-cars did not exist. It also puzzled me that my hospital rooms were sometimes in London and sometimes in France, probably in Paris, though the nurses were always English. No one ever tried to explain to me where I was or what I was doing. It was a long period of bewilderment which I gradually accepted as one of total incomprehensibility. It then just disappeared along with the figures who populated it, including my father and mother. I was sorry to lose him, otherwise I did not worry.

In the last episode of my medical career some of it became clear to me. I recognised that I was in a hospital, though it was not clear to me where – probably London, though it might be somewhere in France. It was also clear to me that wherever it was it was difficult or impossible to get out of it. In the quiet of lunchtime I would pack a small bag and set off for the way out. Sooner or later a nurse would catch me and ask me where I was going. Patiently I would be led back to my own quarters without any explanation. I must have read something during this long and dreary period. But apart from *The Times* every morning, I can only remember reading *The Good Soldier Schweik* in its most extended edition – something over seven hundred pages. It is still an incomparable war book.

One morning, without any explanation, I was told that I was moving out. There was my wife waiting for me. I had to admit that I had spent all this time in University College Hospital, not in France, but I still found many things hard to explain – what had been wrong with me, what treatment I had received, why it should end. The important thing was to be out. I have firmly resolved never to enter a hospital again. If this means the end of my life I shall not care. Anything is better than to be imprisoned in a hospital.

Life has begun to stir since I was released. I opened an exhibition of the works of David Low, which had been locked up since his death. Some years ago I opened a similar exhibition of Low's works which the University of Canterbury had managed to acquire. Now I launched another set which his daughter had at last revealed. It is the finest collection of radical art in existence. A week or two later I attended a commemoration of Bronterre O'Brien, perhaps the greatest of the Chartist leaders. I must confess that I had forgotten about O'Brien until I looked him up. Once I read again his enthusiasm for the radical cause I recognised his greatness. We made something of a pilgrimage to his tomb in Abney Park cemetery, Stoke Newington. This was wild land for us. I had no idea that Stoke Newington was so near the centre of London, still less that Abney Park cemetery was a collection of some historic merit. However, after some toil, we made the journey. The cemetery was much overgrown. Even O'Brien's table tomb was obscured by vegetation. But a way had been cleared. I was glad to praise the great radical even though his memory is somewhat faded. Stoke Newington has an active group of his admirers, mostly Irish, led by Chris Maguire, an Irish electrician whose acquaintance I was glad to make. Of such men were radicals once made.

That ends my expedition. I cannot walk any distance and easily fall asleep. It is a relief not to go to the theatre or a cinema. I miss chamber concerts more than any other form of public activity. One day, perhaps, I shall manage to attend one. One day life will begin again for me. I cannot say that I miss it very much.

2 August 1984

Empson at 68
John Henry Jones

ONE SATURDAY MORNING as I lay in bed, dying of flu, William Empson burst into my room, very sprightly, saying: 'Now come along Jones, you must get up and come to Stonehenge.' I croaked an apology and claimed an imminent, prior appointment with the Lord God Almighty. 'Oh dear. I am sorry,' he said. 'But you would do much better to come to Stonehenge.'

This was Empson at 68, shortly after I had got to know him. My initial acquaintance with him was brought about by an overlap of social circles, and, to my shame, I did not know who he was. As a former chemist turned translator and playwright, I had never had much time for literary criticism or for 1930s poets, nor had I suffered the 'ruination' of a university Eng. Lit. course, a mark in my favour with Empson. I soon discovered his reputation, but had no idea of his stature; and his own manner was sufficiently disclaiming of any personal distinction that one could be excused for failing to regard him as anything more than a most interesting person. So I did not come to him as an Eckermann longing to serve at the feet of greatness, far less did I record our conversations. Indeed it was some time before I could understand much of what he said; quite apart from its occasional gnomic quality, he had a tendency to intone his words and, when he was passionate, to roll his head as he spoke so that what sound there was streamed off in sundry directions, as from Socrates in a basket. He was nonetheless totally engaging.

The Empsons lived in a large, detached house, built in 1880, and set at an angle to the main road from Hampstead into town, on the corner of Hampstead Hill Gardens, one of those circuitous side-roads designed to fit buildings into an existing road network and acting as a short-cut to nowhere. The front is Victorian Gothic, in creeper-strangled red brick, with a pointed, many-faceted, slate-tiled roof which would have served well in Gormenghast, of which there was more than a touch about Studio House. Down below, on a level with the basement windows, was a small front garden separated from the main road by a knee-high wall from which the railings had been removed during the war. Here William's green-fingered wife, Hetta, had made a verdant brief oasis of multi-coloured shrubbery: japonica, Japanese tree peony, clematis, forsythia, almond blossom, euphorbia, a rustic arch of rambling roses, all manner of bulbs, and a dwarf oak cut like a mushroom, a summer parasol for a marmalade cat. There reposed the ashes of a former gardener.

There was a much larger garden at the rear, adequate for a garden party with a marquee, and here in good weather family and friends would eat al fresco while children played on the antique swing beneath the black poplar or tumbled in Hetta's hammock amid laburnum and laurel. Here, too, on sunny days, William would sit and read, stripped to the waist: he loved the open air. Early on (they had bought the house in 1960), Hetta had made a shallow, kidney-shaped pond among the flags and species iris at the back of the lawn, and here, to William's delight, toads came each year to spawn.

The back of the house loomed up sheer, reminiscent of the superstructure of an ocean liner, looking as if it might well be afloat. This was the part occupied by the Empsons, the whole front being let out as rooms and flats under Hetta's management, a task which she undertook dutifully and with loathing: 'I'll die if I ever have to see another plumber' – or words to that effect. Letting was a necessary business as the Empsons were never rich and there had been sons to raise and the house to pay for. The tenants were carefully chosen; they needed to be hardy, resourceful, likeable and interesting, as indeed they mostly were. At the top, virtually in the roof, there was Peter Cadogan, left-wing humanist and champion of lost causes; a typographer, a batik artist and a dress designer, inter alia, occupied the middle floors; and in the basement there lived the late and much lamented Barry Carman, Australian-born author and writer of radio documentaries, a great traveller (fellow of the Royal Geographical Society), the most entertaining raconteur I have ever met, and a very close friend of the Empsons for a great many years. But the geniality, the warmth of the Empsons, Hetta and William, and their sons, made them a focus for friendship and it was scarcely possible to live as their tenant, as I did, without being drawn into this extended family circle, sharing their wonderful hospitality, their lack of reserve, their fullness of living.

Hetta and William complemented one another in a most remarkable manner: fire and water were they both, unpredictable, relentlessly enthusiastic, still and concentrated, effecting slow, planned labours, lashing into flame. Hetta is an accomplished and talented goldsmith and they shared an interest in the graphic arts, yet essentially they inhabited different planets. William was the centre of Hetta's life, but William's centre was his own mind, a place apart to which he had constant resort and where he was to some extent imprisoned. He was emotionally reserved. That they loved one another deeply is beyond question, yet explicit demonstrations of affection were rare. But there was as much love in their breakfast bickerings (better than a sitcom) as in any amount of turtle-dovery.

The domestic and social centre of their home was the long room one entered through a porch, directly from the street. At one end there was an open kitchen, looking out on the garden at eye-level, and here Hetta would cook delicious dinners and William his horrible soup. The main body of the room was dominated by a large rectangular table which was the communal 'hearth' and served for everything. Hetta presided at the top end, nearest the kitchen, and William had his reserved place on the side at her left. Breakfasting here in the middle of the room he could take full advantage of the daylight from a row of high windows behind him, and a single turn would enable him to welcome a visitor. 'Ah, you have made your way,' he would say, before launching into his perspective of some news item which had interested him, or thrusting a jammy *Times* at me with 'I do wish you would finish off the crossword.' (This was something he felt it was necessary to get done with before more serious matters could be broached.) His place would be littered with freshly opened correspondence, books and periodicals, among which condiments, sugar, chutneys and tea hid themselves and dispersed their riches.

Hetta and William rarely dined alone, even if there were no family at home. William would sparkle with good humour as the table-talk flowed and arguments raged over matters as diverse as papal pronouncements and the micturition of titmice. Occasionally there would be *Huo Kuo* (roughly pronounced 'hogwar' = fire-pot), which William particularly enjoyed. This would be a very special occasion and would take place in the vast studio directly above the kitchen and living room. It involved a special copper cook-pot which Hetta had brought back from China: there was a central chimney for charcoal, surrounded by an annular bowl to be filled with seasoned water and some pieces of cabbage. This was placed in the centre of a round table and every guest was supplied with a plateful of raw lamb and liver cut into small pieces. When the liquor was boiling you skewered a piece of meat and immersed it until it was cooked, transferred it to your rice bowl and ate it. Then, when everyone had consumed all their meat, the liquor was served as a soup in the now empty rice bowls.

Unless the dinner were a very special affair, and sometimes even then, William would retire from the gathering shortly after dessert. The length of his attendance at table was a measure of his interest in the company and their conversation; he couldn't bear gossip or dullness and seemed particularly sensitive to a potential outbreak of one or the other. He delighted in active minds, his own being perpetually at work. He thought critically, in the positive sense, all the time. I never once heard him refer to anything that had been reported without illuminating some deeper or unconsidered significance, or demonstrating some stupidity. He was obsessed with thought, and this excluded him from much genial society. By the time I met him the friends of his youth were mostly dead and had proved irreplaceable. He shared Hetta's friends, but though everyone loved William, he had, apart from his family, no great friends.

But he had no time for sentimentality and never complained of loneliness. He was often at great pains to be alone, particularly if he wanted a quiet drink in a pub. He felt himself hounded by bores (and Hampstead has several in the Olympic class) and would seek obscure anonymous haunts, a sequestered backyard, in which to take his pint and papers. I once found him sitting thus in the pouring rain, preferring a wetting to an ear-bending. If he was not visiting libraries, he would spend most of the day in his study bashing at his old Remington; it could be heard still rattling away at three in the morning. His work was his life. He had few recreational interests apart from reading, which he did constantly. He hated noise, displayed no great fondness for music, scarcely ever listened to the radio, and despised television. He distrusted the 'hot' media, knowing they were a con in a way the printed word could never be, for the print stood there to be answered while television led the eye and deceived the mind; television productions of Shakespeare diverted people from the text and delivered them into the hands of a director. Any semi-fictionalised historical documentary was equally suspect as it led to a confusion between known fact and conjecture. He stopped me reading Burgess's reconstructed life of Shakespeare for that very reason.

For light reading he enjoyed pre and early postwar detective thrillers: his main joy was Rex Stout, whose books he would read again and again, until Nero Wolf assumed near reality and figured as a quotable authority in his conversation. All these paperbacks (and many a hardback) suffered a singular fate in his hands, and if you loaned him a book it would be sure to catch the plague: he covered the endpapers, flyleaves, all available space, with trigonometric algebra. It turned out to be a besetting problem from a degree-level rider-book that he used as a diversion, or a kind of patience, a test of his mental fitness. The morning after a serious gastric operation he applied this test and showed me the ten sheets of working with some pride in his recovery. 'I didn't trust myself to try the crossword,' he said. 'They might have put in a difficult one to fool me.'

He would write in the books he read, and edit them, marking them up with 'sordid style' in the margin. Any critical work he found worthy of attention he did to death with scribbles. If he lacked a slip (or the legendary breakfast kipper-bone) he would fold the page. The spine would soon go, folded back for convenient reading in bed. The pages were littered with crumbs and jam, stained with eggs and wine, loosed from their stitchings. The copy of Greg's *Doctor Faustus*, borrowed from the London Library, was returned in such bad condition that he was forced to buy a new one. Keeping him supplied with library books while he was in hospital was not easy: I would take six at a time and on a good day he would only reject four. Biographies were best. Yet there were many books and writers he greatly admired: C.V. Wedgwood's *William the Silent*, Garrett Mattingly's *The Defeat of the Spanish Armada*, Koestler's *The Sleep-Walkers*, and all of Christopher Hill.

He took a strong interest in subjects which intrigued him, notably dinosaurs and stone circles (Stonehenge in particular), cosmology and scientific matters generally (he was an avid reader of the *New Scientist*); and he was keenly interested in current affairs, both at home and abroad. He greatly admired the queen, and would even cut a good picture of her from the paper. He was incensed that the pope was to meet her, maintaining that he was not a fit person to do so, since he had failed to encourage or allow artificial birth-control in Latin America. His accolade (1979) pleased him enormously: 'We must have a boasting party,' and he made a happy progress into Hampstead village, where he was greeted with cheers.

He was fond of walking in company, but was difficult to walk with in town since he would proceed with a gentle bias alternately towards or away from the wall, so that his companion was either distanced to inaudibility or in danger of being crushed or forced into the street. This may have been due to defective vision. He was also obsessed with the directness of the route, which meant crossing busy roads at most awkward places. Seeing a car numberplate XYZ 729 he would point at the car and say, 'There goes a perfect cube.' In town he always used the tube: 'People who travel by bus don't know where they're going.' And he was mischievous to be with: one might say he had an escaping tendency. I was once drafted to accompany him to the Poetry Society at Earl's Court, where he was to give a reading (Hetta was his normal 'bear-leader' – his term – but she was otherwise engaged). He wanted first to visit an exhibition of William Blake's drawings at the National Gallery, so we set out early. I had barely begun to look at a picture when his inquisitive nose carried him off; after ten minutes' anxious search (I was carrying all his poems), I eventually located him engrossed in a Boudin on the other side of the building. 'Over-esteemed, I feel,' he muttered, as if I had been constantly at his side. Hetta has similar tales of his walking off in the African bush.

In the spring and early summer, the garden pond provided him with much entertainment. I would get a phone-call on a blustery March afternoon: 'Jones, the toads will be coming, we must clean out the pond.' The 'we' here was purely diplomatic. I would don my wellies, gather up bucket and shovel, and we would trudge out into the wind like Lear and Fool. The pond would contain a foot of black sludge and decomposing autumn leaves. 'Don't stir it up, it will make a vile smell,' he cautioned, but of course I did, and the first noseful of hydrogen sulphide would send him back to the house with a petulant 'There. You've done it.' Half an hour's hard work and the pond would be clean and bright, sparkling with fresh water and perhaps a couple of early, eager male toads crouching among the stone ruins I had laid at the bottom. Then he would come out, sensing it was ready, and would be delighted: 'You've done very well. You must have a drink.'

The great clumsy females, two or three, each carrying her consort, would straggle in about the first week of April and then there was great excitement and much argument about where they came from and what route they took. The pond would by now be highly popu-lated, and turbulent with activity as the many supernumerary males tried their best to dislodge the incumbent mates, never successfully. They played for all the world like children in a swimming-pool and they were not at all shy of human visitors. If you placed two fingers in the water, one of the boys would mistake them for a female and embrace them tightly, and they would cling on fearlessly while you lifted them out of the water. But, cavorting quite elegantly in their first element, they really did seem to enjoy themselves enormously. Then the real action got underway and the females would take long spawning 'flights' from one end of the pond to the other, discharging the endless twin filaments, spiralled with black dots. Within a few days the now befouled and highly refractive waters were abandoned, except for some forlorn males who perhaps still lived in hope.

When the tadpoles developed William would find new zest. There was a slow leak in the pond, so the water had to be topped up each day, which William mainly attended to. He would hold the end of the hosepipe high in the air and shake it so that the water fell in violent cascades, much of it over himself: 'The tap-water is not good for them, we must get plenty of oxygen into it.' And as the myriad black blobs grew, he began to worry about their food supply. Stealing a skewer from Hetta's rotisserie, he spiked a cork and pushed it to the far end; then he attached some raw liver and floated it in the pond, very pleased with the invention and tickled by his domestic crime. The beasts enjoyed the liver, clustering upon it like gouts of blackcurrant jam, and waxed very fat. As they showed signs of transformation, William became worried about how they could possibly mount the steep sides of the pond. I could foresee no difficulty, but he went to the trouble of arranging a small plank, extending from the water at a gentle angle, as a 'royal road' for them. I don't know if he envisaged a procession of miniature toads hopping their way to freedom, but if so he was disappointed. The entire population was consumed by a pair of mallards, which must have landed one morning and dined at their leisure, and one of the birds knocked on my window on a later morning, as if asking for more. In the years that followed we covered the pond with a net and managed to populate the lawn with so many tiny toads that it was impossible to cut the grass.

He drank freely, sometimes a great deal, even to the point of unsteadiness, but he was no lush. He used alcohol as an essential concomitant to his work, especially when beginning a piece. Having done all the necessary reading and mentally formulated his thesis, he would deliberately make himself 'tipsy' before sitting at the typewriter and dashing out the first few pages (always foolscap): he wanted to establish a flow, to get a 'gut reaction'. Then he would sleep until sober and retype from the beginning, expanding the material but striving not to disturb the line he had set up. More drink was required for each continuation, each new draft being corrected and reworked in sobriety. The labour was prodigious: the drafts accumulated by the quire (some parts of his Faustus essay were reworked as many as fifteen times). As a distraction which would not disturb his train of thought, he would sit on his bed and play patience or work on his algebra problem. Often he would read his work aloud to himself until he was satisfied it was cleared of any desk style. This was the slow and punishing process by which he constructed his lucid, mandarin-free prose.

He was kind and encouraging to young poets who sought his advice or judgment and would sometimes invite them to lunch. If Hetta were at home, the young swan would be sure of an excellent meal, but in her absence things were liable to be different. I might get a midday phone-call: 'Jones, I have a young poet coming to lunch. I'd be very glad of your support.' I would find him in the kitchen in the fawn dressing-gown which he habitually wore over his clothes as a comfort-able housecoat, busily making last-minute preparation and turning a mess in a saucepan. This was Empson soup, a dish which almost defies description. It was concocted from a Heinz tin, to which was added sundry leftovers of vegetables he had tucked away in corners of the fridge, plus the leftovers of yesterday's soup, so that one day's soup would not be noticeably different from the next. There was a large quantity of solids – butterbeans, chunks of celery, slabs of cabbage and bits of boiled egg, and much reduced and recycled gunge, but one would not have been surprised to find anything in it, even false teeth. You could not stir it, you could only turn it over. He ate it every day and Hetta maintained it was the cause of his ulcer.

The young man would arrive, spruced up and serious in the presence of greatness. 'Ah, you have made your way. Do come in. This is Jones. Now, you must have some wine and then we shall have some delicious soup.' The shy fellow would be seated at table, where, smiling affably, perhaps fazed by his reception, he would be served with wine. Then, without pause, the saucepan was fetched and William began to dollop the soup into his visitor's bowl. 'Jones won't eat this,' he says, reassur-ingly, 'but you will find it very nourishing.' 'I'm sure I shall,' says the guest with dedicated avowal, eyeing his portion nervously and perhaps gaining courage from the evident relish with which his host filled his own bowl and sat down to eat. William's lively conversation would be largely lost to me in my fascination with the poet's discharge of his ordeal. Yes, there was the wooden smile of feigned enjoyment betrayed by a fearful expression of the eyes, the horror of fresh discoveries, the shock of recognition, the awful internal query 'What is this?', the urgent need for wine. I would do my best to keep his glass topped up while William kept a firm eye on his performance. When the bowl was empty, or acceptably depleted, William would compliment him: 'Well, you have done very well. Now you must have a delicious fish-cake.'

William's own ordeals were less trivial, and he showed a stoic endurance of pain and discomfort, trying hard to maintain the pace of his work even when seriously ill. Towards the end, he was reduced to dictation, which he hated for its lack of immediate control. He must have known he was dying: certainly the preface to Using Biography, the last thing he wrote, contains intimations of death. With the final silence, the years, the marks of morbidity, fell away from him and he lay serene and quite beautiful in death: one would say seraphic but for the distasteful associations of the word. Lacking any belief in an afterlife, he had never feared death while always battling against it. He was not an irreligious man, although he despised any god who was credited with torturing his creation, and any opinion held in the name of religion. His position came close to that of Huxley in The Perennial Philosophy, a book he had studied closely, with its belief in an intelligent ground for existence. I went to see him on the eve of his last operation; Hetta was to visit him later that evening, but she had been earlier that day and maybe he thought he would not see her again. After a brief pause in our conversation, and without any display of emotion, he said: 'If I die, tell Hetta I love her very much.' Then he squeezed my hand briefly and we parted.

17 August 1989

Too Close to the Bone: Fragments of an Autobiography
Allon White

Faust, despairing of all philosophies, may yet drain a marsh or rescue some acres from the sea.

Edward Dowden

Passionate art, the drowner of dykes . . .

W.B. Yeats

I SUPPOSE THIS is my biography, my life. Fragments of memory. Perhaps even a memorial. Except that I don't believe in biographies and advise you to be especially sceptical about this one, written, one has to say, under the stress of illness and in extreme haste. Self-perception is distorted enough in the healthy, God knows what it is like in those gripped by terminal illness. Don't ask me: I'm terminally ill.

I am 36 years old, a teacher of literature, and I am dying of leukaemia. I have fought the thing for two years, I have had two bone-marrow transplants from my sister and more chemotherapy than anyone should ever have to endure. But it seems I am losing the battle now. Flaccid, diseased cells are swarming and swelling inside my bones and I have little time left. Of course I've waited too long before writing this and now it is late, probably too late. Like beginning to write at twilight with no lamp as the darkness falls. And there is no light now. There was some a little while ago and I should have written then. I also had some within me, a deep blue light the colour of iris which now and then I could see far inside my body and which glowed and gave me great comfort. But it is really dark now, my blue light has deserted me and it is getting very late.

An Old Novel

Several things still puzzle me. I will tell you about the novel and you will have to see what you think – I know that a central knot of my life and unconscious world is tied up in that abortive fiction, but I cannot quite touch it myself. Perhaps the roots of my illness are there in that early attempt to write a novel. Certainly it now seems like it, years later.

It was when I was breaking up with my first wife. One night I was in my room in Norwich (I had been teaching away from home at the university there) and, pained beyond endurance by the break-up, I suddenly began to write – in extremis, you might say (it seems it takes cataclysm to get me to write anything other than scholarly articles). I began to write fast and fluently, pages of the stuff, and though my eyes were full of tears and I normally write with pedantic care and exquisite self-consciousness, this time a coherent story sprang from the end of my pen already formed, the fictional names and the narrative all in place without my conscious mind having any idea that all this had been waiting inside me. In fact, this story, or another story of which this was a strange and displaced version, had been waiting thirty years for its expression, but I was not to discover that until much later. At the time, all I knew was this plangent ecstasy of automatic writing in which a clear, sad story poured out of me, one which I had never known was there.

Even now, as I resume the story for you, new connections come to mind, but they will have to wait a while. The plot was a double-braid: one strand was set in the 17th century during the Civil War and concerned an obsessive, self-absorbed mystic called Nicodemus; the other strand was set in the late 1950s in Sardinia and concerned a hydraulics engineer called Lucas Arnow employed by the Ford Foundation to drain the malarial swamps of the Sardinian coast as part of the worldwide effort after the last war to eradicate malaria. God knows where these names and characters came from, but they wrote themselves immediately onto the pages in front of me and I was surprised to meet them. I knew immediately that they were disso-ciated and egoistic bits of myself split by time and place, but they were also bizarre and unexpected, complete strangers to me. I didn't even know I knew about the Ford Foundation project, but evidently I did because it is perfectly accurate – I must have read it somewhere and 'forgotten'. I think this kind of forgetfulness, this false forgetful-ness where things are lost but not destroyed, hidden but perhaps not for ever, is what this unconventional biography means by 'memory'. Not so much memories as things forgotten and found again. Remembrance.

Anyway, Nicodemus, my 17th-century religious fanatic, was making his way from the Midlands to the Fens – to Ely, in fact, because he had a vision that the fenland marshes were the place of salvation. He had concocted a bizarre and idiosyncratic theology, rather like the wonderful miller in *The Cheese and the Worms*, but in his case it was marshland, and particularly the reeds, which played the central part. The reed is one of the symbols of the Passion, for, on the Cross, Christ had been tendered a vinegar-soaked sponge on the end of a reed. The reed also represents the Just, who dwell on the banks of the waters of Grace. And it represents the multitude of the lowly faithful ('Can the rush grow up without mire? Can the flag grow without water?'). The Evangelists wrote with reeds upon papyrus, another kind of reed bearing the words of God. And the Red Sea (actually Yam Suph, the Reed Sea) had parted to lead the way to the Promised Land. From these and other scraps of insignificant material Nicodemus had stitched together his passionate, crazy faith, and it was now leading him on a pilgrimage, amid the carnage of the Civil War, to Ely and the Great Fens.

His half of the story was thoroughly picaresque. It was farcical – a bit of a carnival I would say now, but I hadn't read about Bakhtin and the carnivalesque in those days (it was 1977). Nicodemus gradually accumulated a motley gang of misfits and outcasts on his slow pilgrimage, including Widow Joan, a vast and wonderful creation, who, in one episode, shows her contempt for a local vicar (who has objected to their overnight stay in his parish) by baptising a huge, squealing pig in the village pond. I forget the other details of this 17th-century part of the plot, which essentially creaked and reeled from one improbable village adventure to another until Nicodemus, having lost all his friends and hangers-on, arrives alone at the Great Fen just outside Ely.

It is evening. Two things have happened which Nicodemus could not have known, and I am unsure whether they could have happened together historically, but they appeared together as the nemesis of his life in the novel. What he beholds when he at last gazes out over the marshland, the goal of months of wandering and years of fervent, private communion, is not the wilderness of the sacred marsh but a drainage channel straight as the arrow of God, leading to the horizon and surrounded by regular fields, ditches, dykes and every sign of new agriculture and hydraulic engineering. A Dutch landscape, in effect, humanised, orderly, patiently raised from the fenland broads by the Dutch engineer Vermeyden and now turning the lost medieval world of the fowlers and fishermen into farmland.

The other thing which Nicodemus could not know about was the iconoclastic destruction of the Lady Chapel in Ely Cathedral, the figures of the saints and the Evangelists and the Virgin having been smashed and broken and hurled into the waters of the fen years before. But with the draining of the fen, the lowering of the waters and the shrinking of the peat beds, on that particular summer evening as Nicodemus falls to his knees at the collapse of his dream, the evening sunlight reveals the broken form of a cathedral statue nearby, half-submerged in the mud of a reed-ditch. Nicodemus does not recognise it for a statue, of course, ripped out from the cathedral. He sees only the figure of Christ, and with this impoverished illusion (the Christ has only one arm and one eye, but Nicodemus does not notice this in his joy) the homely secular landscape of the new engineering is plunged back into a spurious medieval enchantment. It is a moment of treacherous epiphany, at once plangent and ridiculous, returning the world briefly to the darkening, pathless wastelands of Nicodemus's curious vision.

Set over against this medieval and extraordinary mystic at the threshold of the New World, with its technical domination of the hidden places of the earth, there was the other half of the novel. This half concerned a modern Vermeyden figure, the modern hydraulics engineer Lucas Arnow working in Sardinia. I have never been to Sardinia. Come to that, it is only since my leukaemia began that I have developed a passionate interest in the 17th century. So I was breaking the first and elementary rule of the novelist – write about what you have experienced and know about. But then, someone inside me did know this strange fiction, with its names and settings and narratives. It came from my pen with thoughtless fluency. I felt a mere scribe, a copyist.

The second half of this novel which I scribbled out all through the night those years ago in Norwich has a horrid prescience about it now which hurts me to even think about. Lucas Arnow dies of the malaria which he has come to eradicate. He brings the cure to the local people but dies of the disease in the process. Now malaria isn't leukaemia, but the more I begin to unravel this cathartic fiction of mine from the past, the more connections I feel and understand even if it is too late now. Malaria, leukaemia. My novelistic descriptions of Arnow's physical suffering were entirely fanciful at that time, purely imaginary. But since then I have lived through them all. And now, like him, I am dying of a terrible disease. But it is too late now, of course. Too late altogether.

Lucas Arnow is a professional engineer draining the *stagni*, or foetid coastal marshes in which the malarial mosquitoes breed. For many years I have treasured a quotation from Walter Benjamin which may have helped spawn the character of Arnow or, more likely, contributed something further to a figure already compounded of many memories and unconscious sources: 'The slightest carelessness in the digging of a ditch or the buttressing of a dam, the least bit of negligence or selfish behaviour on the part of an individual or group of men in the maintenance of the common hydraulic wealth, becomes, under unusual circumstances, the source of social evils and far-reaching social calamity. Consequently a life-giving river requires on pain of death a close and permanent solidarity.' Lucas Arnow, never having heard of Walter Benjamin, is nevertheless on the side of the common hydraulic wealth. A man of modest and sincere social conscience, a man of *techné*, of the scientific rationalism and practical reason which were so much a part of 1950s optimism and postwar expansion, he works for the common good and with a revulsion against the evils of the marshland – its disease, its mire, its stagnant dangers. He believes strongly in clearing up mess. The foetid pools and malarial reedbeds of the marsh represent, for him, all that civilisation has had to struggle against in order to emerge from the primeval slime. It was the humble digger of irrigation channels, the builders of bridges and dams, who first released mankind from inundation, flood and chaos, not Noah.

Human life only really began to flourish in the deltas and swamps of the Nile, the Tigris and Euphrates, in Kaneh, in the Holy Land of Cane and Tall Grasses when the mud and filth of the yearly floods were tamed with the measuring rod and the simple shovel. Nothing had really changed, according to Arnow's way of thinking. It was still the sewers and ditches, the reservoirs, waterpipes and dams connected and hidden in one vast, intricate network beneath the earth, which held civilisation safe from chaos and disease: the common hydraulic wealth.

I must confess that there was little more to Lucas Arnow than this, and he appears a little small and dry when set beside the fanaticism and inner visionary power of Nicodemus. When I think of Lucas Arnow I see a worthy and anxious man with little humour and even less authority. Even now, by quoting Benjamin and so forth above, I have endowed him with more passion and cosmic vision than he had in the original fiction 11 years ago. Not a particularly attractive person to sustain half a novel – there is something rather abstract and programmatic about him. Indeed, in retrospect, I am astonished at the political symmetry and opposition of these two men, one at the beginning and one at the end (?) of the great arch of bourgeois science and technical control of the world. And what a gulf of time and space I put between Nicodemus the visionary anarchist and Lucas Arnow the progressive rationalist. Three centuries of history and half the length of Europe. This was not a consciously planned or controlled decision, and if I can discover now the links and distance between the two halves of this schizoid fiction then I think I shall have learned something important. Certainly, at the time, the two halves of the novel would not coalesce. They remained obdurately separate and opposed. It was the failure to integrate the two stories satisfactorily into one fiction which eventually prevented me from finishing it. Written in such rhapsodic haste, it just stayed as it was, resistant to any attempt at revision.

Its incompleteness has haunted me ever since. Perhaps now, as I go on, I shall be able to finish with it. Finally.

What obsessed me at the time of writing, however, was not Arnow's mind but his death alone. Very little else got sketched in. I called the unfinished novel 'Gifts' and it began with Lucas receiving one of the workmen from the marsh into his office. The workman had discovered the rare plant *Erba Sardoa*, the Sardinian herb which, when administered as a poison, produces a horrible rictus upon the face of the victim who is convulsed with 'sardonic' laughter. This 'gift' (in German, this also means *poison*) which opens the novel is a portent of Lucas's end. For he is poisoned, not so much by the malarial swamp, nor even by the interminable delays of machinery and parts which in 1950s Sardinia mimic the stagnation and decay of the marsh itself – though both these natural and institutional evils drain his strength and will. It is really within himself that the poison develops. His entirely laudable but quite limited petit-bourgeois sense of purpose and identity are no match for the miasmic forces welling up inside him. It is precisely the *absence* of magical vision and rage within him, or at least their deep and irrecoverable repression, which cankers his soul. His dykes and dams hold back more than the insidious destructive power of nature:

> Soon, soon, through dykes of our content
> The crumpling flood will force a rent
> and, taller than a tree,
> Hold sudden death before our eyes
> Whose river dreams long hid the size
> And vigours of the sea.
>
> Auden, 'A Summer Night'

Lucas's death, which terminates his half of the story and which is paralleled by Nicodemus's epiphany on the margin of the Great Fen, was the most intensely wrought part of the novel. Lucas had been waiting all day for a vital piece of hydraulic equipment (a Bernoulli meter) to arrive from Rome. He is suffering a bad malarial attack, and throughout the long sultry day he drifts in and out of full consciousness, through hallucination, memory and daydream. He becomes superstitiously convinced that his own survival is bound up with the arrival of the Bernoulli meter from Rome. Time and again he asks about it. Towards nightfall he becomes more feverish and ill, and the friend who has been by his bedside in his villa, and his housekeeper, decide that he must be ferried across the bay to the doctor in Muravera (his villa is on a promontory across from the small town, close to the edge of the marsh but also looking out over the sea). The Bernoulli meter has not arrived. As darkness comes, he is carried out to the small fishing boat which also doubles as a local ferry and the boat sets out on the short journey across the bay to the town. Lucas dies before the boat has got halfway across. Strangely, I felt his death in metaphors of communication, a language too modern for Lucas, but that is how it came out:

> Lucas was slumped half sitting and half lying in the bottom of the boat. It was warm even out here on the sea. The sky was cloudy and the air thick as if miasmic fingers of bad air had floated out from the marshes onto the surface of the sea in lethargic pursuit of the small boat. Lucas was on his left side with his knees drawn up tight and his hands pushed down between his thighs. A grey blanket was pulled up over his shoulder. He shook his head to clear it and opened his eyes once to look towards the lights of the town. It was useless. His thoughts drifted again. His head began to fill with noises even though the boat was sliding almost silently through the water with only little waveslaps clapping against the bow now and then.
>
> So this was dying. Nothing peaceful about it. Lucas struggled to stay in contact with the boat and the sky and the water but there was that terrible noise. What was it, that crackle and interference which made everything so far away now. Lucas moved his head from side

to side very slowly trying to clear his head filled with shapeless and indistinct noises. It was becoming so noisy, so busy. Like a city rush hour. So very noisy and busy. Then there was a final subsidence of all clarity and sharpness into a sea of unfathomable sounds, a voice receding just beyond intelligibility like a radio station fading away in the night. And it was getting louder. Lucas groaned in panic. Something seemed to split and slither deep within his belly. It's not silent not silent at all but loud. There was a rush of pure sound through the air like a wind becoming louder and louder crowding out and pushing through him and over him. A gleeful confusion of bugs and babble tumbled and fell upon him like insects swarming in the darkness. Mosquitoes came, filling up his nose and his mouth until at last his mouth, stuffed with the deafening noises, stiffened into a final rictus of defeat.

But Lucas does hear something just before he dies. Across the empty water of the bay a young boy and his father are fishing from a boat anchored near the shore. The young boy is trailing a line from the stern of the small boat and their voices carry clearly across the surface of the waters. As Lucas dies, there is a sudden disturbance and a splash which Lucas hears like an echo from far off. The last thing that Lucas hears, clearly now, with a preternatural clarity, is the excited voice of the young boy in the darkness. 'Look Papa. Look. Look. A fish. I've caught a fish.'

The Village

Cranfield, the Bedfordshire village in which I was born and grew up, is an unappealing place. From very early on I knew I disliked it and wanted to get out. Essentially, it is a nondescript straggle of houses sandwiched uncomfortably between the vast London Valley Brickyard in the Marston Valley on one side, with its hundreds of sulphurous chimneys, and the airfield on the other side, a leftover from the Second World War which has since become a college of aeronautics.

When I was a boy, the village reeked of sulphur for much of the year, whenever the wind blew up the valley from the brickworks chimneys. The sulphur withered the leaf on the trees, especially the elms, and it gave me chronic catarrh. I have a poor sense of smell and blame it on the brickworks. What perfunctory nasal education I received as a child came from my visits to my aunt in Grimsby – at least there the indescribably noxious stink of the Humberside Cod Liver Oil factory, one whiff of which made me vomit, formed something of a counterpoint with the smell of sulphur. In consequence, my olfactory discrimination as an adult splits the whole wonderful subtle world of scents and smells into the codliverish or the sulphurous: reading Proust for the first time I wept in envy and disbelief.

Despite my innate dislike of Cranfield, it is, like my leukaemia, in my bones. It is also, in the most oblique and obdurate way, in my novel, though at first glance the village could not seem further removed from the 17th-century Fens and 1950s Sardinia. But weaving backwards and forwards between childhood memory and recollections of the unfinished fiction, under the duress of my present illness with its closeness of death, I unearth, here and there, bits of understanding and connectedness. It gives me a luxurious sense of indulgent self-archaeology. It also helps to keep me alive, like refusing to die because I haven't heard the end of the story. My Scheherezade.

Cranfield is geographically not the South, nor the Midlands, nor East Anglia – it sits uncomfortably on a small plateau between the three areas, pulled in all directions and blandly unsure of its identity. It is not horribly ugly, which would at least give it a kind of unlovely value. It is indeterminate and forgettable, straggly and ad hoc, like so many of the towns and villages which just fail to be part of the gritty Midlands and also fail to be part of the desolate beauty of East

Anglia. Corby, Northampton, Leicester, Kettering – they all appear part of this grey and undistinguished part of the country, and they all give me the same desperate feeling as Cranfield.

There is something lopsided and one-dimensional about the village, caused by the perimeter fence of the airfield which runs its full length and cuts off its northern side. The airfield was built in 1937 and covered Perryfield, Leanfield and Stillipers, a large area which had once been the common land of the village. Undoubtedly the MoD impoverished and diminished the village with its barbed-wire perimeter far more effectively than the centuries of enclosure had managed to do. Naturally the airfield required the flat land for runways and so took most of the small plateau on which the village is built. The result is that Cranfield feels as if it has been shouldered to the very edge of the plateau and is about to slither down Marston Hill into the valley.

So: to the north the barbed-wire perimeter fence of the airfield; to the south the steep slope of the valley ending in the brickworks. There was nowhere to walk to any more. If now you want to wander around, you are forced to parade up the High Street and back, past the numerous new little housing estates which have filled in the spaces where the farms used to be along the village main street: Moat farm, Glebe farm, Washingleys Manor, Orchard Way, Walkhouse. And of course the Old Rectory, a splendid Edwardian monstrosity the decaying and empty rooms of which I used to explore as a boy, has now become a very smart little estate of 'neo-Georgian' houses over-looking the church. The builders did leave the cedar tree which used to stand on the rectory lawn, but it has to be said that it has lost its lordly splendour and seems a trifle embarrassed now, surrounded by a dozen neat neo-Georgian family homes. Too grand and expansive for its surroundings, the cedar is humiliated by its size, an arboreal Gulliver towering above the Lilliputian privet and suburban forsythia.

When I was a young boy, however, this rather spiritless village had one wonderful compensation. Have you noticed that children, wherever they can, make their own secret pathways and tracks around their neighbourhood by following ditches and waterways, often inaccessible to adults. Waterpipes with nasty spiked collars at each end, stretched across rivers, often prove more popular crossing points for children, especially gangs of young boys, than the bridge down the road. Ditches, streams, ponds and pools, culverts under the dual-carriageway or the railway line – these places form a semi-secret network of tracks, hiding-places and dens which adults half-notice but never see in the way children do.

Cranfield had a rich hinterland of such waterways, particularly old moats and ponds, running through fields and back gardens the whole length of the village. They were alternative, secret byways for the children of the village. Adults rarely strayed there, yet especially during the school holidays the hedges and ponds and ditches were alive with children. This was my world. I seem to have spent much of my childhood playing around these places, trekking from one to the other, building secret camps in the willows, constructing dams and bridges, catching newts, tadpoles and sticklebacks, venturing out onto the ice in winter. One time we built a raft from old oil-drums, and, too afraid to sail on it ourselves, we tethered one of David Luck's hapless chickens to its deck and sent it on a squawking unhappy journey downstream. Another time we constructed an elaborate camp on a small island in the middle of a pond with a rope drawbridge worked by discarded bell-ropes from the church.

I only learned recently that Cranfield has a unique local history in respect of the moats and ditches which were strung along its length. There were dozens of them and the local archivist remarks in his history of the village that 'numerous ponds have long been a common feature of the Cranfield landscape.' In addition to the many natural ponds there are the curious Cranfield moats dating from the 12th and 13th centuries. Evidently most of the farmsteads in the parish were moated or rebuilt within their moats as late as the 19th century and show a remarkable historical continuity from medieval times. Wood End, Moat farm, East End farm, Boxhedge House, Eyreswood farm, Broad Green farm, Perry Hill farm – all had moats, and some of these remained up to a few years ago. The Parish Survey records in 1722 the 'Messuage in Cranfield built by Dr William Aspin, with the moat round it and groves of trees adjoining'. There is no clear explanation for the existence or indeed the survival of these moats, since no other local parishes appear to have them. Moat farm was still completely encircled with water when I was a boy, and almost every old house in the village had a pond or part of a moat somewhere nearby. As children, we could make our way clear from one end of the village to the other by trailing from one pond to another, and they were often connected up with ditches and drainage channels. Our own house, dating from the 1800s, had a curious bridge built into one side-wall, spanning a marshy piece of land, probably too boggy to support the foundations.

It is only now and in the light of my old novel that I see how my childhood imagination was formed in close and unconscious connection with the odd, moated history of my village.

Its abandoned moats and watercourses were a secret domain which filled my days. Concealed by copses of willow, bullrushes and overgrown hedgerow, there was a magical calm and concealment about this marshy realm. There was also something melancholic and a little frightening, too, since the water never flowed. All these ponds and moats were green and stagnant, as still as death. They had long since clogged with weed and flotsam, the drainage pipes smashed and the interconnecting ditch dammed up here and there with mud and undergrowth. And the ponds were a common dumping-ground for village refuse: piles of old bricks, rusting bicycles, even one or two old cars. Whatever their original purpose, as the years went by these moats and ponds were filled in and built over. So in one sense it is clear that Nicodemus, on his slow pilgrimage from the Midlands to the Fens, was in search not only of God and the reeds, but of my own vanished childhood.

As time went on these ponds and pools which so fascinated me as a boy disappeared one by one. The moat system which had lasted from medieval times to the 1950s was buried in less than ten years, first under rubble and landfill, then under new housing and tarmac. Each summer holiday there were fewer and fewer ponds and pools. I felt very sorry for the frogs and the newts crushed beneath the tons of broken brick and earth. These trivial deaths really bothered me. Only a few years ago I wrote a strange and not very good poem about a poor frog, again, at the time, unaware of the origins of my concern. God how the gloomy enchantment of those stagnant places held me in thrall. Yet it was only four years ago, at the age of 32, that I began to learn *why* these marshy moats and stygian pools have exerted such an exorbitant grip upon my unconscious throughout my life.

I came to learn that the most important single event of my childhood was the death of my young sister, Carol. Without the least suspicion, I had lived, worked and loved in the shadow of her death. Its hold on me had been as complete as it was unsuspected. Certainly, when I wrote the novel my drowned sister never entered my head. But all those marshes and swamps, the Great Fen and the Sardinian *stagni*, Nicodemus saved and Lucas Arnow dead, how clearly now they seem displacements of my childhood mourning and terror, my obsessive lingering at the pool's edge summer and winter all the years of my growing-up. But I did not know it then, I thought it was about other things – which it also was, as I shall describe in due course. But I know that the death of my sister Carol was the secret kernel to my marshland fiction.

For it was in one of these village ponds that Carol drowned. It was 1956, and I was five years old. Carol and her twin sister Debbie were three. It was summertime and very hot. Carol simply wandered off down the overgrown garden and squeezed through a hole in the hedge, disappearing within seconds. Her body was recovered the next day when they dragged the pond. The pond had been covered in Canadian pond weed from edge to edge and looked just like a beautifully smooth lawn. She probably walked, or ran, straight into it, thinking it was a garden.

A Screen Memory

I was playing on the back lawn. It was a really hot July afternoon and I was five years old. There was a small sand heap on one corner of the grass not far from the garden swing and the old plum tree. I was a bit bored and listless. I had a white sunhat on and I was idly shovelling sand with a small tin seaside spade, red with a wooden handle. Carol was a bit further down the lawn away from the house. Gradually she began to wander down the garden further and further away from the house and away from me. I knew that she shouldn't go that far down the lawn, and I knew that she would get into trouble, but I didn't say anything. I just watched without speaking, a small boy motionless and silent, no longer digging, but watching his little sister waddling off down the garden into the long grass. I watched until she had disappeared. I knew that she was doing something bad and that she might be hurt or become lost. But I stayed quite still and silent, calling neither to my mother nor to Carol. This memory, carrying with it the full burden of guilt for my sister's death, I experienced with unbearable clarity. I was responsible. I could have stopped her. I knew she was going to lose herself in the perilous forbidden places at the bottom of the garden, but I said nothing. I wanted her dead. I hated her. So I stood silently in the sunshine, five years old, making one or two idle marks on the sand with my seaside spade, watching her go.

This memory, etched into my mind with the clarity of total recall, is false. I was not in the garden at the time when she wandered off. According to my mother, I was elsewhere, playing with a friend in his garden. I couldn't have seen her go. It was impossible. I was not there.

The Realm of Estrangement

Since I contracted leukaemia my father and I have been much closer. There is no chance now of being unfinished with one another. He has held me to him. He cares for me. And after a fashion, we talk to one another about important things. Believe me, it hasn't always been like that. Like so many of my friends, I have spent most of my life feeling estranged from my parents in some vague and indefinite way. And the old clichés about lack of communication and parents just not understanding and children not caring all seemed justified. Up until my illness I felt more and more alarmed that as my parents got older they would die before we had said how much we cared for each other, before we forgave each other. I wanted family closeness and for us all to talk openly to each other. Of course it never quite entered my head that it was not my parents who would die, but me.

It is impossible to say whether my illness is connected with the death of my sister all those years ago. Perhaps, as I sometimes think, it is pure biological malignancy quite unrelated to my spiritual life, a random incident at the level of genetic material and swarming cells as far removed from my unconscious and my history as some galaxy remote in the heavens. Yet the prescience of my fiction disturbs me. Malaria. Leukaemia. Disease of the blood. A life which, at every crisis, turned broodingly to images of shady ponds and stagnant waters, death by drowning. I remember one afternoon not too long after Carol's death when I was wandering aimlessly around the old greenhouse at the bottom of the garden. Again it was a hot summer's day. At the back of the greenhouse there was a waterbutt filled to the brim. I could only just see over the edge. Waterlilies floated silently on the warm still water. It was preternaturally quiet, the day held in suspension by the heat and stillness. I was quite alone and I stood on tiptoe grasping the edge of the rusted butt staring at the water's reflective surface of thick green liquid. Movement came only from one or two mayflies skating back and forth between the lilies. I seem to be held there for ever, even now, peering into the depths of the water, trying to get down beneath the surface, among the coiled stems of the lilies and the shoals of tiny white wireworms wriggling and disappearing into the green depths.

In the early days of my leukaemia two years ago I was convinced that this death wish, this identification with my drowned sister, was responsible for my illness. Three things, tangled up together but separate, seemed involved. The first was identification: inside me somewhere Carol actually constituted a part of my being, she was me. Not as a part of my personality, but as something much more physical, a hysterical body, a violence which terrifies me even when expressed as mere words here on the page. I can hardly begin to approach this level of my being: Here Be Monsters. Nothing can be held steady enough for language in this place, things flicker and slide, shapes loom and melt away. There is none of that elegiac lyricism of drowning and summer afternoons here – gentle kaddish for the dead. Here it burns and hurts. It is violent, spasmodic, monstrous. There is no wholeness. I am not *myself* here. I can bear to stay here no longer.

But there is a second thing, a second way in which Carol's death is inside me – less exorbitant, a little more approachable, perhaps. I took upon myself, at the age of five, complete and sole responsibility for her death. It hardly matters that in fact so did everyone else in the family, each one of us taking up the burden alone, never dreaming that we had all done the same. Nor did it matter that I didn't 'understand' death at that age. I understood enough to know that a terrible crime had taken place. There were policemen standing awkwardly in the kitchen, anguished tears from my mother carried sobbing round to Grandma's house, whispers, knots of people gathered outside the house, groups of men from the village coming and going throughout the day late into the night. How a child takes on the guilt of death and separation I don't know, but before the body had been found something inside me had already decided that I was responsible for the crime, that I had a dreadful guilty secret that I would henceforth carry with me unknown to myself for thirty years. And like the scene of seduction in Freud, the truth or falsehood of the matter was utterly irrelevant.

The third element in Carol's death was the childhood puzzle of death itself and my unresolved mourning for her sudden, permanent disappearance. I did not attend the funeral and until last year she remained somehow unburied for me. I could not 'put her away', too many unfinished and importuning emotions remained.

The fact of my leukaemia intervened across all this with an extra-ordinary new possibility of resolution. After some months of acute illness it became clear that the only thing which might save my life was a bone-marrow transplant. This still remains the major hope of cure for most people with the disease. Sadly, it requires a closely matched donor for the marrow, and by far the most important group of donors are siblings – the brothers and sisters of the victim. The chances of a sibling possessing a suitable marrow are about four to one. This means that, taken with those patients who have no siblings, less than 15 per cent of leukaemia sufferers will have a marrow-donor.

There seemed something marvellously providential when we discovered that my sister Debbie was a perfect match. A real prospect of cure was suddenly available. My sister would save me. She was delighted. She was proud and happy to be able to help fight for my life. Always somewhat distant from each other in the past, we were suddenly brought really close. We laughed at the curious fact that the transplant would change my blood-group to hers, that we should indeed become blood relatives.

Remember that Debbie was Carol's twin sister. They were identical. Gradually the symbolic force of it all began to dawn on me. The marrow of twins is perfectly matched. If, somehow, my morbid identification with Carol were in some complicated way connected to my falling ill, then how perfect that her marrow, her blood, in Debbie, should be used to save my life. It could not fail. I felt no religious redemption involved, but the poetic logic of it was over-whelming. I felt joyful and confident that such a pattern had emerged. It just seemed impossible that it would not work. Debbie would give me life just as Carol had threatened to take my life away. Carol had made me ill, Debbie would make me well again.

I passed the summer months before the transplant in a largely confident and happy mood. I set about trying to settle the account with Carol. I needed to rid myself of all that stagnant water and muddy morbidity, shake it off once and for all. I needed to be able to bury her at last, peacefully and permanently. I needed to let go of her. I went to a therapist and worked through all that I have told you and I slowly and carefully tried to find good ways of ending her mournful tyranny over my life.

When the twins were born, my father had planted two lovely juniper trees either side of the path in the garden. Tiny saplings, they had been intended to grow with the twins as they grew up. When Carol died, either my father deliberately dug up one of the trees or it died: in any case, only one tree was left, Debbie's tree, after Carol's death. It remained on the left-hand side of the pathway guarding the way down to the bottom of the garden and the orchard. In one of my therapeutic sessions I had a clear and purposeful vision of Debbie's tree, now very tall and straight, over thirty years old, and I knew that it symbolised life and hope for me. I also knew that I should replant Carol's tree, a new tree in the position of the old one, and that this, too, would give me life and strength. I also felt that, at last, I should be able to symbolically bury Carol for myself in the planting of this tree. And it was not enough merely to have this vision. I must actually do it, actually buy a juniper sapling and go back to the old house and plant it as it had been.

My brother-in-law thought I was crazy, Debbie said she understood but had her doubts, my parents seemed to think that anything which helped was all right. So I planted the tree. I dug the hole in the earth, but before I put the tree into it I placed a small wooden box beneath the roots with a rose inside it and a short prayer to Carol asking her to help me. The tree looked beautiful. Shortly afterwards I went into hospital and had the transplant, which seemed a great success. For six months I grew strong again until the following May when, suddenly, I relapsed. The leukaemia was back. The transplant had failed.

Great-Grandma and the Well

The Whites have lived in Cranfield for at least two hundred years and for most of that time the men of the family were village artisans and craftsmen. The family business seems to have covered a variety of skilled trades, but for most of the 19th century the Whites were gunsmiths and watchmakers. By the turn of the century my great-grandfather was also running the local post and telegraph office as well as selling and repairing bicycles, making and repairing guns, clocks and watches. Omni-competent, occupying sprawling premises in the centre of the village, by the time of the Great War the Whites were a village institution, one step down in importance from the vicar and one step up from the local farmers and other tradesfolk. However, when my great-grandfather died, my great-grandma did a curious thing. She took all the guns and clocks which he had in his workshop, all the spare parts and bits of mechanism which he had needed for his trade, and she threw them down the well in the back yard. From that moment on, the family gunsmithing and watchmending were at an end.

It gives me a most peculiar feeling to imagine that moment when the guns and clocks, pendulums, cogs, and tiny fragments of mechanism, were hurled into the well. They must all have rusted to nothing by now deep beneath the back garden. My father says that great-grandma did it because she was afraid of the guns in the house, but that doesn't account for the clocks and the bits and pieces. She certainly didn't want her son following his father's trade, that's for sure. From that time on, the post office and a heavier kind of engineering – agricultural vehicles and such – became the mainstay of the family.

Indeed, the skills and abilities of the Whites closely followed the technical and engineering developments of the century: from guns and clocks to bicycles and early farm machinery in my great-grandfather's time, through to lorries and finally cars in my father's time. By the time I was born 'Allon White & Son' had been moving quietly with – or just behind – the times since before the First World War and was a small but modestly successful village garage. A quiet local business, it was as ready to mend bicycle punctures and pull farm tractors out of ditches as it was to sell Morris cars, repair lorries and taxi Mrs Malsher to hospital on the third Thursday of every month. The post office and the garage were run side by side. Between the wars Great-Aunt Tess used to run the village telephone switchboard where each phone had a jack-plug of its own and the operator listened in and personally relayed every call (there is a splendid and hilarious example in the Ealing comedy *Whisky Galore*). Every Saturday morning great-grandfather used to open the back parlour as a barber's shop. He bought a special barber's chair with a high back and neck-rest which swung down for shaving, and each week men from the village would gather round the back of the house for a haircut, a shave and a gossip. I don't know exactly when the Whites ceased to be village barbers – probably on the death of great-grandfather along with the gun and clock repairs, I suspect. The post office and the garage became more and more important over the years. Practical, hard-working, unpretentious, without wide ambitions, the men of the family from great-grandfather down to my own father carried the business on generation after generation.

A certain timidity and caution marked these men despite their innovations and diversity of skills. They kept out of controversy just as they seem to have kept out of the pubs (of which there were at least nine in Cranfield in great-grandfather's time). The family had some status in the community and was well respected, partly because of the very centrality and diversity of its functions, partly because of a reputation for scrupulousness and fair dealing, and partly because of its long history in Cranfield. Despite a near hegemonic monopoly on every village activity – post and telegraph, barbering, agricultural machinery and blacksmithing, taxi and car repairs, guns, clocks and watches – the men had an unassuming and down-to-earth quality which well suited local people.

I think the women of the family have always been somewhat more ambitious and class-conscious than their husbands. In part, this is because they have come into the village from outside – and my mother's story is an extreme case of this which I shall come to presently. But grandfather married a bit above himself when he courted my grandma – at least so she was fond of hinting to me as a child, and indeed she was of gentry stock and introduced a new level of social accomplishment into the family. She had studied music in Paris, spoke some French, played the piano extremely well and tirelessly corrected the rustic manners of her husband, children and grandchildren. In the 1930s grandfather briefly became the owner of a Rolls-Royce, which he hired out for all the local weddings and used as a taxi to ferry local people to Bedford on market day. In the 1950s my father's sister married the vicar's son and a little later the other sister married an air force officer; grandfather was chairman of the Harter Trust which administered the almshouses.

My great-grandfather was called Allon White and I am named after him. The family firm has been called Allon White & Son since just after the Great War – indeed I have a photograph taken in 1920 of the post office and bicycle shop with 'Allon White & Son' displayed boldly across the front. This shop sign tells two stories, one about the distant family past and one about myself.

The first story is just a speculation of mine and there is no one left alive to confirm it or deny it. However, I possess an even earlier photograph than the one I have mentioned. This earlier photograph was taken around 1910 or 1912 and the whole family stands informally in the garden in front of the post office: great-grandfather with his full-length white apron, my grandfather aged about 12 sitting on the fence beside his brother Alwyn, aged about 14; great-grandma in a full-sleeved silk blouse, and her two daughters; finally the two village postmen in their uniforms holding their bicycles, with Tinker the dog sitting alert and watchful in one of the front baskets. Between the two photographs the First World War intervened. Uncle Alwyn, grandad's elder brother (14 years old in the picture), was called up for active service and contracted TB in the trenches. He was invalided home and, since it was thought that fresh air was helpful for TB, lived and slept either in the washhouse or in a tent in the back garden throughout the winter. He died in 1919. Since my grandfather was two years younger than Alwyn he only got called up at the end of the war (he always maintained that he was the last man in England to go into the Royal Flying Corps – the day following his enlistment it became the Royal Air Force). The second photograph was taken about a year later, about 1920, and whereas the shop sign before the war read simply 'Allon White', the sign after the war has added '& Son'. There was only one son left now, my grandfather, and he was taken up onto the shop sign very shortly after Alwyn's death – in defiance, or pride, or compensation, who knows: 'Allon White & Son'.

The second story concerns me. My name is Allon White. Throughout my childhood and growing up it was my name on the sign over the garage and over the post office, on the letterheads and the envelopes. From long before my birth I was enchained in that *Allon White & Son* as thoroughly as young Paul in *Dombey and Son*. It was as if both the past and the future were already firmly in place, me to replace grandfather, my son to replace me in an endless, preordained chain of signifiers. My prescribed destiny seemed written up on the housefront for all to see. How cruelly, how closely the convention of '. . . & Son' can bind business and genealogy together: the old family firm. If you had wondered where all those engineers were coming from in the novel, it should now be apparent. Lucas Arnow the hydraulics engineer was in part the man I should have been had I not broken with my own 'proper' name. The novel was not simply about my attempts to escape from Carol and the miasma of marshland and drowning. It was also about my breaking away from a preordained class and family history, which in my case meant ending that history since I was the only son, the final son, and the history carried my name. In retrospect, I see that this wrench away from my ascribed place in the chain of names was both more protracted and traumatic than I realised at the time. But this came gradually. At first it did not weigh upon me.

The Garage

As a boy I loved the garage. It was a magical place. The English, unlike the Americans and the Italians, have never understood the romance of the garage. To understand what 'Allon White & Son's' garage looked and felt like when I was a young boy in the 1950s you have to go to Italian or American films – to that dusty village garage in Visconti's *Ossessione*, with its one tall petrol-pump and piles of old tyres and rusty parts and a lorry jacked up waiting to be repaired. Or you have to go to those lonely gas-stations in the Midwest of the Hollywood 'road' films, miles from anywhere, with a line of telegraph posts disappearing across an empty plain to the horizon. Of course I'm romancing a bit, but garages have changed so much since the 1950s that they have become completely transformed and it is hard to imagine what they were like just after the Second War. Now they tend to be full of *new* things: brightly coloured pieces of machinery, lifts, Krypton testers, the noise of high-technology machinery competing with transistor radios. They have to be *busy* now, and rather colourful like shops (they become more and more like little supermarkets every day, or they perish).

Colour and pace are relatively recent in garage life. The garage of my boyhood was like a wonderful, quiet museum. Everything was old. There were two large workshops, several storerooms, attics, a few sheds and an office. The whole premises were crammed with parts and tools and spares going back decades, much of it completely out of date. Valve radios, blacksmithing equipment, anvils, even bits of old tack and harness. Boxes and boxes of curious 'things' stored everywhere, of no conceivable use any longer but never cleared out. The place was a secret store of fascinating, inexplicable bits and pieces to play with. Old engines and gearboxes were stored in the pigsty. An orchard surrounded the workyard at the back and lorries sometimes broke branches of blossom from the apple trees as they were wheeled in for repair.

Even with four or five mechanics working there it was usually peaceful with only occasional bouts of rhythmic hammering or the revving of a motor. There was an old red air-compressor in the corner of one workshop and it was switched on at eight every morning. It had an uncannily human bronchial condition and began each day uncertainly with an impersonation of chronic whooping cough. For the rest of the time it intruded rather quietly on the day and then only at long intervals. The pace was very, very slow. Each mechanic usually worked alone, and so for most of the time, absorbed in separate tasks under cars or lorries, rarely spoke. My father and grandfather, as well as two uncles, worked alongside the other mechanics in their oily overalls, and I suppose it was because they were there that I was allowed to spend so much time in the workshops even as a small child. An old brown bakelite radio played away, apparently to itself, in one corner of the main workshop every day.

I remember my father's dirty, oily hands. They are calloused and cracked, with the grime deep black in the cuts and grazes round his knuckles. His hands are so large and dirty. I am very small. They are rough and smelly when he touches me. I don't want hands like that. I never want hands like that. Dirty and oily. He puts his fingers into a Dundee marmalade pot which he keeps on the kitchen windowsill. It is full of a slimy red oil-jelly to clean off his dirty hands before lunch. The oil-jelly smells of paraffin. His hands have black cracks all over the palms.

Nevertheless I am gradually drawn into the world of the workshop. Little by little, imperceptibly moving from play to errands and small tasks and then to work. At first I squatted beside a car or sat on the anvil and played with welding-rods or a huge box of old motorbike spokes stored in the corner. The petrol-pump attendant was a young woman called Janet and she used to look after me. On sunny days I could play with my matchbox toys on the dusty forecourt between the petrol pumps. So few cars called for petrol in those days that I could trace out elaborate roadways in the gravel and play all morning there without having to move out of the way for customers. Most days I returned home covered in oil. I can remember one summer day when I was sitting on the kerb in front of the garage so covered in grease and dirt that all the village women who went past laughed and told me that I'd be for it when my mother saw me.

Sometimes the garage frightens me. Horace Riddy is trying to lever a punctured tractor tyre from its rim. The rear wheel of the tractor, orange and covered in mud, is huge and takes three men to wheel into the workshop before they let it roll forwards on its own to crash down on the floor. I like Horace. He stands on the wheel and drives a great steel ram again and again into the edge of the tyre to break the seal. I put my hands over my ears but he continues, smashing the ram against the steel rim. It is winter, and his breath hangs white in the air. There is ice round the hub bolts. Horace has skinned the flesh from his hand with the ram, but he continues to pound at the unrelenting tyre.

As I got older, I began to run small errands for the mechanics. Their morning tea-break was at ten and they used to send me down to Sampson's grocery to buy them fruit pies: Lyons fruit pies at sixpence each. These pies came with a bewildering number of different fillings and the mechanics were very particular about this, specifying and listing with great care who was to have which filling – apple and blackberry for Sam, apricot for Ken, blackcurrant for Paul, and so on. Time and again they would make out the list and slip in a request for some quite impossible fruit filling which they had concocted, warning me that I really mustn't get it wrong. Off I would trot down to the shop clutching a handful of sixpences in one hand and diligently running through the list in my head. 'And Sam wants a plum and marmalade pie,' I would say to the shoplady, who was in on the conspiracy. 'Well, we're out of those love, but why don't you just run back up to the garitch and tell him we've got a fresh batch of damson and peanut – lovely they are.' So back up the High Street I would run, perhaps half a dozen times, willing and completely unsuspecting, chasing imaginary fruit pies with impossible fillings throughout the day – a fruitless task.

The same thing happened with errands to the spares department. It didn't take me long to cotton on to dire warnings that the screws *had* to be 'left-handed and headless half-inchers'. But I spent many an hour scouring the shelves for a 'Vauxhall Vicar's Rubber Gaiter (screw thread only)' or some other such marvellous spare part.

The mechanics increasingly adopted this playful and teasing attitude towards me as I became more involved with serious jobs in the workshop. In some ways it was the beginning of my political education. I was the boss's son, bright, innocent, and definitely not one of the workshop mechanics however much I tried to please. None of them was ever cruel, and indeed often they were friendly and generous, but there was at bottom a mistrust which I could never appease. I was compromised. They sometimes let me know, with a broad wink, that they were 'borrowing' a gallon of oil or some tool or other for home. They knew that I wouldn't betray the theft and they also knew it made me feel awkward and ashamed. They took advantage of my youth to revenge themselves upon my grandfather, father and the firm itself. At dinnertime my dad would sadly and bitterly recount how this or that was missing, how he knew that someone was thieving. I felt his hurt and hated the theft but sat silently, unable to betray the men for whom I was now a kind of occasional apprentice.

Ken

Ken had pale, slate-grey eyes and his forehead sloped back severely so that when he stared at you it looked as if his head were thrown back in contemptuous laughter. His teasing was more violent than the others' and yet he fascinated me. He taught me dirty. 'Go and tell your mother to "fuck off",' he would whisper to me, winking at the other mechanics (did I? I don't remember). He put on little acts of deliberate vulgarity: excavated his huge nose with his oily fingers crooked like crow's feet, his strange pale eyes rolling and his teeth gritted in a manic grin. He could fart prodigiously and at will – sometimes it was his only contribution to a conversation and invariably the last word. Sometimes if I asked him for something he would look at me slyly and give a long, thin fart as his only reply. He would drink Tizer and belch magnificently. I could do neither. His scornful play lives within me still: he suddenly arches forward and ambles towards me, rounding his shoulders and dropping his knuckles to the floor, neanderthal now, grunting and staring, cigarette smoke billowing from his nostrils as he chases me shrieking round the workshop. He taught me to swear and I still do – his sinister, hilarious lessons in fuckpissshit have become an unstable, eruptive substratum to my cultured university language. He used the grotesque and the lower body and dirty orifices and taught me all the Bakhtin I know.

Welding

My father said, 'I can weld spiders' webs,' and I believed him. No one could weld like my father. I loved working late in the darkened workshop beside him, holding a clamped piece of metal or a lamp. At the core of the oxyacetylene flame there was a tiny cat's tongue of liquid silver which had to lick the metal. It was the hottest part of the torch, sheathed both by a violet spear and an outer orange plume of flame. My father would slowly play the different colours of the flame against the metal until suddenly it would sigh and fuse with itself, the crack gone, the gap filled. I often stood by his side watching him do this, filled with excitement and envy. Perhaps there was also a kind of Oedipal longing, for welding was a man's job in the garage and learning to weld was a rite of passage – one which I never accomplished. And I really regret that I never learned to weld: it remains for me a kind of alchemy mixing the magic of the workshop with childhood time with my father. It might even have made a man of me. But by the time I was old enough and strong enough to wheel about the huge gas cylinders of oxygen and acetylene I had already begun to lose interest in the garage.

The Bernoulli Meter

I have been reflecting on that piece of equipment – the Bernoulli meter – which Lucas Arnow was waiting for in the novel. It flickers in and out of his consciousness during the long day of malarial fever and becomes a sort of talisman or fetish, connected in his mind with his own illness. If the meter arrives then he will live. By the early evening the fever clears a little and he wakes to find his friend Fabrizio beside his bed:

Lucas awoke suddenly. The flood had subsided within him and the swelling of his upper arms and mouth seemed to have gone. He rubbed his hand across his forehead and felt the drying salt of his sweat sticky against his palm. He felt thirst, but calm at last. He could move his head. Fabrizio still sat beside the bed in the twilight waiting for the return of Marietta with the doctor. As the light faded, the mosquitoes on the marsh rose up in silent clouds to greet the darkness and began softly to invade the margins of the shore. Fabrizio flicked down the netting around Lucas's bed and sat back, shifting his weight in the wicker chair which creaked once.

– Fabrizio?

– Yes Lucas.

– The fever has left me. Now I am alone.

– You're not alone Lucas, I am here, over here, look at me. Marietta is fetching the doctor. You are all right.

Lucas turned towards his friend and attempted to raise himself on his elbow but his arm would not move properly. He did not smile.

– But I am alone Fabrizio.

Fabrizio did not know what to say. There was a long silence. The mosquito netting shivered and shifted silently with the last exhalation of the day.

– Yes Lucas, you are alone.

– And the Bernoulli meter did not come?

The rate of flow will not be determined the valve will not be connected and the measurements will not take place. Bernoulli's theorem, on which the simple and highly efficient measuring device of the meter is constructed, will not, here on the coast of Sardinia, find its place in the hydro-metric control of the world. *Stagni stagni stagni.* Let them die. Lucas turned back to stare across the dark bay.

Fabrizio leant forward and covered his shoulder with the sheet patched damp from the fever.

– No the Bernoulli meter did not come, Lucas.

What disappointment of desire, beyond mere superstition, is imagined in that Bernoulli meter? It is precisely a measuring device, the measure of all desire, inflated by Lucas's desperation into a symbol to ward off not only his death but the entropic degeneration of the earth. But that's not the half of it. In reflecting on the novel so closely over these last days I have discovered an over-intensity of connectedness to the Bernoulli meter which astonishes me. Of course it shouldn't surprise me at all: for years I have taught my students about Freud's theory of condensation, in which every symbol condenses within it not one but a number of different contents. It has an unconscious economy which brings different desires or fears into one concentrated image. And so indeed it proves with the meter.

The science of hydraulics was born in 1738, when Daniel Bernoulli published his *Hydro-dynamica*. The Bernoulli meter as such does not exist, and at first I called it a Venturi meter, which was invented in 1887 by an American, Clement Herschel, for measuring the flow of liquids and was named in honour of the Italian scientist Venturi. The Venturi meter depends on Bernoulli's theorem for its operation, and I changed the name from Venturi to Bernoulli to celebrate and retain the symbolic history of hydromechanics from its origin. It is interesting in view of what follows that both names signify a certain 'Italian-ness', which is relevant to my story.

What was the Bernoulli meter doing in the novel? Last week it suddenly occurred to me as so obvious that it made me laugh out loud. Throughout my youth I had listened, day after day, to a single lament from my father: why hadn't the — arrived from Bedford yet? The — was some spare part or other needed for the completion of a job in the garage, a carburettor cable or a clutch plate or a tyre or valve spring or something without which the job remained unfinished. Day in, day out, lunchtimes and teatimes, my father would ritually butter his bread while intoning his litany of frustrations, this job held up, that job pushed aside, because the distributors hadn't delivered such and such a spare part. Or, as happened with unbelievable frequency, they had delivered the wrong part (sometimes three or four times) which had to be returned costing yet more delay. The customers complained and got angry, jobs drifted on for days, sometimes weeks, and my father drifted into migraine and depression.

So, the Bernoulli meter was the condensation of a thousand spare parts spread over a decade and a half which had worn my father down with their delays and confusions. Its very triviality as a small measuring device was significant. Trapped between the large distributors and irate, impatient customers, my father suffered acutely from these minor travails. A quiet and gentle man, he hated 'scenes', and whenever there was a delay he could sense impending trouble and shrank back. Like so many men worried at work, he brought his anxiety back to the privacy of the family dinner table and turned it into a set narrative, automatic after a while, which I must have heard hundreds of times. It confirmed me in my hardening decision that I would never work as he had done, that I would never suffer the same helplessness and frustration, that I would never work in the garage. This became obvious to both of us as I entered my teens and he began to look around for other people who might take my place in Allon White & Son.

The finest mechanics by far whom my father had employed were two Italian brothers, Giuseppe ('Jo') and Louis. After the war thousands of Italians had been brought into Bedford and the surrounding area on work contracts at the brickworks. They had to work for about four years and then, if they wished, they could take other jobs. Most of these Italians came from the Mezzogiorno around Naples and stayed on – Bedford has the highest number of Italian immigrants in the country and even has an Italian consulate. I grew up with the second generation of the original migrant workers and Jo and his brother were a few years older than I was. At school several of my friends were second-generation Italian and by the 1960s Bedford had a thriving Italian subculture.

Jo in particular was an outstanding mechanic. He started work in the garage when he was about 17 and quickly proved to be a better mechanic than Sam the foreman. After some years he was ready to set up a workshop on his own but lacked the capital. Meanwhile my father was becoming more and more convinced that I wasn't going to join the firm and began to think that he would take Jo into partnership, which he finally did in 1965. Jo effectively became my substitute, my replacement, and I felt a mixture of guilt and relief at the arrangement.

At first the idea worked well. Jo was able to persuade many Italians from Bedford to make the ten-mile journey out to Cranfield to have work done on their cars, and so the number of customers at the garage grew. Jo became foreman/manager and my father largely ceased manual work in the garage and took to his office to run the expanding business.

One day my father came down from his office to discover six large cases of Chianti in the middle of the workshop. For some months the accounts had been going awry and the Chianti was the first ominous sign that another mode of exchange than the official one might be taking place. 'Non ti preoccupare, Eric,' smiled Jo with an airy wave of his hand, 'don't worry about it. It's from Roberto, for the worka we done on the Jaguar.' My father did worry about it. As the weeks went by, two separate and competing economies grew up in the garage side by side, one rooted in the exchange-and-favour system of Southern Italy, the other rooted in the scrupulous petit-bourgeois accountancy of the English Protestant ethic. The accounts were chaotic. Half of the work passing through the garage now had no paperwork to it at all: Jo kept a note of it in his head to exchange against present or future 'favours'. We started eating Italian bread. Strange Italians would arrive unexpectedly to do plumbing jobs or mend the fence. Hundreds of tins of tomato puree would suddenly appear from nowhere.

I think the crisis finally came during the wine-making season. By the late 1960s the Italian community in Bedford was importing lorryloads of grapes from family back in Southern Italy so that they could produce their own wine locally – which they did, in abundance. That year it seemed as though most of it ended up stacked in the workshop of Allon White & Son in payment for services rendered. We had our own wine lake. My father was in despair. Money – real money – had dwindled to almost nothing despite the large increase in trade. The garage began to resemble a customs warehouse at Villafranca or Torino, full of unidentifiable and perishable Italian foods. 'Mozzarella,' my father would moan into his dinner plate at night. 'We haven't got any,' replied my mother. 'Haven't we though,' said my father. 'Haven't we though.'

The partnership was dissolved amicably and Jo went back to Naples to set up his own garage there. He returned to Bedford a few years later having been driven out of Italy, so he said, by violent demands and extortion. 'Perhaps the mozzarella was a blessing,' murmured my father.

4 May 1989

Confessions of a Poker Player

Paul Myerscough

O N THE LAST Sunday before Christmas, I drove to Blackpool to play poker. You wouldn't have got me there for any other reason. When I was young, my family used to take day trips to Lancashire's beach resorts. Each of them – Fleetwood, Cleveleys, Lytham and Morecambe – was desolate in its own way, but none provoked so many tears as Blackpool, all that giddy anticipation disappointed by damp amusement arcades, flea-ridden donkeys, filthy beaches and filthier seawater. I arrived in the mid-evening, and parked at the southern end of the Golden Mile beneath the silhouette of the Big Dipper. There were no signs of life. Most of the hotels and restaurants were closed for the season; the rest were boarded up. The illuminations were switched off; the only sound was the incessant thunder of the sea. This part of town is currently rated one of the most deprived areas in the country. An eerie, desperate place. The perfect place for a casino.

The poker room in Blackpool is at the back of the casino, as it has been everywhere I've played, from Barcelona to New Orleans. In poker the players win money from each other, so the casino's cut is limited to the hourly rate it charges players to sit at the tables, or to the small, capped percentage (the 'rake') they take from players' winnings.

Casinos are arranged so that poker players have to weave their way through the blackjack, craps and roulette tables on their way to and from the exit. In these games, the house has a small, irreducible edge: players can beat them in the short term, but in the long term the house will win. Poker brings prestige, new customers, perhaps even television coverage, but the game itself is fundamentally against the spirit of the casino, in which people are supposed to have fun losing their money to the house, not to each other. Most casinos do without it, having decided that the space would be more profitably filled with slot machines, but even if they do have poker rooms, casinos try to lure players away from the game on their way in, or tempt them into spending their winnings on the way out.

I haven't played a hand of blackjack in my life, and the hopeless flirtations with chance in roulette and dice don't interest me. There may be a thrill to be had playing those games in Monte Carlo or Las Vegas, but it requires some suspension of disbelief to feel the glamour 'doing your money' amid the plastic fittings and bus-seat upholstery of a casino in Wolverhampton or the Edgware Road. For every person you see having fun playing roulette, you will see two more unsmilingly handing over one £20 note after another until all their money is gone. I try to avoid casinos whenever I can. Until just a few years ago, that would have made it difficult for me to play poker in London, unless I had an introduction to a private game; for a long time, I played all my poker either in a room above a pub on the Farringdon Road, or in a side street in Tooting, where twenty strangers would turn up to play every Saturday night at the green baize tables a couple had set up in their front room. But in recent years, an explosion in poker's popularity has made it possible to find games on the high street. In 2004, a restaurant and internet café called Gutshot opened in Clerkenwell. The name was as unappealing to outsiders as it was transparent to those in the know – a 'gutshot' is a particular kind of chancy play in poker. The only people eating were the people who turned up in scores to play the poker tournaments laid on in the basement every night.

Other clubs followed, scattered across London in Walthamstow, Purley, Stanmore, Royal Oak, but Gutshot was the biggest and the least hole-and-corner. I played there, week in week out, until the club closed at the end of last year. Gutshot had always been operating outside the law, and everyone knew it. The gaming laws made no distinction between poker and other games of chance; anyone who wanted to make money by laying on poker games would need a prohibitively expensive licence, which the authorities in London are, in any case, very reluctant to grant. The police and the Gambling Commission turned a blind eye for a while, but their hand was forced when Rank, the owners of Grosvenor Casinos, commissioned private investigators to play undercover at Gutshot and report their findings to the Commission. In September 2005, one of the club's owners, Derek Kelly, was charged with offences under the 1968 Gaming Act.

I was with the poker players who filled the public gallery when Kelly appeared at Snaresbrook Crown Court four months later. Kelly didn't deny what he'd been doing, just that he'd been doing anything wrong. Poker, he argued, was not a game of chance, but a game of skill, and shouldn't therefore be covered by the Gaming Act. The case was hopeless, and not just because the only people who knew anything about the game were either in the gallery or in the dock (at one point on the third and final day of evidence, the judge interrupted to ask for clarification of one of the most basic rules of the game). Under the 1968 act – and even less ambiguously under the Gambling Act of 2005 – games of chance are defined as also including those which combine skill and chance. Given that even a game like chess, which most people regard as a game of pure skill, involves an element of chance – the players draw for the white pieces, an enormous advantage between two players of similar ability – it isn't clear that the law's definition of a game of chance defines anything at all. But the court didn't see it that way. The prosecution contented itself with pointing out, over and over again, that the cards were shuffled before a hand of poker, that the distribution of cards between players was therefore dictated by chance, and that that should be the end of the matter. The jury saw no reason to disagree, and found Kelly guilty; the judge, evidently sympathetic, declined to send him to jail or even to fine him, requiring only that he pay £10,000 towards the prosecution's costs. London's remaining unlicensed cardrooms, meanwhile, have been keeping their heads down.

If the only time you've seen poker played is in The Cincinnati Kid, you'll have watched Steve McQueen lose everything to Edward G. Robinson in one hand of five-card stud; if your family played around the kitchen table when you were a child, it's likely the game was five-card draw. But if you have played poker for real in the last five years, it will almost certainly have been a variation called Texas hold 'em. In hold 'em, each player is dealt two cards which no one else sees (their 'hole cards'). The two players to the left of the dealer make small forced bets ('blinds'), and each player in turn must decide whether to fold their hand, match ('call') those bets or raise them. Next, three cards are dealt face up in the middle of the table (the 'flop'), then another card (the 'turn') and a final one (the 'river'); there is a round of betting at each stage. Players must make the best five-card hand they can from their two hole cards and the ones in the middle, which they all share; the quality of your hand can change dramatically as the flop, turn and river are dealt. A hand doesn't always reach the river – if every player but one has folded by then, the last player standing takes all the money in the pot without showing his cards – but if it does, the remaining players turn their hole cards face up and the one with the best hand wins.

Ten years ago, you would have struggled to find a game of hold 'em outside American casinos; now, it is probably the most popular card game in the world. It isn't surprising that the poker boom has coincided with a time in which speculation has been so recklessly encouraged, but few cultural phenomena gather this amount of momentum unless they can be cut to the cloth of television and the internet. I first played with friends in 1999 after seeing *Late Night Poker* on Channel 4. By putting cameras under the table so that you could see the players' hole cards, the programme demystified the game at a stroke: the commentators would explain how players' betting, their actions and their table-talk related to the cards they held; crucially, you could tell when they were bluffing. It was an education. Now, after a certain time of night, it can be difficult to escape poker on television; there is coverage on all three commercial terrestrial channels and a dedicated poker channel on cable; you can watch novices play celebrities, celebrities play professionals and professionals play one another in high-stakes cash games. Hardly any of this is at all educational, though there's nothing like watching a soap stars' poker showdown after midnight on Five to make you realise how thoroughly a game once confined to window-less rooms and the tough-guy part of men's self-imaginings has been democratised under the sign of cheap entertainment.

Around the time *Late Night Poker* began, internet entrepreneurs also came to see what a dream opportunity poker presented. Simple soft-ware has made possible a proliferation of online cardrooms in which players' avatars meet at virtual tables to play poker for real money. At peak time on the biggest site, PokerStars, late enough in the evening for American players to have returned from work but not so late that the Europeans will have gone to bed, there might be 200,000 players at 30,000 tables, playing for stakes ranging from a few cents to hundreds of thousands of dollars. PokerStars takes a very small 'rake' from each pot won, and last August it dealt its twenty billionth hand; the market value of the site has been estimated at $2 billion.

The game is much quicker online: you don't need to know any of the etiquette or worry about body language, you can play at any time of day or night and you can play at as many tables as you like without leaving your sofa. An online professional might play as many hands in a year as a grizzled veteran of the live game will have played in a lifetime. Quite a few of them write blogs: some to set down their thoughts on strategy, some to write their Bildungsromans as poker players, others to chart the daily rollercoaster of wins and losses. The numbers can be shocking. I have followed 'Milkybarkid's Poker Blog' since 2004, when its author, Ben Grundy, started out as a small-stakes online player. Three years later, this is the sort of thing you could find there:

> $100/$200 6-handed no limit hold 'em on Betfair. I have $60,000. I make it $700 to go with AK. One caller in small blind. Loose aggressive player with big stack. Flop AAK. How does this become a $120,000 pot? Ridiculous. He checks . . . I check. Turn 5. He checks . . . I bet $1600, he calls. River a Q. He leads for $2000. I make it $8000. He makes it $24,000. I push all in expecting a split pot. He calls and mucks. Yikes.

A few clicks, a few hundred grand. In Grundy's latest blog entries, you can see graphs tracking his winnings for 2008 – more than $3 million – and a photo of his new car, which isn't a Volvo.

Few successful online players are happy to remain superstars in their own bedrooms; they are hoping to gain access to the celebrity and crazy financial rewards of the live game at the highest level. At the annual World Series of Poker in Las Vegas, the main event is a $10,000-entry Texas hold 'em tournament, in which each player starts out with the same number of chips and play continues until one player has all of them. The collected entry fees are divided between the players who survive longest – usually the top 10 per cent of the field – and the winner takes the biggest prize, about 30 per cent of the total. For a long time the stiff fee for the World Series meant that only the very serious and the very rich would step up. But in 2003, Chris Moneymaker (the jokes have all been made) beat 838 other players to become the champion. He had won his ticket in an online tournament that cost him $39: his prize for winning the World Series was $2.5 million. Three years later, there were 8773 entrants, the overwhelming majority of whom had qualified online; the top prize that year was $12 million.

I tried playing online for a while, but it felt too much like data processing. The few desultory attempts I made ended in failure: fits of undisciplined betting provoked by boredom, and pique at what I was too quick to see as my bad luck or someone else's bad play. The future of poker no doubt belongs to the adolescent millionaires of the online game, which means that I belong to its past. 'Pass me the cards young man,' one of the older players at the table said to me at the beginning of the game in Blackpool. 'He doesn't look so young to me,' growled another. The streets may have been deserted, but inside the casino a hundred people had gathered to play a cheap hold 'em tournament, just £30 to enter, the winner of which would get about £900 for six or seven hours' work. I hadn't played in this casino before, but felt completely at home. The tactile pleasures and protocols of the game – drawing for seats, the ritual of the deal, the riffling of chips, the feel of the baize, the rhythms of the game and the rise and fall of tension – are the same everywhere. So is the strained sociality, the banter that insulates the players from the game's inherent aggression.

In time, these things become second nature: while you are at the table, the world falls away and the game is all that remains. For some, it can come to replace the world altogether. I have left games on Friday night and returned to find them still going on Sunday afternoon; the players have been eating at the table and sleeping at the table. Perhaps they play poker for a living: this is a workplace, too. Such players live a harsh second life. The elements of poker are those of a tough negotiation. Someone bets as an announcement of strength, you raise to tell him he is weaker than you; he bluffs in an attempt to deceive you, your call tells him he's a liar. It can be salutary to discover how poorly, or how well, you are able to adapt. Unless you have it in you to change your persona at will – a useful asset at the poker table – your playing style will be inextricably bound up with your character. In theory, any style – passive or aggressive, straightforward or devious, quiet or flamboyant – should have its strengths, but at the higher levels of the game, the will to dominate is indispensable.

I played tournaments for years, but my career ended abruptly one night in August 2006, when I came up against a player called Dave Shallow. The entry fee for the tournament was £500, which I'd won in a smaller game; Shallow, a high roller with a notorious contempt for money, had bought in for the fun of it. He sat on my left, stared me in the face and held a handful of chips over the table whenever I looked as if I might bet, and speculated constantly, with unnerving accuracy, about the cards I was holding. The experience was crushing: I couldn't think clearly, and in the end lost the capacity to make decisions of any kind; after just two hours of a tournament scheduled to last three days, Shallow had taken away my dignity, my will to survive in the game, and every chip I had. Usually, losing is a sickening feeling; that night, it was a merciful release.

Shallow was schooling me in the importance of being able to play poker not only as if the game were a simulacrum of the real, but as if the money were too. These days I play in very few tournaments, but I do play in cash games, in which the chips, like notes or coins, represent real money: you buy chips to sit down in the game, and cash out your chips when you leave. Whoever invented the poker chip understood that it is considerably easier to take risks with money if, each time you throw £50 into the pot, you aren't thinking about the rent or your children's Christmas presents. Poker players have to distance themselves from material concerns if they are to make cool decisions. Television commentators on high-stakes cash games repeatedly invoke the real-world value of the bets made – '$60,000? That's a new luxury sedan for you or me . . . $150,000? That's a down-payment on a condo in Boca Raton' – but the players think of the money merely as a way of keeping score, no more real than the sums shuffled about by futures traders. (I know one trader who got his job after producing a printout of his online poker records at his interview, which perhaps throws as much light on the degeneracy of the City as it does on the economic rationality of poker.) But like traders, poker players know, or should know, that losses can become all too real when they cash out at the end of a session. I felt I was seeing signs of the financial lull last autumn when the loose money (players who have fun gambling and are happy to lose) and the dead money (players who aren't any good, and will lose whether they're happy about it or not) began to dry up. The faces I see at the moment are all familiar; we're passing money around among ourselves.

The cash games I play in are small: each hand begins with blind bets of £1 and £2. Even so, single hands regularly generate pots of hundreds of pounds, and players will typically sit down in the game with at least £200. However, even to play in a game this small, you should be drawing that £200 from a bankroll – the money you keep aside just to play poker – of, say, two or three thousand. The reason is what statisticians call 'variance', which measures the degree to which the possible outcomes of a given event are dispersed around the expected outcome. If you pick a ball, blindfold, out of a bag containing three white balls and one red one, your chance of picking white is 75 per cent. But what if you hit the one-in-four chance and get red? You would be happy to get your money into the middle in a poker game as a 75 per cent favourite, but one in four times you are going to lose, and to continue playing you will need more money. The more times you pick a ball out of a bag containing three white balls and one red one, the closer the overall number of times you pick white will tend to 75 per cent. But along the way there will be points at which you pick two red balls in succession: that's two lost buy-ins to the game. Occasionally you will come up with red three or four times on the trot. The odds of picking red ten times running are one in 1,048,576, but keep picking for long enough and you will see that happen too.

The point is that even in a normal probability distribution, there are sometimes clusters of unexpected results. In poker, you could make the correct decision every time and only ever invest in winning positions, but until your opponents have folded or the river is dealt you will remain exposed to the risk that the next card will spell disaster. Consistently making the correct decisions will win you money in the long run, but you need the £2000 bankroll to play even in a small game so that when a cluster of bad results comes along, you can ride it out. Play with too little behind, and you increase your 'risk of ruin'. To go broke as a poker player is to have to play with money drawn from the real world, from your wages or savings, or loans from 'backers' – with all the real-world anxieties that brings. (Players try not to think too much about the effects that losing might have on their opponents; I was once at the table when, oblivious of the roomful of men watching her, a woman came to plead with the cardroom staff not to let her husband play any more.) Needless to say, only a tiny proportion of players have any kind of bankroll at all, which means that even the smallest game in town is too big for most of the people playing in it.

Nonetheless, once players have a little success, the temptation to 'move up' can be irresistible. The higher the stakes, the larger the potential rewards, but since bigger games require bigger bankrolls, the risk of ruin remains about the same. The sense of risk is one of the pleasures of poker, but also a necessity: unless you have something at stake, it is difficult to take the game seriously. In the Big

Game at the Bellagio in Las Vegas, the blinds are typically $2000 and $4000, and the players buy in for hundreds of thousands of dollars, drawn from bankrolls of millions held in the casino's vaults. But these amounts are just as vulnerable in that game as a few thousand pounds are in mine; no player could ever be comfortable living off his bankroll because it could always, suddenly, be gone. And although, after just one good day at the office, any of the players in the Big Game could retire and live off the interest, they don't, because this, after all, is the only life they know.

Hold 'em is an easy game to pick up, and its simplicity is seductive: there doesn't appear to be much to master, so there should be easy money to be made. But poker is a zero-sum game: whenever one player wins, another loses, and while an inexperienced player may do well at first, over the course of an evening the money will tend to drift towards the skilful. Every player of any experience knows the basic arithmetic of the game: how to weigh the probability of any given outcome against the cost of investing in a hand. More advanced players might use mathematical modelling and game theory to confound orthodox play and to insulate their decision-making from their emotions. Others put great store in their ability to 'read' other players, to pick up from their betting patterns and their physical 'tells' how confident they feel about their hand, whether they are bluffing, how likely they are to fold under pressure. What such players call 'instinct' is, no doubt, mostly a matter of accumulated experience: they are recognising situations they have been in many times before.

There is an irreducible element of chance in poker, but the skill lies precisely in minimising the role it plays in the outcome of your decisions. You can play poker as a gambler – chase every longshot, enjoy the glory when they come off, moan about your luck when you run out of money – but you can also play it as a mathematician, a strategist, a psychologist or a logician. The ceaseless restaging of the encounter between reason and chance, the struggle of intelligence and imagination to overcome dumb luck is, for me, the chief pleasure of the game. Not that I'm much good at it. In the last two years, I have put a total of about £25,000 in play (I keep careful records), over more hours than I care to count, and turned a profit of less than £500. That makes me a break-even player, solid enough and canny enough to stay on top of the variance, not single-minded or gifted enough to make real money. If this were a job, it would be a stressful way to earn slave wages.

Poker, fundamentally, is a game of representation: what you have in your hand is one thing; what you represent yourself as having – in the way you behave, in the way you bet and the way you respond to other players' bets – is another. You need to think not only about what you have or what your opponent has, but also about what he thinks you have, and what he thinks you think he has. The skill in the game lies in finding your way through this hall of mirrors, while misdirecting your opponents so that they bump into their own reflections. Good players sometimes entertain themselves by seeing how many hands they can win without even looking at their cards. This is one of the many things the jury in the Gutshot case was given no opportunity to understand. An inexperienced player may do well when he first sits down at a table full of old hands: since he doesn't know what he's doing himself, he is difficult for anyone else to read. But to last an hour at that table, still less survive a whole evening, he will need to get lucky. I don't use the word casually. You hear a lot about luck at the poker table. Players take pride in their luck; they would 'rather be lucky than good'; they curl their lips when other players 'get lucky'; they like particular dealers because they have been lucky for them in the past, and protect their hole cards by placing lucky charms on top of them. I like to be at the table with players who let superstition cloud their reasoning. Luck isn't a commodity, or a quality that people possess. What looks lucky or unlucky is just a cluster of unlikely events, an effect of the variance.

Half an hour into the game in Blackpool, I was dealt two nines, a good starting hand, but not so good that you would want to risk everything to defend it. I raised, and was called, falteringly, by a blushing boy of barely twenty. I watched him carefully as the flop was dealt; he looked at his cards once more, then expectantly at me. The flop was perfect, a two, a seven and a beautiful nine, giving me three of a kind, the best possible hand at that stage. I bet; the blushing boy raised; I pushed all my chips into the middle of the table. He looked at me once more, less sure now than he had been; but eventually he called and turned over his cards: two kings. He had made the novice's mistake of falling in love with a good hand, without thinking hard enough about what his opponent might have. With only the turn and river to come, I was a 90 per cent favourite to win: only another king could beat me. It came immediately on the turn, a one in ten shot – just part of the variance. 'This is my first time,' he said as he raked in his winnings, 'I only came with a mate.' The game is full of fresh humiliations. I tapped the table and left quickly so as not to meet the peculiar mixture of sympathy and embarrassment you sometimes find in the eyes of the remaining players. But I needn't have worried: they'd forgotten me already.

29 January 2009

What's Left of
Henrietta Lacks?
Anne Enright

I DON'T KNOW where I heard of her first: a woman whose cells are bred in culture dishes in labs all over the world; a woman whose cells were so prolific that there is more of her now, in terms of biomass, than there ever was when she was alive.

It seems to me that she is one of the saints who multiplied in reliquaries after their death, to produce, as Ian Paisley's website reminds us (in an essay called 'The Errors of Rome'), the many prepuces of the infant Jesus, and the variously coloured hair of His madly trichogenous mother. Perhaps, in these days of cloning, or in future days of cloning, we will look to the evangelical Protestants and say that they were right all along: no miracles please, scientific or otherwise, no icons, and a Just Say No approach to reproduction.

Is there such a thing as an unconscious saint – a saint who didn't know that she was in some way chosen, or even holy? I would like to put this woman and her cells in a story, but what kind of story would it be? What kind of epiphany would grace her ordinary afternoons?

My-sister-the-doctor says that what I heard was a reference to the HeLa cell line – a popular choice with medical researchers. They are, disgustingly enough, the cells of a woman's cancer. What is the difference between a woman's own cells and the cells of her cancer? They are normal body cells that have suffered a genetic alteration, that is all. The question is moot: the closer you get to the body, the harder it is to see. On a cellular level, we are each a community, or several communities, and the relationships are not always clear: some cells 'commit suicide', for example, but the question of intention must be a false one. Under the microscope, the question of 'self' is so diffuse and so complicated that it might as well not arise.

This is all unlucky talk. I am pregnant for the first time, the bump just beginning to show. I don't know what my pregnant self is, either. The pregnant body has been through a lot of law courts but I have never seen it properly discussed or described. I don't know what I am. Am I twice as nice? Am I twice as alive now as I ever was?

On the internet, I look up 'HeLa' on Yahoo and find, within minutes, that the woman's name was Henrietta Lacks. So what is she missing, I wonder, what does Henrietta lack? What does she want *now*? I type her name into AltaVista, and get 52 replies. The first site, 'The Immortal Cells of Henrietta Lacks', is illustrated with a photograph of a cell. It looks like a ball of maggots. Is this her? No. It is a duly credited picture of a 'cultured rat bone marrow cell', magnified 19,500 times.

According to the anonymous author, the HeLa line was begun when cells were taken from the cervix of a 31-year-old Baltimore woman, for tests. The woman died of cancer eight months later but in the meantime some of the cells found their way to the lab of John and Margaret Gey of Johns Hopkins University. They were trying to find a method of keeping human cells dividing in a culture outside the body and had turned to cancer cells for their ability to divide essentially unchecked. These particular cells, named HeLa for the first two letters of the first and last names of the 'patient', proved spectacularly successful. Henrietta's cells were the first human culture to survive beyond the 50th generation and they are still growing: 'Although Henrietta is dead her cells live on in research labs around the world! In fact, some biologists believe that HeLa cells are no longer human at all and consider them to be single-celled micro-organisms!'

The exclamation marks are some kind of exhortation – but to what? The webpage goes on to say that HeLa cells grow so aggressively they cause problems by invading other cultures during routine lab transfer procedures. The result is a lot of bogus data – papers written on the biology of various cell types are in fact about the biology of good old HeLa. I'm delighted, of course, and note the recommended book by Michael Gold, *A Conspiracy of Cells: One Woman's Immortal Legacy and the Medical Scandal It Caused* (1986).

As so often on the internet, the easy information comes first. This is perhaps all I need to know about HeLa, but if I want to get a fix on Henrietta I will have to pick through the rest of the websites the search engine has thrown up, in all their glorious irrelevancy. I will have to judge by the quality of the writing whether the people who wrote them are educated or intelligent or honest. Through various inaccuracies, I will arrive at a sort of consensus of fact – the facts will probably be the same ones as on this first website, but somehow richer and more known. And somewhere along the line, an accident will give me my own fictional Henrietta, or the relentless concatenation of near-relevance and irrelevance will smudge her, and possess her. There is a danger that information will kill Henrietta Lacks. I sit at the computer, growing all the while, wondering about the differences between reproduction and creativity; between either of these and what you might call *spawning*.

Click. The same rat bone marrow cell, this time tinted sepia, with a drop-shadow added for dramatic effect. It is not credited, and the (of course, anonymous) author claims it to be 'a HeLa cell'. This is a typical infiltration of electronic content from one site to another – until everyone has a scanner, they will steal their illustrations and graphics from other websites, and the same pictures will turn up again and again. Everyone robs on the internet. The more often a piece of information is used, the more likely it is to mutate: I suspect, though, that it mutates towards, rather than away from, the expected ('Of course it's not a rat, why would we put a picture of a rat cell on a page about HeLa?').

I'm in a series of sites that show me, if I want to know, how to detect the papillomavirus type 18 DNA in HeLa cells (using some nifty gel and a PCR machine). I *think* this means that Henrietta Lacks had genital warts. I *think* this means that she slept around.

Click. A picture of Henrietta Lacks. A woman looks down at the camera: hands on hips, smiling, as if to say: 'Is this the way you want me?' It is a confident, intimate picture. She has a strong chin, her hair is in a Victory Roll, she is wearing a short fitted jacket and is standing in front of a brick wall. The text announces a documentary called *Ihre Zellen leben weiter* ('Her Cells Live On'), to be shown on Swiss television. In the accompanying blurb, Margaret Gey is dropped from the Johns Hopkins research team, leaving 'Dr Gey' to lonely late nights in the lab, watching the petri dish where Henrietta Lacks's cells were nurtured in a solution of placenta (it doesn't say whose) and hen bone marrow. HeLa was apparently vital in the development of the polio vaccine; it was used to test cosmetic products and the effects of the atom bomb. Henrietta's cells were the first 'piece of human life' ('*das erste Stuck menschliches Leben*') in space. Go girl.

Click. Wait. Wait. Error.

I don't know where dead websites go. Perhaps they are not dead in any real sense, just lost, or inaccessible. This worries me – if the internet is to evolve, surely it must both reproduce and die. Do websites do either? They certainly cross-fertilise, or cross-infect. But when people say 'what will the internet turn into' maybe it won't 'turn into' anything, it will just spread (get less accurate at the edges, more stodgy in the middle).

Click. High School Biology. Students are asked what they would do if they were dying of cancer and a doctor asked them to donate some cells. 'Your cells are the first success! This could be a medical break-through – your approval could allow researchers to evaluate drugs in a test tube before administering them to patients.' More exclamation mark ethics. No one asked Henrietta Lacks for permission, that much seems clear.

Click. Wait. Another biology module, a different school, or college. 'This is not so much concerned with the choice HL made, but with the speed at which information flows. The actions of the editors of scientific journals, the interaction of politics and science.' There follows an interesting list of words. 'Money. Mistakes. Contamination. Spontaneous transformation. New parameter. Invalid data. Tainted literature.' The class will work from a copy of a *Reader's Digest* article, which I do not have. At this point I should look up the *Reader's Digest* site. It takes an effort to be passive on the internet, but I hold the line. I am pregnant. I am not looking for information, I am looking for Henrietta Lacks. I am looking for an accidental insight into her red-brick, Baltimore, smiling afternoons.

Click. 'Dresses for Henrietta Lacks', an installation by Brisbane-based artist Jill Barker. 'Dresses made of silver contact paper have been adhered to the windows. Each contains intricate structural patterns, like the DNA and other molecular structures of which we are all composed.' A picture of a metal dress. In the text, John Gey has mutated to John Grey and Henrietta, for the first time, is black. (I do go back now, in a hurry, to the photo and find that this is indeed so.) Furthermore, 'Henrietta's family were never told of the research. Dr Grey [sic] claimed the donor's name was Helen Lane or Helen Larson (supposedly in order to protect her anonymity). In the 1970s Henrietta's name was released and the Lacks family were shocked . . . to them a part of their mother is still living and is being made to live on.'

Click. 'Behind the façade of big hospitals, many African Americans can only see one big medical experiment.' The internet often provides its own narrative like this: the story 'becomes' one about race and therefore starts to move away from me. The cells in the petri dish are black cells, they are no longer universal, they are certainly not Irish (as I am). It bothers me that I did not notice what colour she was, it makes me feel foolish, or virtuously blind.

The website brings us on a quick trot through, among other outrages, the Tuskegee experiment, where, between 1932 and 1972, in a study funded by the US Federal Government, 400 black men were intentionally denied treatment for syphilis so researchers could track the effects of the disease.

Click. For sale: various growth media and cultures. For a mere $55 I can buy a litre of media for Chinese hamster ovary cultures. There are also 'various magnetic goat antibodies' for $79–$89 (50 ml) and 'a laser tweezers micromanipulator' for $25,000–$40,000. Snap on those latex gloves.

Click. 'Why Cells Die'. A very technical discussion. As far as I can make out, the problem is this: free radicals are generated in the mitochondria as part of the normal metabolic process. They cause somatic mutations and deletions of mitochondrial DNA, which in their turn produce more free radicals. An overload contributes to cellular necrosis and apoptosis. The cells die or self-destruct, in other words, and other cells replicate in order to replace them.

Every time a cell replicates, its telomeres get shorter. Telomeres bind the bottoms of chromosomes together, like the aglets on shoe-laces, and after, say, fifty replications they wear out. This is called the Hayflick Limit. After it is reached, the cell can't replicate and simply dies. Cancerous cells somehow 'express' telomerase and therefore avoid this problem – but don't ask me how. As I say, this was a very technical essay, complete with footnotes, which, in the world of the internet means that every single word is True True True.

Click. A personal diary. A trip to the Blijdorp Zoo to visit the Surinam Toad. Some musings about small information appliances (like an intelligent fridge) and how attached people still are to their large information appliances (like their computers). A discussion of difficulty and reward (the VCR v. the violin). A description of the sense of foreboding the writer had before witnessing an accident. Entry ends: 'Took half a melatonin before I went to bed and slept very soundly.' There is no mention of Henrietta Lacks.

Click. The American Congressional Record.

IN MEMORY OF HENRIETTA LACKS –
HON. ROBERT L. EHRLICH, JR
(Extension of Remarks – 4 June 1997)

Henrietta Lacks was born in 1920 in Clover, Virginia. At the age of 23 she moved to Turner's Station, near Baltimore, Maryland, joining her husband David. She had five children, four of whom – Deborah, David Jr, Lawrence and Zakariyya – still survive. Ms Lacks was known as pleasant and smiling, and always willing to lend a helping hand.

Because it is the Congressional Record (unless it is not) we know that John Gey, or Grey, is in fact Dr George O. Gey, though his wife Margaret (though perhaps she was called Mary, who is to say?) has gone the way of all female scientific flesh. The citation ends: 'I sincerely hope her name will also be immortalised as one of courage, hope and strength, and that due recognition will be given to her role in medicine and science.' Well so do I. But what was extraordinary about her particular courage, and in what sense was this unknowing contribution to science 'hers'?

Click. Click. Click. Repeat of Swiss TV timetable, more biology classes, mitosis, meiosis, all that. Click. *Der Tanz ums Grab*. Henrietta reminds someone of the 'Toraja', a tribe perhaps, who carry their dead around with them for many years, like so much hand luggage. Click. Causes of cancer: 1. Infection by an oncogenic virus. 2. Chromosomal abnormalities. 3. Exposure to chemical carcinogens. Click. 'How to use micro-organisms as vector cells in genetic engineering'. A fairly detailed guide. This, along with 'Nuclear Bombs Made Easy', I download and save for later.

Click. Error. Click. A man in California, I am warned, sued his doctor for marketing a cell line derived from his cancerous spleen. Click. 'Twenty years later a disturbing factor came to light, the HeLa cells had the ability to infiltrate and subvert other colonies of alien cells.' Now this is my favourite space on the internet, the paranoid place, where people use words like 'infiltrate' and 'alien' to produce questions like: 'Would the human immune system be capable of dealing with such an invader? Could the tales of vampire and werewolf bites have some basis in fact?' I didn't trust this site to start with because the background was pink. I think this means that I didn't trust it because I knew it was written by a woman. Oh well.

Click. 'Diana's Bodyguard Conscious and Well Enough to Talk'. Scroll down through a local newspaper to find 'Cancer Victim's Family Receives Plaque'. Good old Congressman Ehrlich has awarded the Lacks family a plaque recognising her contribution to science. 'A foundation named for Lacks plans to build a $7 million museum in her honour.' I wonder what will be in the museum. Horrors, I assume.

Click. 'Death Wish – Do Our Cells Want to Commit Suicide?' A harmlessly inaccurate essay about living for ever. Of Henrietta Lacks the writer says: 'We want the immortality of a god, not of a tumour.' Quite. He hints at future resurrections: 'Each cell contains a genetic blueprint for constructing Henrietta Lacks – who died back in 1951.'

Click. But – and there are often 'buts' in the gaps between websites – 'by now the cells have mutated so much that it's questionable whether they can still be considered "human" tissue.' So if our previous author got his wish and reconstructed Henrietta, then the human being cloned from the cell would be perhaps unpleasantly different from the original, perhaps unpleasantly different, indeed, from the human.

Click. Wait. Now what? On the internet, the meaning is so often in the gaps, and poor, mutated Henrietta is slipping between the cracks. I am waiting for the argument to continue; for something unexpected to clinch it or make it silly. This is the pleasure of browsing, and probably the trap. I used to teach multimedia students and found that they were almost exclusively interested in synchronicity and the random. This is not a kind of meaning that can be generated by a single author, it exists between authors. These students had plenty to say, they just thought it uncool to say it – all significance had to come from the group. There is nothing new about this, but it will always be frightening (and this time the group is global).

Click. 'Life Itself. Exploring the Realm of the Living Cell'. By Boyce Rensberger. There is nothing better than coming across a whole chapter of a book on the net, a proper book, especially on a page reassuringly hosted by washingtonpost.com.

The story is of the American Type Culture Collection, where 20,000 frozen ampoules hold about 40 billion human cells in suspended animation. These cultures are routinely 'resurrected' and shipped off to researchers around the world. They include skin cells taken from a little girl who died of a birth defect in 1962, and brain cells of a 76-year-old man.

Rensberger quotes the cell biologist Matthias Schleiden's insight into what we are, what our cells 'are' – they 'lead double lives, their own and that of the organism of which they are a part'. He goes on to say that 'the human body is a republic of cells, a society of discrete living beings who have, for the good of the society as a whole, sacrificed their individual freedoms.' I am not sure what individual freedoms my cells possess, though I know they can go on strike, especially the ones in my ex-smoker's lungs. But my child, when still very small, made itself known to me – first in a dream (this is only true, I am only reporting what is true) when it was under a hundred cells 'big', and then in a craving for Japanese seaweed. I have no idea how small a hundred cells are, but their impulse was, from the very start, not so much republican as despotic.

As evidence of this cell 'republic', Rensberger cites the mechanism known as 'programmed cell death'. If a cell goes 'wrong' its neighbours will order it to self-destruct. This is what is supposed to happen with cancer cells, but sometimes, of course, doesn't. It also happens to the webbing between my child's fingers. At least I hope it does.

Rensberger worries that we may find the world of cells 'miraculous' – though he allows wonder. Most wondrous of all is the cells' tendency towards self-assembly. Skin cells will form a sheet in the dish, breast cells will manufacture and secrete milk protein, and 'muscle cells will sometimes weld themselves into large fibres that spontaneously begin twitching in the dish. When cells of the heart muscle do this, they begin twitching rhythmically.' Perhaps the body is just a yearning. Every good scientist tries to rid his prose of all hint of intention, and fails. They love their cells and molecules as fiction writers love their characters, they watch them and will them on. Rensberger celebrates the 'glory' of a mechanistic view of life, quoting Jacques Monod, another important cell biologist, who says: 'No preformed and complete structure existed anywhere: but the architectural plan for it was present in its very constituents.' It seems that what molecules, and later cells, contain is information. This is not how I understand the word 'information', which, after all, can be either correct or incorrect. It is information as an imperative, information as a seed. 'The necessary information was present, but unexpressed, in the constituents. The epigenetic building of a structure is not a creation; it is a revelation.'

So I am pregnant. I am busy building bones, in an epigenetic sort of way. The child is being revealed inside me, but not yet to me. The child is being revealed to itself, but slowly. I wonder if it is lonely: I find pregnancy to be a vastly lonely state. This child cries already, or so I am told. I fancy that it likes the sound of its father's voice, that it kicks at songs by Nina Simone. I have no idea what might cross its mind, as different expressions cross its face. I have no idea what it is like to be of recently specified sex, to have webbing between my fingers and toes and then to lose it. And of course I have every idea what these things are like.

I surf the net and grow, my belly pushing towards the keyboard. I should work, but I would rather lie on the sofa and be. Sometimes, for hours at a time, I do nothing but exist. I find it quite tiring. I say to my-sister-the-doctor that my brain is gone. She laughs and says: 'You'll never get it back.' I panic and download an IQ test from the internet. I have never done an IQ test before, I don't believe in them. The test tells me that, on its terms, I can think perfectly well. It is just, perhaps, that I can't be bothered. I grow large and swim like a whale through all this information. There is a part of me now that is entirely happy. I sit and listen to my own blood, or to someone's blood. 'I am no more your mother,' said Sylvia Plath. 'I am no more your mother than . . .'

As for Henrietta – I am pregnant. I cannot conclude. I am lodged at AltaVista 44, a site called 'What Happens': it's the story, among other things, of her revenge. Everything on the internet is about what someone else said. There are so few primary sources, I sometimes feel that the whole thing is just a gossip factory. 'What Happens' contains a summary of Michael Gold's *A Conspiracy of Cells*, which is, of course, unfindable, out of print.

The book says much about HeLa's ability to overwhelm other tissue cultures in the lab and how it led to widespread and unacknowledged contamination of data. Researchers shared their cultures around like gardeners do clippings, and as HeLa took over in dish after dish, papers about skin cells and lung cells were in fact based on the cancerous cervical cells of Henrietta Lacks. The problem reached unbelievable proportions – in 1966 Stanley Gartler compared 17 cultures of ostensibly different tissue types and found that they were all, in fact, HeLa. In 1968 the American Type Culture collection tested all its line of human cells, and 'of these 34 cell lines, 24 proved to be HeLa.' In 1972 Russian scientists supplied American scientists with six different cancer cells taken in different parts of the Soviet Union and 'all six turned out to be HeLa.'

The author of this site, Louis Pascal, is more interested, however, in the refusal of the scientific community to acknowledge that mistakes were made. He traces the relationship between the whistle-blower Walter Nelson-Rees, who worked at the cell bank at the University of California, and the various journals which refused to publish him. Nelson-Rees, he says, was 'effectively forced to retire' in 1981. Pascal claims a similar history for his own attempts to expose the truth about the source of HIV. There follows a passionate and plausible essay about the possibility that HIV crossed over from SIV (a variation of the virus in chimpanzees) via the polio vaccination project in Central Africa in the 1950s – in which HeLa also played its part. This is the earlier, underground version of the argument put forward by Edward Hooper in *The River: A Journey back to the Source of HIV and Aids*, but when I stumble across it, it's all news to me.

Here is the apotheosis of the internet: forbidden information, a conspiracy against the truth. Overturning my prejudices, Pascal is all content and fiercely political. But the fact that he uses copious footnotes, and is prefaced with a note written by a professor from the University of Woolagong, does not mean that I know he is sane. I find myself involved in a drama of verifiability. My ignorance makes the information urgent. I have no scientific training, I am ordinary and sometimes frightened and I have no reason, finally, to disbelieve him.

Click. 'A Crime of Manners'. Blurb for a romantic fiction with a cast that includes a Lady Fuddlesby and a parrot called Sir Polly Grey. The hero, Giles, Duke of Winterton, decides to pay attention to an earl's daughter who has many bountiful charms that the heroine, 'Henrietta, lacks'. So here is my saint: a woman who, according to the Congressional Record, was like all saints in that she 'was known as pleasant and smiling, and always willing to lend a helping hand'. A woman whose womb carried five single cells that became children and one single cell that killed her. A minor martyr in an as yet unspecified cause. I think I should leave her alone.

Out at my sister's I ask a dinner table of doctors who owns the placenta, me or the child. Legally, I am told, it is a 'waste product'. Hospitals sell placentas all the time, sometimes to the cosmetics industry. This seems all right to me, though I worry about the lipsticks. Everyone loves scaring me about having babies. There is much gleeful talk of epidural and episiotomy. When it came down to it, none of the men actually wanted to be in the labour ward with their wives, but they gritted their teeth and sat it out anyway. All of them play golf.

13 April 2000

Working Methods
Keith Thomas

I T NEVER HELPS historians to say too much about their working
methods. For just as the conjuror's magic disappears if the
audience knows how the trick is done, so the credibility of
scholars can be sharply diminished if readers learn everything about
how exactly their books came to be written. Only too often, such
revelations dispel the impression of fluent, confident omniscience;
instead, they suggest that histories are concocted by error-prone
human beings who patch together the results of incomplete research
in order to construct an account whose rhetorical power will, they
hope, compensate for gaps in the argument and deficiencies in the
evidence.

Perhaps that is why few historians tell us how they set about their
task. In his splendid recent autobiography, *History of a History Man*,
Patrick Collinson reveals that when as a young man he was asked by
the medievalist Geoffrey Barraclough at a job interview what his
research method was, all he could say was that he tried to look at
everything which was remotely relevant to his subject: 'I had no
"method", only an omnium gatherum of materials culled from more
or less everywhere.' Most of us would say the same.

But how do we deal with this omnium gatherum when we have
got it? We can't keep it all in our heads. Macaulay claimed that his
memory was good enough to enable him to write out the whole

of *Paradise Lost*. But when preparing his *History of England*, he made extensive notes in a multitude of pocketbooks of every shape and colour.

Scholars have always made notes. The most primitive way of absorbing a text is to write on the book itself. It was common for Renaissance readers to mark key passages by underlining them or drawing lines and pointing fingers in the margin – the early modern equivalent of the yellow highlighter. According to the Jacobean educational writer John Brinsley, 'the choycest books of most great learned men, and the notablest students' were marked through, 'with little lines under or above' or 'by some prickes, or whatsoever letter or mark may best help to call the knowledge of the thing to remembrance'. Newton used to turn down the corners of the pages of his books so that they pointed to the exact passage he wished to recall. J.H. Plumb once showed me a set of Swift's works given him by G.M. Trevelyan; it had originally belonged to Macaulay, who had drawn a line all the way down the margin of every page as he read it, no doubt committing the whole to memory. The pencilled dots in the margin of many books in the Codrington Library at All Souls are certain evidence that A.L. Rowse was there before you. My old tutor, Christopher Hill, used to pencil on the back endpaper of his books a list of the pages and topics which had caught his attention. He rubbed out his notes if he sold the book, but not always very thoroughly, so one can usually recognise a volume which belonged to him.

A more brutal method is to cut the pages out of the book and incorporate them in one's notes. More than one Renaissance scholar cut and pasted in this way, sometimes even from manuscripts. It enabled them to accumulate material which it would have taken months to transcribe. Nowadays, we have less incentive to carve up books because we have photocopiers and digital cameras, and can download material from the internet. But historians still make newspaper cuttings. At breakfast, I often take a pair of scissors to the LRB, the TLS or the *New York Review of Books*.

Another help to the memory is the pocketbook in which to enter stray thoughts and observations: what the Elizabethans called 'tablets'. John Aubrey tells us that Hobbes 'always carried a note booke in his pocket, and as soon as a thought darted, he presently entred it into his booke, or otherwise he might have lost it. He had drawn the designe of the book into chapters, etc, so he knew whereabout it would come in.' The National Portrait Gallery has a fine snapshot (taken by Colin Matthew) of the architectural historian Howard Colvin in the ruins of Godstow Abbey: spectacles pushed up on his forehead, camera dangling from one hand, he looks down intently as he makes a neat entry in the notebook he has just fished from his pocket. I have always been impressed by those academics who can sit impassively through a complex lecture by some visiting luminary without finding it necessary to make a single note, even a furtive one on the back of an envelope. They'd lose face, no doubt, if they were seen copying it all down, like a first-year undergraduate.

In the end, we all have to make excerpts from the books and documents we read. In the 16th and 17th centuries, scholars tended to read books in an extrapolatory way, selecting passages to be memorised or copied into commonplace books. Sometimes they kept their excerpts in the order in which they came across them. More usually, they tried to arrange them under predetermined headings: virtues and vices, perhaps, or branches of knowledge. Properly organised, a good collection of extracts provided a reserve of quotations and aphorisms which could be used to support an argument or adorn a literary composition. As the historian Thomas Fuller remarked, 'A commonplace book contains many notions in garrison, whence the owner may draw out an army into the field on competent warning.'

These compilations were not necessarily a preparation for writing, but could become ends in themselves. They were the predecessors of those anthologies of memorable sayings, anecdotes, jokes, eloquent passages and 'gems from old authors' on which publishers for the Christmas trade still rely. But they also enabled students to organise and retrieve their data. The art of making excerpts (*ars excerpendi*) was an essential scholarly technique.

The great limitation of the commonplace book was its inflexibility. Since each excerpt was entered in the book under a single heading, it could not be moved around thereafter. Noel Malcolm has described the system invented by the country clergyman Thomas Harrison, who explained it to Charles I during a two-hour conversation in 1638. It involved writing excerpts on small pieces of paper, which were then stuck onto hooks attached to metal plates bearing alphabeticised subject headings. This was a great advance, because it meant that the excerpted passages could be repeatedly rearranged to fit different conceptual schemes. In his book on *The Footnote*, Anthony Grafton quotes a letter by the great Swiss historian of the Renaissance Jacob Burckhardt, reporting that he had just cut up his notes on Vasari's *Lives* into 700 little slips and rearranged them to be glued into a book, organised by topic.

From this practice of making notes on separate slips of paper there emerged what became the historian's indispensable tool until the electronic age: the card index. By using cards of uniform size, punching holes in the margin and assigning different categories to each hole, it became possible, with the aid of a knitting needle, to locate all cards containing material related to any particular category.

These various techniques were codified in the guides to research which proliferated with the rise of academic history-writing. In one of the most influential, the 1898 *Introduction to the Study of History* by the French historians Charles Langlois and Charles Seignobos, the authors warn that history is more encumbered with detail than any other form of academic writing and that those who write it must have those details under control. The best way of proceeding, they say, is to collect material on separate slips of paper (*fiches*), each furnished with a precise indication of their origin; a separate record should be kept of the sources consulted and the abbreviations used to identify them on the slips. If a passage is interesting from several different points of view, then it should be copied out several times on different slips. Before the Xerox machine, this was a labour-intensive counsel of perfection; and it is no wonder that many of the great 19th-century historians employed professional copyists.

Prescriptions of this kind reached their apotheosis in the little essay on 'The Art of Note-Taking' which Beatrice Webb included in *My Apprenticeship* (1926). It propounded the famous doctrine of 'only one fact on one piece of paper'. In his delightful autobiography, *Memories Migrating*, the late John Burrow records his perplexities when this injunction was conveyed to him by his graduate supervisor, George Kitson Clark: 'I brooded on this. What was a fact? And what made it one fact? Surely most facts were compound. How would I know when I had reached bedrock, the ultimate, unsplittable atomic fact?'

Nobody gave me any such instructions when I began research in the 1950s. I read neither Beatrice Webb nor Langlois and Seignobos until many years later, by which time my working habits had ossified. When I did, though, I was reassured to see that, in a slipshod sort of way, I had arrived at something vaguely approximating to their prescriptions. En route I had made all the obvious beginner's mistakes. I began by committing the basic error of writing my notes on both sides of the page. I soon learned not to do that, but I continued to copy excerpts into notebooks in the order in which I encountered them. Much later, I discovered that it was preferable to enter passages under appropriate headings. Eventually, I realised that notes should be kept in a loose form which was flexible enough to permit their endless rearrangement. But I recoiled from uniform index cards: my excerpts came in all shapes and sizes, and there was something too grimly mechanical about card indexes. Since Anatole France's description in *Penguin Island* of the scholar drowned by an avalanche of his own index cards, it has been hard to take them seriously. I still get cross when reviewers say that all that I have done is to tip my index cards onto the page.

When I go to libraries or archives, I make notes in a continuous form on sheets of paper, entering the page number and abbreviated title of the source opposite each excerpted passage. When I get home, I copy the bibliographical details of the works I have consulted into an alphabeticised index book, so that I can cite them in my footnotes. I then cut up each sheet with a pair of scissors. The resulting fragments are of varying size, depending on the length of the passage transcribed. These sliced-up pieces of paper pile up on the floor. Periodically, I file them away in old envelopes, devoting a separate envelope to each topic. Along with them go newspaper cuttings, lists of relevant books and articles yet to be read, and notes on anything else which might be helpful when it comes to thinking about the topic more analytically. If the notes on a particular topic are especially voluminous, I put them in a box file or a cardboard container or a drawer in a desk. I also keep an index of the topics on which I have an envelope or a file. The envelopes run into thousands.

This procedure is a great deal less meticulous than it sounds. Filing is a tedious activity and bundles of unsorted notes accumulate. Some of them get loose and blow around the house, turning up months later under a carpet or a cushion. A few of my most valued envelopes have disappeared altogether. I strongly suspect that they fell into the large basket at the side of my desk full of the waste paper with which they are only too easily confused. My handwriting is increasingly illegible and I am sometimes unable to identify the source on which I have drawn. Would that I had paid more heed to the salutary advice offered in another long forgotten manual for students, *History and Historical Research* (1928) by C.G. Crump of the Public Record Office: 'Never make a note for future use in such a form . . . that even you yourself will not know what it means, when you come across it some months later.'

My notes are voluminous because my interests have never been very narrowly focused. My subject is what I think of as the historical ethnography of early modern England. Equipped with questions posed by anthropologists, sociologists and philosophers, as well as by other historians, I try to look at virtually all aspects of early modern life, from the physical environment to the values and mental outlook of people at all social levels. Unfortunately, such diverse topics as literacy, numeracy, gestures, jokes, sexual morality, personal cleanliness or the treatment of animals, though central to my concerns, are hard to pursue systematically. They can't be investigated in a single archive or repository of information. Progress depends on building up a picture from a mass of casual and unpredictable references accumulated over a long period. That makes them unsuitable subjects for a doctoral thesis, which has to be completed in a few years. But they are just the thing for a lifetime's reading. So when I read, I am looking out for material relating to several hundred different topics. Even so, I find that, as my interests change, I have to go back to sources I read long ago, with my new preoccupations in mind.

Christopher Hill believed in reading everything written during the period (provided it wasn't in manuscript), and everything subsequently written about it. He used to buy every remotely relevant monograph when it came out, gut it and then sell it. Like him, I try to soak myself in the writings of the time, particularly those I can find on my own shelves or in the Oxford libraries, or in Early English Books Online (EEBO) and Eighteenth-Century Collections Online (ECCO). In G.M. Young's famous words, my aim is to go on reading until I can hear the people talking. Anything written between roughly 1530 and 1770, whatever its genre, will have something to offer. If I peruse a 17th-century letter or skim through a monograph by a modern historian, I am likely to pick up half a dozen quite separate points relating to a variety of different subjects. Because I am as interested in the attitudes and assumptions which are implicit in the evidence as in those which were explicitly articulated at the time, I have got into the habit of reading against the grain. Whether it is a play or a sermon or a legal treatise, I read it not so much for what the author meant to say as for what the text incidentally or unintentionally reveals.

When the time comes to start writing, I go through my envelopes, pick out a fat one and empty it out onto the table, to see what I have got. At this point a pattern usually forms. As Beatrice Webb rightly said, the very process of shuffling notes can be intellectually fertile. It helps one to make new connections and it raises questions to which one must try to find the answer. So after scrutinising my scraps of paper, I set about reading more systematically, often discovering in the process that somebody somewhere has already said most of what I thought I had found out for myself. If not too discouraged, I add my new notes to the old ones and try to create some coherence out of these hundreds of pieces of paper. This involves dividing the topic into a great many subheadings, writing each subheading at the top of a page of A4, stapling the relevant slips onto the appropriate page, and arranging the sheets in a consecutive order. Only then do I start writing. Compared with the labour of making, sorting and arranging notes, this is a relatively speedy business. But it is followed by a much more time-consuming task, that of travelling round the libraries to check the references in my footnotes, only too many of which, thanks to poor handwriting, carelessness and an innate tendency to 'improve' what I have read, turn out to be either slightly wrong or taken out of context. I wish I possessed the splendid insouciance of David Hume, about whom a Scottish friend said, 'Why, mon, David read a vast deal before he set about a piece of his book; but his usual seat was the sofa, and he often wrote with his legs up; and it would have been unco' fashious to have moved across the room when any little doubt occurred.'

When all my mistranscriptions have been sorted out, the task is finished. Months later, the proofs arrive, by which time more books and articles have been published and I have found several more delicious passages which cry out to be inserted. By then, of course, it is too late.

It is possible to take too many notes; the task of sorting, filing and assimilating them can take for ever, so that nothing gets written. The awful warning is Lord Acton, whose enormous learning never resulted in the great work the world expected of him. An unforgettable description of Acton's Shropshire study after his death in 1902 was given by Sir Charles Oman. There were shelves and shelves of books, many of them with pencilled notes in the margin. 'There were pigeonholed desks and cabinets with literally thousands of compartments into each of which were sorted little white slips with references to some particular topic, so drawn up (so far as I could see) that no one but the compiler could easily make out the drift.' And there were piles of unopened parcels of books, which kept arriving, even after his death. 'For years apparently he had been endeavouring to keep up with everything that had been written, and to work their results into his vast thesis.' 'I never saw a sight,' Oman writes, 'that more impressed on me the vanity of human life and learning.'

Living, as I do for much of the year, in Shropshire and following a routine uncomfortably close to Acton's, I find this account distinctly painful. The unread books pile up and I know that I shall not live long enough to use all the references I have accumulated. Those who come after me will almost certainly be unable to read what I have written or interpret my abbreviations, leave alone discover what purpose the excerpts were meant to serve in the first place. As Francis Bacon warned long ago, 'One man's notes will little profit another.'

The truth is that I have become something of a dinosaur. Nowadays, researchers don't need to read early printed books laboriously from cover to cover. They have only to type a chosen word into the appropriate database to discover all the references to the topic they are pursuing. I try to console myself with the reflection that they will be less sensitive to the context of what they find and that they will certainly not make the unexpected discoveries which come from serendipity. But the sad truth is that much of what it has taken me a lifetime to build up by painful accumulation can now be achieved by a moderately diligent student in the course of a morning. Moreover, today's historians don't make notes on pieces of paper. They have computer programs for filing and indexing. Even as I write, an email message informs me that 'wiki software can be used to develop a personal research knowledge base.' My methods are in no way an advance on those of Burckhardt and now appear impossibly archaic. But it is far too late to think of transferring this accumulation onto some electronic database. When I look at my cellar, stuffed with cardboard boxes and dog-eared folders, and littered with loose slips which have broken free from overstuffed envelopes, I envy my colleagues who travel light, with their laptops and digital cameras. But, as Gibbon said, where error is irreparable, repentance is useless.

Yet as I pick my way through my accumulation of handwritten material, I don't feel depressed. The thousands of used envelopes themselves give me a good deal of nostalgic pleasure; they remind me of old friends, of institutions with which I have been associated and of the secondhand booksellers who have sent me catalogues over the years. Admittedly, they also remind me of many false starts: topics I began on, tired of or discovered were being written up by somebody else. But that is a challenge to reorder my materials as the world moves on and my interests change. In his essay 'On Intellectual Craftsmanship', appended to his The Sociological Imagination (1959), C. Wright Mills reassuringly remarks that 'the way in which these categories change, some being dropped and others being added, is an index of your intellectual progress . . . As you rearrange a filing system, you often find that you are, as it were, loosening your imagination.'

I feel sympathy for Robert Southey, whose excerpts from his voracious reading were posthumously published in four volumes as *Southey's Common-Place Book*. He confessed in 1822 that,

> Like those persons who frequent sales, and fill their houses with useless purchases, because they may want them some time or other; so am I for ever making collections, and storing up materials which may not come into use till the Greek Calends. And this I have been doing for five-and-twenty years! It is true that I draw daily upon my hoards, and should be poor without them; but in prudence I ought now to be working up these materials rather than adding to so much dead stock.

In fact, Southey published a great deal, including three-volume histories of Brazil (1810–19) and the Peninsular War (1823–32), in both of which, the ODNB tells us, 'the curious reader can still find much engaging anecdote and odd information.' Unfortunately, these works are said to show poor narrative grasp and a lack of perspective. For without a clear conceptual plan, an accumulation of excerpts, what Milton called 'a paroxysm of citations', can rapidly become a substitute for thought. 'What tho' his head be empty, provided his common-place book be full?' sneered Jonathan Swift.

It is only too easy to misapply excerpted passages by taking them out of their original context. Ideally, I should have followed the technique, recommended as long ago as 1615 by the learned Jesuit Francesco Sacchini, of always making two sets of notes, one to be sliced up and filed, the other to be kept in its original form. That way, I could have seen at a glance where the passage I wanted to quote came in the author's argument. Failing that, there is nothing for it but to look at the source once again and check that I am not misrepresenting it. This may involve return visits to distant record repositories and can be very time-consuming.

Even when all the necessary precautions have been taken, the result will still lack anything approaching scientific precision. For what my method yields is a broad-brush impression of beliefs and behaviour over long periods of time. I am a lumper, not a splitter. I admire those who write tightly focused micro-studies of episodes or individuals, and am impressed by the kind of quantitative history, usually on demographic or economic topics, which aspires to the purity of physics or mathematics. But I am content to be numbered among those many historians whose books remain literary constructions, shaped by their author's moral values and intellectual assumptions. When writing history, there are rules to be followed and evidence to be respected. But no two histories will be the same, whereas the essence of scientific experiments is that they can be endlessly replicated.

In a report for the publisher, an anonymous reader of the manuscript of my recent book *The Ends of Life* described my way of working as an Oxford method, which I associate with the work of Christopher Hill, as well as with Keith Thomas. There is always a line of argument, but it tends to be both contained and artfully concealed in a great many references to and citations of a generous selection of (mostly printed) texts and documents, which account for a high percentage of the text. According to strict and even censorious critical criteria, these materials cannot stand as proof of any argument, since the reader is in the hands of the author and of what he has chosen to serve up as, strictly speaking, illustrations of his own contentions, it being, in principle, always possible to build up a different picture with the aid of different examples. The last thing one will find in this kind of social-cultural history is the allegedly knock-down evidence of statistics, but the wholly justified implication is that these matters are best understood with the aid of what German social scientists and theorists call the faculty of *verstehen*.

That, I think, is a very kindly account of what I try to do: to immerse myself in the past until I know it well enough for my judgment of what is or is not representative to seem acceptable without undue epistemological debate. Historians are like reliable local guides. Ideally, they will know the terrain like the backs of their hands. They recognise all the inhabitants and have a sharp eye for strangers and impostors. They may not have much sense of world geography and probably can't even draw a map. But if you want to know how to get somewhere, they are the ones to take you.

10 June 2010

My Mad Captains
Frank Kermode
remembers the war

I could give you the names o' three captains now 'oo ought to be in
an asylum, but you don't find me interferin' with the mentally afflicted
till they begin to lay about 'em with rammers an' winch-handles.
Kipling: 'Mrs Bathurst'

CALL TO ME all my mad captains. The first of my mad captains
was mad in a quite different way from the others. He was
unlucky as well as crazy, certainly worthy of a better deal
than he got when he found himself consigned, as I was, to service in
a sort of parody-navy, though he would have been quite at home in the
real one, whereas I would not have found there, any more than in
this grotesque doppelgänger, a climate that suited me.

On a certain day, every other Friday perhaps, I can't remember and
it doesn't matter now, the troops got fell in to claim their pay. When
his name was called, the sailor stepped briskly forward, saluted, took
off his cap and placed it on the table. His pay would be placed on the
cap. The sum would often be less than he had expected because of
various deductions, especially what were called 'mulcts'. This was
the archaic word the Navy used to mean 'fines'. Whenever authority
was irritated or distressed by something a rating had done, it would

award him a mulct. Ignorant recruits sometimes found it hard to understand that somebody who was professing to give them something was actually taking something off them. It might be a day's pay or more, and what with one thing and another, it wasn't difficult for a man to be awarded so many mulcts that he got no pay at all. When that happened an officer, or more likely his writer (the Navy word for a 'clerk': the only writers in the Navy were of inferior rank) would cry 'Not Entitled!' and put nothing at all on the cap. The relevant entry in the ledger that lay open before the writer was 'NE', meaning, of course, 'Not Entitled', but decoded by the troops as a North-Easter. The mulcted man would then put on his cap, hand out a parting salute as lively as the one which signalled his approach, about turn and impassively withdraw, unwilling to risk any more such awards by a display of chagrin, dissidence or even surprise. He would then tell his comrades that he'd got a fucking northeaster. The epithet was applied not only to circumstances of disappointment such as this, but also to more agreeable awards like Liberty or what sailors called 'Leaf'. It was used less frequently in connection with what you might hope to be doing when you got your leaf, and never if the person you were likely to be doing it with was a wife or a steady friend. Worn though it was by over-use, it was especially apposite to northeasters. Sometimes simply to be in the Navy was to be in a fucking northeaster that never stopped blowing. Sometimes it seemed that to be alive at all was to have been born in the teeth of such a gale.

The summer of 1940 might have been a sombre time for a twenty-year-old, for it seemed that, unless the war quickly ended in national disaster (as seemed quite probable), the future consisted of indefinitely prolonged military service. But I remember it as a pleasant time, offering many satisfactions to which, for imperfectly examined reasons, I felt myself to be entitled. As for the future, let that come when it comes. Meanwhile, there were parties, tennis, bathing, love and the ordinary terrors, such as the gamble against the disaster of pregnancy, worrying, naturally, but at the same time enlivening.

In September, during the first daylight raids on the docks, I was summoned from the North to London, and, trotting naked from booth to booth, was examined by a team of perfunctory doctors and then interviewed by an amiably rough-tongued civilian who asked me if I had the power of command, was I a leader of men? This was a topic new to me, and I had never had occasion to form an opinion about it, but I assured him I had this power, and believed that I was telling the truth, for like many people at twenty I assumed that my powers were virtually without limit, though I lacked any notion as to how I might have acquired them – hardly from my father, four years a private, the dispossessed owner of a small off-licence, an amiable man, much liked in his own circle precisely because it would never have occurred to him to lead anybody anywhere; or from my education, small grammar school and redbrick, in which such leading as had to be done was done by other people, who would never have dreamed of asking me to join them. However, in the omnipotent summer of 1940, I felt sure I must have leadership tucked away with all my other unused capacity.

Taking me at my word, the brisk, overworked interviewer sent me to Liverpool to be interviewed again, this time by a scholarly captain, a paymaster captain, his sleeves encrusted with bands of gold lace separated by bright white stripes, his breast bemedalled. This was my first encounter with persons of such high rank, though I soon discovered that in the eyes of 'executive' officers, paymasters, or 'pussers' as they were called even if captains, were not quite the real thing, despite their being regarded with a touch of superstitious awe because of their overdeveloped literacy, their familiarity with an arcane compendium called King's Regulations and with the insane naval system of accountancy. But then I was to learn that the real thing was, and perhaps is, not often to be met with.

This captain seemed a rather sympathetic figure, but said nothing, and it took some time for me to realise that this was less because his thoughts were on more important matters, which I would have understood, than because he couldn't think of anything to say. So I said I supposed he would tell me where I should be sent to be trained. He waved this remark aside impatiently, as if there were neither time nor need for such peacetime luxuries. Then, hitting on a subject, he asked me why I wasn't in uniform. 'I have no uniform, sir.' 'Well,' he said, 'that will hardly do. Very little can be done without a uniform. You must get one at once.' It seemed certain that there was more to be said, and I sat still while he continued to ponder. Eventually he walked over to his safe, unlocked it, and took from it what looked like quite a lot of money. This he handed to me, saying, 'Go to Gieves and order yourself two uniforms, one of doeskin and one of serge. On the serge tell them to sew only half a ring. It is for everyday wear and lace all round would fray the cloth. The doeskin is for number ones. Better buy a greatcoat also.' He warmed to the subject and speculated that the tailor was unlikely to be able to execute my order in less than a fortnight. It occurred to me to say in jocular mode that the troops recently extracted from Dunkirk had not looked particularly well turned out, but his mind was on the future. 'So you'll need two weeks' leave,' he said. He unlocked the safe again and gave me more money as an advance of pay, which he correctly assumed I should need to see me through this painful interval. I signed receipts and departed, puzzled but reconciled to the fact that in worlds other than mine they did many things differently.

Accustomed as I had been to living on £180 a year, I had never had so much money all at once, about four months' normal supply; and I had no intention of giving most of it to the expensive tailor nominated by the captain. Instead, I went to a meaner establishment in Paradise Street and bought a ready-made uniform – in doeskin, the silly choice – and had the gold lace sewn on all the way round. I added a few other things, including a greatcoat weighing about twenty pounds which I was still wearing fifteen years later when I was much poorer. Then I went off to see my girl, which is what in those days we called young women, and we went to the seaside, where we stayed in a small boarding house. Every night the landlady and, as we supposed, her husband, made clamorous love on an unstable bed. This struck us as the right way to behave in these difficult times. I don't think we were conscious of any worries at all, unlikely though that must seem.

Returning scrupulously on the due date, I sought out my pale, elegant paymaster captain. He seemed abstracted and hardly knew who I was; perhaps, after all, he had other cares, greater and more martial responsibilities. As before, he was stuck for something to say, so he asked me if I'd like some leave; but the money was all spent, and I felt unreasonably sure that if he were once again to unlock the safe that very action would remind him of our past relationship; so I honourably declined the offer, and instead asked if there was any place I could go to in order to learn my job.

After some deliberation he told me to go down to the Huskisson Dock, find a ship called the Sierra, and report to a Lieutenant Taylor. 'Tell him I sent you to learn the ropes.' He sat at his desk and reluctantly wrote a letter of introduction. As I was leaving the room he stopped me and examined my uniform.

'Where did you get it?' he asked.

'At Gieves, sir.'

'You did well to go there,' he said.

As I walked out of the building, haughtily returning the salutes of passing sailors, I was wondering about HMS Sierra and suspecting that it was unlikely to be the educational establishment I'd have chosen myself, but one thing I knew was that, as I had never had any choice in such matters, it was absurd to expect to have one now. As a matter of fact I was to spend the next two and a half years in that ship, and if I did learn anything I wanted to know I can't now remember what it was. I did pick up some things I didn't want to know: to drink far too much; never to speak of women (except of a wife if you had one, or of the wives of colleagues) without innuendo or obscenity; and to deal with the madness of captains.

As things fell out, instruction in this last art began immediately. I found the ship, a bestially ugly thing rearing its bow coarsely above the dockside, held there by cables with rat-guards positioned, I noticed, to deny entry rather than to prevent flight from the vessel, which belonged to a company trading in West African cocoa. It had a top speed of about nine knots and in peacetime had carried back and forth as supercargo a dozen or so passengers in reasonably lavish colonial style. The officers, taken over with the ship, were professionals of a different caste from regular naval officers; a closed society or guild, but more amiable than the passed-over naval officers who emerged from early retirement to supplement and advise them – 'dugouts', they were called, heavy-eyed and gin-glazed, mostly useless but keen on their privileges.

The Merchant Navy officers nearly all had malaria and from time to time would collapse and lie in their cabins shuddering. Once established, I took to visiting them and offering unwanted conversation. They could offer me a few insights, reduce my ignorance of their world, perhaps even of the world more generally considered. For instance, I hadn't known that in the tropics a man should always put on a jockstrap at sundown and wear a cummerbund at dinner. After a hot day shifting cargo you of course needed a bath, but then you gave yourself the giddy pleasure of the uplift provided by the jockstrap; it was like floating for a moment in the cool of the evening. The tightly-wound cummerbund presumably sustained this effect.

These people also shared certain esoteric jokes which came in series, and when intelligible were clearly obscene. One series featured two characters called Mr Saccone and Mr Speed, names which happened to be drawn from the name of the firm which at that time was the principal supplier of booze to the Fleet. For some reason Saccone and Speed were represented as monkeys in colloquy, with dago accents and an interest in unusual sexual practices. Because I could never join in this game, had never had malaria, never worn a jockstrap, and no doubt for many other reasons, this confederacy of ailing, amiable and experienced officers found me, despite my willingness to please and to visit the sick, quite uninteresting, odd and green, which of course was true. I could understand why they did, which at least was evidence of maturation.

These discoveries lay in the future. As I picked my way across the cluttered dockside and approached the *Sierra*, I entered a world about which, without admitting it even to myself, I knew nothing. All around were inactive workmen, some evidently responsible for fitting a First World War gun on the poop, others sitting among scattered bits of ancient anti-aircraft weapons, while others wandered about the deck or the dock, manifestly unproductive.

In those early days the authorities were still unsubtle about air-raids. Liverpool had suffered some serious night attacks, but the sirens also sounded at intervals through the day, when there was nothing around except perhaps a plane sent over to have a look at the damage inflicted on the previous night. When these daytime alarms went off, the air-raid wardens rushed about blowing their whistles, and in the docks the noise of riveting and the beat of hammers at once ceased. Since it was by now assumed that no raid was likely to follow, the workmen did not move from their places but got out their cards and played till the all-clear sounded, while the public at large simply went on with their usual business. The workmen apparently had it in writing that they should cease work and take cover during an alert; they scrupulously observed the first part of this order and ignored the second. It wasn't difficult to understand this – every concession, every petty benefit, had been achieved by laborious union action, and to work when ordered not to would have struck them as treacherous or crazy. It would have been useless to explain to them that this was not the right way to behave when the Empire was under serious threat and the bastions of democracy were crumbling. If the all-clear came just at the moment when an official tea-break was due, they ran the one into the other and sat on in the sun, enjoying the dusty, leisured scene.

One of these unalarming alerts was in force as I reached the ship. A large sheet of steel dangled in its slings, while its handlers reclined on sacks. The crane-driver dozed in his high cab. I had one foot on the gangway when there was a sudden commotion and an officer whom, ill-informed as I was, I could already identify as an RNR commander, hurried down the gangway. I removed my foot. This man had a sharp red face and cornflower eyes – it seems, in memory, that my mad captains all had cornflower eyes. He looked excited but authoritatively angry. Marching up to a group of card-players, he ordered them to get up and return to work, pointing out that there was a war on, that ships were desperately needed, and so forth. He said something about Churchill, something about the Hun. The men turned towards him, eyed him curiously, and invited him to fuck off. As if he had foreseen this degree of resistance the Commander now took a pistol from his pocket and pointed it at the group. 'Get back to your work,' he said. 'And for God's sake try to behave like men.' At this the men rose, backed away, and as soon as they'd opened a certain distance from the Commander, ran like hell to the dock gate. A cordon of civilian functionaries now appeared from neighbouring offices, smiling nervously at the officer and hinting that such gestures, however well meant, would not in fact advance the war effort, since their likeliest outcome was a full-scale dock strike. He was calm but disappointed. Later, sharing with me a moment of self-reproach, he said he regretted not having 'winged' one of them. 'Then the rest would have pretty quickly toed the line.' He had been in similar situations before.

He went back on board and I followed. I explained to the officer of the watch that I had been sent to see Lt Taylor. The gunman, who was still there at the head of the gangway, said: 'Why the devil do you want to see him?' I sketched a salute and explained my mission. 'You'll probably find him in the wardroom,' he said. 'And don't let me see you again with a button undone.' I was hurt by this because I had spent a lot of time and trouble getting myself up for the part. 'That's exactly the sort of thing we have to get right if we're going to win this war,' he added. I suddenly realised I was being told off by the captain of the *Sierra*. I surveyed with distaste the unspeakable mess over which he presided, feeling only slightly ashamed to have added to it.

This was Commander Stonegate, a mad captain, but a gallant fellow who as a midshipman had fought with Keyes at Zeebrugge and more recently won a DSO on the Dunkirk beach. His conduct on the dockside was perhaps partly explained by his having taken part in these bloody actions. He was said, falsely no doubt, to have witnessed the killing by a British officer of 38 out of 40 men who had tried to surrender to the Germans, presumably to encourage the other two. In any case he had seen some bad things. He was just the man for the summer of 1940, an expert in lost causes and forlorn hopes, a leader of men, of men often too cowardly or too stupid to follow him; perhaps he needed to be a bit mad but he was a shade madder than he needed to be. Very likely what pushed him over the top was the extraordinary quantity of pink gin he drank. Of course, there may have been other more private incitements to mania.

Threading my way past the card parties, I eventually found the wardroom, actually a passenger saloon on the upper deck, designated 'wardroom' by a freshly painted sign, still unfinished and no doubt waiting, like the rest of the vessel, for the all-clear. Behind the bar was a man who turned out to be Taylor, acting as his own steward. Perhaps the regular barman had taken cover. Taylor was a tall thin man with a very white face, middle or late thirties. He looked quite refined but gloomy. He had been purser of the ship before it was taken over and was now responsible to their Lordships for its supply and secretarial requirements.

He gave me a pink gin and offered me a lamb's tongue, which he pulled out of an open tin. He explained that he had some time before decided that what suited his constitution best was an exclusive diet of lambs' tongues. He pointed to several cartons of them, stacked against the wall. 'They should last me a good while,' he said, but added that he was worried about maintaining his supply if the ship was sent to inaccessible foreign parts. He carried an open tin everywhere he went, from time to time popping a pale pink leathery strip of the meat into his mouth and slowly chewing it. He told me in his quiet, depressed voice that he knew nothing whatever about the Navy; he found its methods of accounting and even its manner of conducting correspondence quite unintelligible. He complained that he was the very last person the Paymaster Captain should have sent me to. I took to him at once. In his office he pointed to a great unsorted heap of books and papers. King's Regulations, Admiralty Fleet Orders, Confidential Admiralty Fleet Orders, handbooks explaining how to carve a duck. 'You'll find everything in there, I daresay,' he told me sadly. For his own part he proposed to account for stores, pay and so on, in an ordinary human way. His accounts would be in order, though not in the order recommended, indeed commanded by their domineering Lordships. Probably he would have liked to feed the ship's company on lambs' tongues, washed down with pink gin, for this would have made for simpler accounting procedures than the fussily varied diet demanded. Sighing rather attractively, Taylor now said he must get home to his wife. We walked together to the gangway, he carrying gloves and a tin of lambs' tongues. We saluted and went ashore.

I never saw him again; he died two days after our only meeting, presumably of malnutrition and cirrhosis. He got a rather early and blustery northeaster. By another brilliant expedient of the Paymaster Captain, Taylor's deputy, a Sub-Lieutenant Hewlitt, was promoted to the vacant place and I took his. Hewlitt was about thirty-five, a grey, clean-linened, brushed sort of man, of most cautious demeanour. He was still deciding whether to marry a woman he had been courting for fifteen years. 'You need to be sure with women,' he would say. 'There's mistakes that can't be corrected.' That was also how he ran his office, checking and double-checking far into the night, unwillingly impressed but also alarmed by the careless pace at which I worked. It was he who gave me that advice about the jockstrap, and he also told me that I must always dubbin new shoes and never entrust their care and cleaning to anybody else.

Our first official duty together was to attend Taylor's funeral and condole with his astonished wife. It was a quiet affair and was just ending with sherry and cake when Stonegate suddenly turned up. He had been in London for a few days, possibly summoned to explain to his superiors why he had threatened civilian dockworkers with a pistol. Drunk to the point beyond which more alcohol can make very little difference, he approached the widow, took her hand, and said in a grave, confident way: 'My dear, he can't really be dead, you know. If he were I should have been officially informed.' Mrs Taylor looked slightly more amazed than before, but neither wept nor spoke. 'I suppose eating all that tinned lamb upset him a bit,' Stonegate continued, as if nothing more was at stake than an unusually prolonged *crise de foie*. He next explained that to his regret he had urgent business requiring him to leave without more delay, thus, for the moment, denying the widow any further consolation, but he turned at the door and promised to have the remaining cartons of lambs' tongues sent round to her house.

Next day I took up my duties as his secretary. My main job was to insert a filling of intelligible prose asking for something, or offering humble compliance with some peremptory demand, into the sandwich of grandiose salutation and valedictory obeisance insisted on by their Lordships. We rubbed along fairly well, Stonegate having what I came to recognise as the usual awe felt by naval officers at what they took to be the superhuman powers of otherwise negligible people who, though presumed incapable of anything else, could write letters easily. The rest of the work was more difficult, since no more than Taylor could Hewlitt or I understand the byzantine naval system of accounting. You entered not the true cost of anything but an arbitrary figure selected by authority. The price of beef, for instance, was always the same unless you were told to alter it, and the figure, which memory says was 7d a pound, bore no relation to what we paid for it. In this way it was possible to feed a sailor on 6d a day, as their Lordships required. Of course the real cost had to show up somewhere, and the relation between the two figures was deeply problematic. Hewlitt added everything up, down and sideways, over and over, in a hopeless attempt to resolve the discrepancies, while I swashbuckled across the ledger, alert to imaginary indications of sensemaking, seeking occult rational structures. We made a bad pair.

Meanwhile the ship was somehow patched together and provided with a crew that called for the pen of a Conrad: the sly greaser, the rusé steward and the genuinely naval bosun. There was the dugout lieutenant-commander who recognised in this vessel nothing that reminded him of the Navy except the gin at twopence a shot. Officers had a large daily allowance of spirits, which was nevertheless greatly exceeded. Some would spend most of their pay on booze, sitting all day long in the dark wardroom, smoking duty-free cigarettes and speaking bitterly of the Geddes Axe, that infamous instrument of government which, after the First War, had, in what seemed to them a frenzy of cost-cutting, prematurely lopped off their jobs.

With such helpers Stonegate, inappropriately on Trafalgar Day, got his ship to sea, wearing the white ensign for the first time, its weird crew at their stations. He headed North, spending the long night on his bridge, all dressed up with a white collar and a tie, a gold-spangled cap and a greatcoat. At Lamlash on the Isle of Arran we stopped a while and were given too much drink at too many parties involving eightsome reels and the like, by people who mistook us for hardy adventurers requiring rest and recreation. Then Stonegate was again summoned to London, not, this time, to return. His replacement was signalled. A few days later we heard that, ready as ever with his pistol, he had shot himself. So he got his northeaster. We were never officially informed.

20 October 1994

A Part Song
Denise Riley

i

You principle of song, what are you *for* now
Perking up under any spasmodic light
To trot out your shadowed warblings?
Mince, slight pillar. And sleek down
Your furriness. Slim as a whippy wire
Shall be your hope, and ultraflexible.
Flap thinly, sheet of beaten tin
That won't affectionately plump up
More cushioned and receptive lays.
But little song, don't so instruct yourself
For none are hanging around to hear you.
They have gone bustling or stumbling well away.

ii

What is the first duty of a mother to a child?
At least to keep the wretched thing alive – Band
Of fierce cicadas, stop this shrilling.
My daughter lightly leaves our house.
The thought rears up: *fix in your mind this*
Maybe final glimpse of her. Yes, lightning could.
I make this note of dread, I register it.
Neither my note nor my critique of it
Will save us one iota. I know it. And.

iii

Maybe a retouched photograph or memory,
This beaming one with his striped snake-belt
And eczema scabs, but either way it's framed
Glassed in, breathed hard on, and curated.
It's odd how boys live so much in their knees.
Then both of us had nothing. You lacked guile
And were transparent, easy, which felt natural.

iv

Each child gets cannibalised by its years.
It was a man who died, and in him died
The large-eyed boy, then the teen peacock
In the unremarked placid self-devouring
That makes up being alive. But all at once
Those natural overlaps got cut, then shuffled
Tight in a block, their layers patted square.

v

It's late. And it always will be late.
Your small monument's atop its hillock
Set with pennants that slap, slap, over the soil.
Here's a denatured thing, whose one eye rummages
Into the mound, her other eye swivelled straight up:
A *short while only, then I come*, she carols – but is only
A fat-lot-of-good mother with a pointless alibi: 'I didn't
Know.' Yet might there still be some part for me
To play upon this lovely earth? Say. Or
Say No, earth at my inner ear.

vi

A wardrobe gapes, a mourner tries
Her several styles of howling-guise:
You'd rather not, yet you must go
Briskly around on beaming show.

A soft black gown with pearl corsage
Won't assuage your smashed ménage.
It suits you as you are so pale.
Still, do not get that saffron veil.
Your dead don't want you lying flat.
There'll soon be time enough for that.

vii

Oh my dead son you daft bugger
This is one glum mum. Come home I tell you
And end this tasteless melodrama – quit
Playing dead at all, by now it's well beyond
A joke, but your humour never got cruel
Like this. Give over, you indifferent lad,
Take pity on your two bruised sisters. For
Didn't we love you. As we do. But by now
We're bored with our unproductive love,
And infinitely more bored by your staying dead
Which can hardly interest you much, either.

viii

Here I sit poleaxed, stunned by your vanishing
As you practise your charm in the underworld
Airily flirting with Persephone. Not *so hard*
To imagine what her mother *had gone through*
To be ferreting around those dark sweet halls.

ix

They'd sworn to stay for ever but they went
Or else I went – then concentrated hard
On the puzzle of what it ever truly *meant*
For someone to be here then, just like that
To not. Training in mild loss was useless

Given the final thing. And me lamentably
Slow to 'take it in' – far better toss it out,
How should I take in such a bad idea. No,
I'll stick it out instead for presence. If my
Exquisite hope can wrench you right back
Here, resigned boy, do let it as I'm waiting.

x

I can't get sold on reincarnating you
As those bloody 'gentle showers of rain'
Or in 'fields of ripening grain' – oooh
Anodyne – nor yet on shadowing you
In the hope of eventually pinpointing
You bemused among the *flocking souls*
Clustered like bats, as all thronged gibbering
Dusk-veiled – nor in modern creepiness.
Lighthearted presence, be bodied forth
Straightforwardly. Lounge again under
The sturdy sun you'd loved to bake in.
Even ten seconds' worth of a sighting
Of you would help me get through
This better. With a camera running.

xi

Ardent bee, still you go blundering
With downy saddlebags stuffed tight
All over the fuchsia's drop earrings.
I'll cry 'Oh bee!' to you, instead –
Since my own dead, apostrophised,
Keep mute as this clear garnet glaze
You're bumping into. Blind diligence,
Bee, or idiocy – this banging on and on
Against such shiny crimson unresponse.

xii

Outgoing soul, I try to catch
You calling over the distances
Though your voice is echoey,
Maybe tuned out by the noise
Rolling through me – or is it
You orchestrating that now,
Who'd laugh at the thought
Of me being sung in by you
And being kindly dictated to.
It's not like hearing you live was.
It is what you're saying in me
Of what is left, gaily affirming.

xiii

Flat on a cliff I inch toward its edge
Then scrutinise the chopped-up sea
Where gannets' ivory helmet skulls
Crash down in tiny plumes of white
To vivify the languid afternoon –
Pressed round my fingertips are spikes
And papery calyx frills of fading thrift
That men call sea pinks – so I can take
A studied joy in natural separateness.
And I shan't fabricate some nodding:
'She's off again somewhere, a good sign
By now, she must have got over it.'

xiv

Dun blur of this evening's lurch to
Eventual navy night. Yet another
Night, day, night over and over.
I so want to join you.

xv

The flaws in suicide are clear
Apart from causing bother
To those alive who hold us dear
We could miss one another
We might be trapped eternally
Oblivious to each other
One crying *Where are you, my child*
The other calling *Mother.*

xvi

Dead, keep me company
That sears like titanium
Compacted in the pale
Blaze of living on alone.

xvii

Suspended in unsparing light
The sloping gull arrests its curl
The glassy sea is hardened waves
Its waters lean through shining air
Yet never crash but hold their arc
Hung rigidly in glaucous ropes
Muscled and gleaming. All that
Should flow is sealed, is poised
In implacable stillness. Joined in
Non-time and halted in free fall.

xviii

It's all a resurrection song.
Would it ever be got right
The dead could rush home
Keen to press their chinos.

xix

She do the bereaved in different voices
For the point of this address is to prod
And shepherd you back within range
Of my strained ears; extort your reply
By finding any device to hack through
The thickening shades to you, you now
Strangely unresponsive son, who were
Such reliably kind and easy company,
Won't you be summoned up once more
By my prancing and writhing in a dozen
Mawkish modes of reedy piping to you
– Still no? Then let me rest, my dear.

xx

My sisters and my mother
Weep dark tears for me
I drift as lightest ashes
Under a southern sea
O let me be, my mother
In no unquiet grave
My bone-dust is faint coral
Under the fretful wave

9 February 2012

Germs: A Memoir
Richard Wollheim

A S A CHILD, I loved lists of all sorts, and found that all sorts
of things could be listed. I listed the sails on a windjammer,
not knowing how they worked, and the names of philoso-
phers, not knowing what they were, and, a particular source of
pleasure, the names of royal mistresses and of royal favourites, not
knowing how they earned their keep. I listed the flags of the different
nations, and their capital cities, and the rivers on which these cities
stood. I listed butterflies, and the names of Napoleonic marshals,
and shirtmakers in London, in Paris, in Venice. When on a journey I
had, as a matter of singular urgency, to list in what became a succes-
sion of small red notebooks the names of the places we went
through, often with a pencil that went blunt when I needed it most,
I learned out of necessity countless ways in which place names could
be discovered by a small boy sitting in the back seat of a car, and
craning his neck so as to see out of the window. There were the wasp-
coloured AA signs, there was the writing over the local post office,
there were ancient milestones, and, in many counties, signposts had
a finial, cone-shaped or circular, giving the name of the nearest
town or village. To grown-ups, or those I met, these clues were
unknown, or were so until the war came and they were ostentatiously
swept away so as not to give assistance to enemy parachutists, but to
a small boy, always in doubt that he had been anywhere unless he

could write the name down with a pencil in a notebook, these signs had a value born of desperation. And, of all these lists, the most necessitated – though, even if I could have, I never would have entrusted it to paper – was a catalogue of the various ways in which the unreliability, the incontinence, of the body forced itself on my attention. I memorised the different shapes, and colours, and outlines, sharp or blurred, with which scabs, and bruises, and grazes, can mark the skin, nor was I content until I also had a mental list of the yet more formless stains that shame a child's underclothing as the secretions of the body spread outwards, and I would try to commit them to memory even as, in the sanctuary of the lavatory, I endeavoured to remove their physical traces.

I was born on 5 May 1923, in a London nursing home, which occupied a house in an early 19th-century square. The square, Torrington Square, was destroyed in the war. One side of it still stands as a terrace, but I do not know whether this includes the house where I was born, even though I know the number of the house, and, if the house still stood, it would not be more than two or three hundred yards from the university department in which I taught for over thirty years. And, if I add that, for the last twenty of those years, my department was in the very square, and more or less directly across from the very house, where my mother was born, and where she lived for the first five or six years of her life, and I never went to look at the house, it might seem as though my life has had a unity to which I have been indifferent. I can only say that coincidences are not unity.

My mother was much impressed by coincidences: these and others. She treated coincidence as a fact of life, and she tended to think of it as the most powerful link that could unite two lives. She asked me if I didn't think it a coincidence that someone had been to the same school as my brother, or that I shared my initials with a friend of hers. She would say to me sometimes, 'Do you believe in coincidence?' meaning, did I accept the importance of coincidence. If, in later years,

I asked her something about the Russian ballet, or about my father's life, she was likely to say, 'That's a coincidence, for last week I over-heard someone talking about the Russian ballet,' and she might add, 'Has the Russian ballet come back into fashion, because I have a lot of things I could tell people?' or, 'That's a coincidence, I was thinking about Daddy only today, and you couldn't have known about that,' and she might add, 'Or could you?' and these coincidences she then took, and expected me to take, as more interesting than what I had asked her. Certainly she never gave me the information I asked for. But she never answered any question that I put to her. She did not like it if one person talked to another.

My parents, once married, always lived outside London. This was a decision of my father's. Before he married in 1920, he had, from the time he arrived in England from Paris in 1900, with just one exception, when, during the Great War, as we called it in my child-hood, he had evacuated himself to Aylesbury, always lived in London.

Marriage, he thought, required a change. A family needed fresh air. I paid dearly for this decision, but it was what he would have thought had he worked in Paris or in Berlin, and, once I recognised the un-Englishness of the thought, I was willing, at least intermittently, to forgive him for it. I colluded by trying to think of the roads, and the houses, and the woods where I grew up as part of some leafy French or German suburb, Neuilly-sur-Seine, or Wannsee, or Schwabing, where the air is perennially fresh. Where I actually lived was the first issue over which I asked myself whether reality mattered, or how much.

As to what the decision meant for my father, I do not know. It certainly gave him freedom from the family for whose sake he had made it. Weekends apart, he dined at home at most eight or nine times a year. Generally he returned from London well after midnight. He rose after a breakfast in bed of stewed apple, toast melba, tea, a glass of hot water and some pills, and left the house briskly at 8.20.

His face was delicately shaved, he selected his overcoat with great care, put one arm in the sleeve, shook the coat up onto his shoulders, inserted the other arm, picked up his letters and a newspaper, and ran the short distance from the front door to the waiting car. The only friends he had were friends who came down from London.

That I was born in London came about because my father thought that, at least for a matter as serious as birth, there was no reliable doctor outside London. Indeed it was only for us, us English as he must have thought of us, my mother, my brother and me, that an English doctor would do at all. For himself, until history put a stop to it, he always went to Berlin to see his doctor, and, when his doctor came to London for a few days, my father would take him out to an expensive restaurant, and there order for both of them all the rich food he had travelled several hundred miles to hear himself forbidden. In two other respects, he tried somewhat harder to follow his doctor's orders. Every summer he started a cure at Marienbad, or Carlsbad, or Pau, though he invariably broke it off after a week, and spent the rest of his holiday on the Lido or the Riviera, or at Biarritz. And every morning, he stood on a pair of scales, and, taking out a gold pencil from his dressing-gown pocket, wrote down his weight in fine German numerals, on a pad which was attached to a metal ashtray.

Shortly after I was born, I was circumcised. It was done by a rabbi, and with, I was led to believe, a cigar cutter. I was circumcised for health reasons, though there might have been other vestigial reasons. I imagine that my father was circumcised, but I never knew for sure. I do not believe that I ever saw my father naked, even though I often watched him dress in the morning. These levees, to which I was certain to be invited within a day or so of my father's return from one of his frequent trips abroad, when he would lay out at the end of the bed the dozen or so ties he had brought back, were almost the total of the moral education that I received from him. However, from them

I learned many things which I value highly. I learned how to choose a shirt in the morning, I learned how to hold up my socks with garters, I learned how to use the forefinger of the right hand to make a dimple in the knot of my tie, I learned how to fold a handkerchief, and to dab it with eau de Cologne before putting it into my breast pocket, and, above all, I learned that it was only through the meticulous attention to such rituals that a man could hope to make his body tolerable to the world. But, as to the body itself, what I learned was strictly limited by the fact that, at a certain moment, my father invariably turned his back to me, and, manipulating the long tails that shirts had in those days, passed the back of his shirt between his legs, and so deftly pulled it up towards his waist, that, by the time he turned round to face me, the lower part of his body was completely swaddled in linen shirt and silk underwear.

It was another thirty years or so before I came to realise the loss that I, and perhaps both of us, had suffered through my father's reticence. We were on holiday in North Wales, where we had taken for the summer the upper part of a rambling 19th-century castle, and, one late afternoon, various members of a large and famous Bloomsbury family, children and grandchildren of the old lady to whom the house belonged, had settled down in deckchairs under the window where I was trying to write. Some of them had been swimming in the sea, some reading, one had been writing in pencil in a large notebook, and now they had gathered, with bottles of white wine standing on the grass between them, and they were settling down to discuss a member of the family whose arrival had been delayed. Was he a contented person, or a discontented person? Did he really belong to the town, or to the country? Would he have been more at home in Tolstoy or in Turgenev? What painter could have done justice to his appearance? How did he look at his best? On all these matters conflicting views were expressed, and, when it came to the last question, a dry, shrill voice, coming from a young man, rose to a peak: 'I think Dad looks best stark naked.' There were restrained cries of 'Oh, yes, yes,' and generous applause.

As these words reached me, sitting at my desk and writing a partly confessional work, which I recognised at the time would never, on one pretext or another, be allowed to see the light of day, I was made to feel how different my life would have been, what a happier fate my manuscript at least would have had, had I only been in a position to make that remark, or had my father, just once, turned to confront me as he was arranging himself within his trousers. I am not suggesting that my father was emotionally reserved with me. Indeed I never felt him to be more himself than when, leaning forwards and taking off his spectacles, he tickled my cheeks with his eyelashes, and gave me what he called 'butterfly kisses'. With me, he was, I suspect, more bored than reserved. It was the thought of having, within the dullness of his own house, exposed to a young boy the vagaries of life, the excitements that awaited him in later years or in foreign cities, that he found so daunting.

When I was somewhat less than two we moved house, and this house, like the last, my father rented. The truth was that there were only certain things that my father liked owning. He liked owning paintings, and, to a somewhat lesser degree, he liked owning books. He liked owning the things that he turned out of his pockets at night and laid out on the dressing-table. These were the gold pencil, a gold case for a toothpick, a very thin Swiss pocket watch in a shagreen case, which, when pulled open, became a small bedside clock, a special key for opening first-class compartments on the Southern Railway, a silver cigarette lighter, a few carefully folded five-pound notes, printed, as they were in those days, on the finest transparent paper and held in place by a gold clip, some spare coins, and a small pearl tiepin, which smelled permanently of eau de Cologne. My father liked owning suits, and he liked owning ties, in both cases in profusion, and the latter passion he communicated to me, though, in loving ties, I possibly loved the shirtmakers they came from, or at least the names of the shirtmakers, even more. In time I came to believe that, through associating my father's ties with the labels sewn inside them, I would, when expensive foreigners came down to lunch on a Sunday, be able, by observing how the silk was ribbed, or how the dots were formed, or the precise shape of the knot, to know one of the most important things about them, or the shirtmaker they went to. Another thing my father liked was paying for everyone when he ate out: he liked owning, for a brief while, his own airy portion of a restaurant or a grillroom.

At about the time when I came of an age to notice novelty, and no longer assumed that the world as I now looked out on it had witnessed all the events recounted in the history books which I was just beginning to devour, the first new thing to break in on my vision was the cinema. At one moment the cinema did not exist, and, the next moment, these generally square buildings were all over. Made of the thin, dark red bricks of the period, they were faced with white stucco grooved to look like stone, which, with great artificiality, introduced the bright look of the seaside into land-locked suburbia. Behind the cinema was the car-park reserved for the patrons – *cinema, car-park, patron*, all being new words – but soon there were few more familiar, more welcome, sights than the string of small coloured lights looped over the entrance to the car-park, or the two chromium-plated boxes that were screwed to the brickwork of the cinema, through the glass fronts of which, when they were not too dirtied by the rain, passers-by could make out from the sepia-tinted stills, the high points in the movie that was currently showing: when one of these shots came up in the course of the movie, a low gasp of recognition was involuntarily released into the crowded darkness of the hall. If the film was a western, or a war film, another form of preview, which I loved, was a sand table that would be set out in the foyer of the cinema, re-creating the high sierras and canyons of some unknown land, or the battlefields of Flanders with their water-filled trenches and blasted trees, or the skies above them where fearless aviators were locked in single combat.

In every cinema, a patrons' book was placed next to the kiosk where tickets were sold, and those who signed their names in the book would then receive free a monthly programme, printed in violet ink on shiny paper so that the lettering was always slightly blurred. Each double bill had a page devoted to it, and it was a rule of our family, originating probably from my mother, who liked rules without reason, that only on a Thursday morning, and then with her permission, and under her direct supervision, could the programme be picked up, and the page turned, turned and then very precisely folded back onto itself. When my mother turned the page of the programme, she let out a low hiss. Ordinarily the programme lay on my father's bedside table, along with the miscellaneous books he brought back from his travels: some Tauchnitz volumes, a work of Freud's in German, a novel by Joseph Kessel in French. My mother had no need for a bedside table.

Half turning the page, or looking round the corner into the future, was, without some very special excuse, forbidden, and not until I was fourteen or fifteen, by which time I was grappling in my mind with the ideas of Raskolnikov, did it seriously occur to me to breach this rule.

For each film, the programme gave the title, listed the characters and the actors who played them, said whether the film was a U certificate or A certificate, and provided a brief synopsis of the plot. I loved the words *character, cast, plot, synopsis*, and I wanted to learn the precise distinctions that they embodied. I did well with some of these words, but with the last of them I made the least headway. The word itself was obscure, and so were many of the synopses themselves, particularly so when the film was A certificate, or was judged unsuitable for children to see, for the management went on the assumption that the synopsis, though it had to be fair, must be suitable for all to read, with a result that was very far from that intended. Even as I began to read the three or four lines, I fell into a state of dread that I had read, or was just about to read, something that, innocuous enough in itself, would nevertheless inform me, particularly if I allowed my mind to wander, of something that I was not supposed to know about, and, though I had no desire to preserve my innocence, what I did not want was to lose it through someone else, and least of all through someone else's carelessness or oversight, for then I would inadvertently be tied for ever to the shame from which I desired to escape.

The regime under which I grew up reserved the cinema for two sorts of occasion: winter, and rainy afternoons. Winter came round with its own relentlessness, and it began on the day when the clothes I had been wearing for the past few months (aertex shirts, khaki shorts, cotton underpants) were, without any discussion, taken out of my chest of drawers and cupboard, and replaced by another lot (Viyella shirts, tweed shorts, woollen combinations) which were stored on shelves of wooden slats surrounding a metal boiler held together by rivets, in a small, steamy room called 'the airing cupboard'. At first the winter clothes were painfully rough against the skin, the one exception being my balaclava, which, because it was made out of the very coarsest wool, had, on the suggestion of some friend of my parents, been lined with silk. However, one great glory of winter clothes was that, once the sharp smell of mothballs had worn off, they were aromatic, and, as they were laid out first thing in the morning, most powerfully when there was snow outside, they gave off the delicate smell of warmed flannel, which, merging with the smell of eau de Cologne, which illicitly I dabbed myself with as soon as my father left the house, stayed with me all day. The end of winter was left more to chance than its arrival, and it roughly coincided with the sound of the first cuckoo, and, a week or so later, winter and summer clothes were reversed.

Rain, by contrast, was unpredictable, and it remained all my child-hood the object of a deep conflict. On the one hand, there was the knowledge that only the sight of rain spitting against the windows, or battling with the wipers as they raced across the windscreen, could convert what was a shadowy promise written in violet ink into the warm reality of the cinema. Entry into this reality was gradual, and it was the richer, the darker, the more deliciously oppressive, for the three or four stages into which it was broken up. First, the car had to be parked. My mother, like many drivers of that period, had some difficulty in 'backing back', as it was called, and often I could feel my bladder fill in response to her slowness. Then there was the run across the car-park in wellingtons and a stiff mac, crunching the cinders underfoot as I went, and already feeling that the world in which anything might happen was taking me over. Jumping the puddles, I was a horse leaping a swollen stream as we, the cavalry, moved up into the attack, or I was a steeplechaser taking in its stride a particu-larly vicious hurdle, or, cut out the horse, and now I was my own awkward self who hadn't seen the puddle, and waded straight through it, or who had seen it but hadn't noticed how deep it was, and slammed down, first one foot, then the other, to make the water splash up over the top of my boots. For a minute or so, I became the rough boy I never wanted to be. Next there was the delay as the tickets had to be bought, and the small violet or cherry-coloured pieces of paper curled up through the carefully etched slab of steel that lay just the other side of the ornamental grille, and were torn off and handed to us. Certainty descended, and we progressed through the foyer, up the steps, into the cinema itself, unless there was a necessary detour through the long curtains into the chamber grandiosely marked 'Gentlemen'. My prayer was always the same: it was that we should arrive just before the lights went down, and the torches of the usher-ettes, flickering like fireflies in the night, were needed to direct us to our seats. For, once darkness fell, couples who had nowhere else to meet started to find comfort in the warm smell of each other, and, for me to be certain that I could withstand the excitement with which the cinema began to creak, it was best to have looked on the faces of the audience while they were still distinct under the ceiling lights. Indeed I could see no reason why my mother should not imitate the punctuality that my governess showed every Sunday when she took me to church, and why we should not time our entry to perfection so that we would walk down the aisle at the very moment when the organ, which always gave me a headache if I had to listen to it for any period of time, had stopped, and the organist had taken his bow, and organ and organist had descended into some uncertain depths. If only my mother would co-operate with my wishes, then no sooner would I have been got into my seat, and my mac folded on a neighbouring chair, than the great miraculous event, half sunset, half sunrise, with the intervening night displaced, would start to unfold. The lights dimmed, a hush, like the end of the day, fell on the audience, and the first titles came up on the screen, and they could, just for a moment, be seen on the far side of the gauze curtains, as clear as pebbles through still water. Then, as the curtains slid open, and the gauze was gathered up into pleats, it was as though a light wind had started up before dawn, and made ripples on the surface of the stream, and now, from one second to the next, as fast as that, the lettering became blurred, until the curtains passed across it, and then, one by one, the words again became legible, and the screen took on the unbounded promise of a book first opened.

All this I longed for, but, against this, there was another sight, and the deep-seated dread I had of it. It was that when, at the end of the film, still blinking at the light, still trying to resolve the loyalties that the film had stirred up in me, who was good, who was bad, and, as a separate issue, which side was I on, I would find myself standing by the heavy glass doors that led back to reality, and not only would the rain have stopped, but the sun would have come out. By now the water that had clung to the trees, or that had collected on the lamp-posts and on the tiled roofs and on the undersides of the gutters, would, at first slowly, but with gathering momentum, have dripped down, and now lay on the road, where the first rays of pale sunlight hit it, so that, looking out, I could see the tarred surface glint and sparkle in the late, departing glory of the evening. To many a natural cause of joy, this sight stirred in me the deepest, darkest melancholy. Local sunlight after rain had, quite unaided, the power, not just to make my spirits drop, many things did that, but to convince me, beyond anything that hope could counter, that life would never again have anything to offer me. Even today, when in actuality the sheen on a bright, wet surface has more or less lost its terrors for me, I have only in imagination to take myself back in years, and I can once again understand the full dismal power that the experience had over me. But my inability to convey this terror to others, like my inability to convey the far worse horror of the smell and sight and touch of newspaper, has sometimes made me feel a mute among mankind. One evening, while I was an undergraduate at Oxford, about the time I first got to know Lord D.C., and he had given me the sense, which I had barely had up till that moment, of how easy it might be to talk to someone, the conversation after dinner turned to the differences between melancholy, and sadness, and nostalgia, and to what Turgenev, and what Jane Austen, and what Hardy, could tell us about these things, and I, after a silence that I had kept for twenty minutes or so, plucked up my courage to bare my soul to the company around the table, and I said that I knew nothing more melancholy than sun after rain on a suburban road. D., who was my host, turned to look at me, screwing his head around in a very characteristic way, and blurted out his answer in a fast, high-pitched voice. 'Richard,' he said, 'I think I see exactly what you mean, and it's fascinating, but really I don't see why "suburban". Aren't you trying to be too – specific? I don't see why suburban has anything to do with it. I really don't think it has.' At that moment, I believe, though I have not fully appreciated it until now, the certainty that I had had interesting experiences, and that one day I would be able to convey their poignancy in words of great precision, died. Over the years it was to die many deaths, none altogether fatal.

Someone might ask why could I not have wanted the rain to come down enough that I could go to the cinema, but to clear up enough that, the film over, I would look out on dry streets? I convey nothing about my childhood if it is not clear that I could never have formed such a desire, for I always found one thing worse than having too little, and that was having too much. To a superstitious child, which I was, it was like being God. To a young boy unruly with socialism, which I was soon to be, it was like being rich. It handed life over to boredom.

The sight that so distressed me brought me closer to the sense of death than anything else that I experienced at that time of my life: closer even than seeing, as I once did, from the front seat of my mother's car, around six o'clock on a Saturday evening, a man in white flannel trousers, who had been walking home after an energetic game of tennis, and had collapsed just where the road was crossing an expanse of gorse and fern. At the moment we passed, two ambulance men were drawing a sheet over his face. A tennis racquet lay beside him, out of its press, which, I knew, was the final neglect.

Over the years, sunlight after rain on suburban streets has been overtaken as an intimation of mortality by another sight. This is the sight at evening of large orange tail-lights, dipping and rising, rising and falling, as the cars and the taxis, one after another, slowly recede down Park Avenue, bumping over the potholes and the large metal panels, past the expensive apartment blocks and their doormen, past the neon-lit coffee-shops where small elderly ladies in fur capes dine early, past the street-vendors and the stores where cheap cigars are sold, until they eventually disappear into the electric blue of the dusk.

At Lower Halliford, there was a big, rambling hotel, part Tudor, part improvisation out of corrugated iron and ill-fitting panes of glass. It was there that parties of fishermen stayed, and, one stifling August evening, when most likely I was ten or eleven, my father, quite uncharacteristically, proposed that we should go there and dine as a family, perhaps to celebrate the unlikely fact that he was in England at that time of the year. How the meal passed, and who spoke to whom, and the measure of my father's disappointment, are things I find it impossible to imagine. What followed an hour or so after I had gone to bed was of a kind that punctuated my childhood.

At dinner I had ordered what was at that time my favourite food: a grilled Dover sole on the bone. Whether the fault lay with the fish, or with the way it was cooked, or with the suppressed excitement inside me, I do not know, but, after saying my prayers and sleeping a short while, I woke up. I rushed myself to the bathroom, and there, crouched over the washbasin, I began a long agonising vigil. Hour after hour passed: for much of the time my governess, with whom I shared a bedroom, stayed with me, and once my father came in and cooled my forehead with eau de Cologne. Craning my head forward, I wondered why, knowing that things would be better if I could stick my finger down my throat, I could not do so: was it the love of life, or was it the lure of death, and why could I not achieve the result I desired by merely pretending that my finger had gone as deep down as I could want? I prayed to God, and promised that, in return for a respite from terror, I would give up this, I would give up that. Never again, as the bathwater grew cold, would I tell myself stories about the courts of distant royalty, which had, I noticed, the power to wrinkle the skin on my scrotum.

Some time in the early hours of the morning, I managed, against all odds, to raise my head, and I suddenly caught sight of the moon, and I tried to offer up my stomach, and the dreadful taste of rotting fish in my mouth and around my teeth, and all my feverish thoughts, to this sudden vision of beauty. To see the moon in her entirety, I placed my forehead against a pipe, and rolled it to right and left, so as to catch now this refraction, now that refraction, as the image passed through the pane of fluted glass, and, years later, during and just after the war, in nightclubs, or bottle parties, or small homosexual clubs where my friends took me, I would, in response to frustration, or uncertainty, or fear, get up from the table where we were sitting, excuse myself from the predatory attentions of the cigarette-girl with her beestung lips, and walk falteringly to the lavatory, and there I would rest my forehead against the cream-coloured pipe that brought the water down from the cistern into the lavatory bowl, and slowly rotate my head in that old way, to right and left, from side to side to side. Without benefit of the moon, I sought solace from the cool of the pipe, and from the words of the crooner as they filtered through the flimsy door. On such occasions, a single line of poetry, which had become like a rune for me ever since I first read it at the age of 15, appeared in my head, repeating itself over and over again, night after night, frustration after frustration, lavatory after lavatory. 'Elle passa sa nuit sainte dans la latrine.' It has been my companion, this vagabond line, this present from the voyant voyou, for over sixty years.

What happened with the Dover sole repeated itself with every favourite food of childhood. First, I loved it; then there was one occasion too many, and I was sick all night; then the next morning, I had turned equally against the thing, the thought of the thing, and the word for the thing. The foods were in turn Dover sole; flapjacks; unripe plums, which I preferred to ripe plums; tinned sardines; fried tomatoes; and, most fallen from grace in that I cannot eat them to this day, sweetbreads.

Once a week there were seven ties of my father's, plus one or two black bow ties, to be taken to the dry-cleaners to be steamed and pressed. I always tried to be the one who gathered up the ties from the stair-rail on which they were set out, so that, running my thumb into the heavy silk of the lining, I could find the name of the shirt-maker from whom they came. For some years I used to think that I would come of age when my ties too were pressed every time I wore them. But, by the age of eleven or twelve, I changed my mind on this subject, and for a reason that was to have far-reaching consequences. By this time, I had pored over photographs of poets and avant-garde composers, and I had noticed that they favoured large loose knots, whereas my father instructed me that a well-dressed man, though he tied his tie at its widest part, pulled it as tight as he could, at the same time puckering it in the middle with the help of his index finger, and then slid the knot up so that it concealed the collar button. It was, of course, only if in life I continued to follow my father's instructions that my ties too would need to be so frequently ironed, and, not only did the photographs I loved tell me not to, but increasingly my deepest wish was to break him too from the habit, even if I had no idea how a flowing knot would look as it swelled under his well-tended double-chin. The reality was that my father had, after all, known poets and avant-garde composers, and, in quarrelling with him, as I did in the early years of adolescence, and bitterly too, I was above all things trying to recall him to a sense of who and what he really was. When I was sixteen, I found the phrase I needed to describe what my father had turned his back on: it was 'the buried life'. My father had turned his back on a life he had buried, and, by turning his back on it, he buried it deeper, he buried it from me. I found the phrase in the poetry of Matthew Arnold, which I loved at this stage, and which was one of the few tastes I had that bound me to the 'official' culture of the school, and two things made the discovery more poignant. One was that Arnold's poetry was itself the poetry of a buried life, and the other was that, underneath some exterior that I was starting to form, there was a buried life of my own, another 'stripling Thames'.

As to my mother, one of the strongest memories I have of her is of late afternoon, after riding, or on being collected from school, going with her to a nearby town of some size, where, in the market-place, behind iron railings, there was an ominous block of dark grey stone on which the kings of Wessex had been anointed: it was said that you could still see the stains where the oil had poured off their heads. We would park outside a small dress shop, which was ahead of its time in that its owner ordered dresses from Paris. I sat on a hard chair, while Suzy, a vivacious woman, thirty or somewhat more, with pretty earrings, and smelling of cigarettes, brought out dress after dress for my mother to try on. Each new dress she held up for inspection, tucking it under her chin, or breaking its fall by draping it from the waist down over the back of a small sofa, and she would say, 'I think this is going to be perfect for you', 'I had you in mind when I got this from the collection', 'I've been keeping this one back for you', or, as we came to the end of the line: 'This, Connie, is you.' Sometimes my mother rejected a dress out of hand, but, if she didn't, and tried it on, she was always, when asked whether she liked it, less than fully positive, though to different degrees, and in consequence the dresses were sorted into rejects, probables, possibles, and those which needed to be tried on again. I remember one particular dress vividly, made of very fine, very dark blue cashmere, with a little sprig of daisies woven on it, and underneath the daisies the word 'margue-rite', spelled with a small 'm', had been handstitched in pale blue wool. Every so often, I would pick up a dress out of the pile to which it had been assigned, and examine with great care the stitching, and how the shoulders were cut, and how the buttonholes had been made, in an attempt to see whether an incontrovertible way of reaching a decision could not be thought up. For a period I wanted to be a dress designer. After an hour or so, my mother had settled for three or four, which she would take home on approval. If in the car my mother did not start to regret one in particular, she would be in high spirits. She would say to me conspiratorially, which I loved: 'Don't say anything to Daddy about this.' She would add, 'I can never make up my mind,' and further add: 'You know me.' The truth is that I didn't: but I knew that she couldn't make up her mind.

Rarely did my mother talk about the one occasion, decisive for me, on which she had made up her mind. When she did, she would say, 'I could have married many people,' or: 'Many people wanted to marry me.' And then she was likely to add: 'And I could have done much better for myself.' It was an odd thing for her to say, since she cared so little about doing well, let alone better. After my father died, leaving precisely £186, she felt that she must find work for herself, and only one test counted: whether what she did would bring her into contact with people who would admire her. Of the various possibilities of marriage that she had foregone, she always returned to the son of the Dutch ambassador, and sometimes she showed me photographs of his house in the Hague, and of his Hispano-Suiza, and of herself in a long fur coat and boots, leaning against the bonnet, and laughing with her large grey eyes. The sticking point, she explained, had always been her mother, and this was where my father won. She could have married only someone who could accept her mother, which my father could. She spoke to her mother on the telephone perhaps twice a day, and they met frequently, but, as I recall things, every conversation, every meeting, was a quarrel, and they quarrelled as two people might who truly hated one another. My father accepted his mother-in-law in that she could come to the house whenever she or my mother wanted, and he paid all her bills. But they found nothing to say to one another.

Until I was thirty or so, I experienced life as traversed by a series of boundaries, which, once crossed, could never be uncrossed, for their passage left an indelible mark: some knowledge was acquired, some experience gained, innocence lost, a new shamelessness entered into.

A painful number of such transitions were connected with the loss of faith, but the earliest, which was different, I experienced in the upstairs lavatory. It was when, for the first time, I was allowed, not just to go to the lavatory alone, but to leave it alone. Up till that moment, I had been required, when I was ready to do so, to get off the lavatory seat, hobble to the door, open it and shout: 'Ready.' But, if the sweeper was being used, or worse the hoover, I could not be heard, and, though I felt ignored, I had, as for much of my childhood, my own resources.

My father, who was not a tall man, had legs short for his size, and he had had a footstool made, painted white, with a cork top, to ease the situation. My father sat there and smoked, but, when I sat on the lavatory, and put my legs up on the stool, I was a king, King Canute, or a great prince, though also a bard. The stories I told myself were of tournaments, and of knightly encounters in which the combatants were represented by the tassels at either end of my dressing-gown cord, which I bashed together until the cleaning outside stopped, and help was on its way, and then one of the combatants took off his helmet, and capitulated with honour. Sometimes, not often, I told myself stories of shipwrecks, and other disasters at sea, which tracked more closely the movements of my bowels.

But one evening I was taken by surprise. I was told that I could clean myself, that I would be initiated into the mysteries of how, and that from that time onwards I would be on my own. First, I was asked to observe how the roll of lavatory paper was divided into separate sheets with perforated lines between them. Then I was instructed how to hold the roll, and told that I must first tear off three sheets in one, then fold them so that the fold ran through the middle of the middle sheet, and then I wiped myself. Then I folded that whole piece in two, and wiped myself with it a second time. Then I tore off just two sheets, and folded them along the perforated line, and wiped myself with them. When I tore off two sheets, there was no second folding, no second wiping. I was to go on using just two sheets until I was clean, and I was shown what a clean piece of paper looked like.

Then I stood up, and, for the first time in my life, I could take it on myself to pull the chain: it was my decision. If I did, I mustn't pull too hard, or too gently. I could, if I liked, turn round, and watch the paper go down the lavatory, and in Australia it would rotate the other way.

This small incident was probably the single greatest increase in personal responsibility that my childhood had in store for me. It is what I think of when I hear moral philosophers discuss responsibility.

My father, Eric Wollheim, was born in Breslau on 13 December 1879, the son of Eugen Wollheim and his wife, who was his first cousin, but whose name I do not know. Indeed I know of the name Eugen only because my father used to recall with such delight that, when he visited St Petersburg before the Great War, he was called Eric Evgenovich.

I knew two facts about my father's childhood. One was that his family doctor was the doctor of Friedrich Lassalle, the famous socialist and enemy of Marx. The other was that, when he had to walk to school in the bitter cold, he prepared himself by swallowing a mouthful of goose fat, and wrapping a sheet of brown paper across his chest under his shirt. I never knew what religion he was brought up in, though I believe that he was educated in a Catholic school. At some point after he came to England, it would have seemed to him inevitable that he should behave as a member of its established church. He was married in St James's, Piccadilly, and sometimes he accompanied me to church. How deep this went was not a question that either of us was disposed to pursue, though for different reasons: I because, though, when I went away to school, I encountered boys who were Jews by religion and were thus, like Roman Catholics, excused from going to Abbey, it was not until very much later that I knew of the Jewish religion as a serious possibility of belief, he because his real views were those which he exposed to me only when, after having insisted that I should have a religious upbringing, he took me, by now 16, out to supper in the restaurant of the Savoy, told me that all religion was folly, asked me if I had read Freud's *The Future of an Illusion*, and suggested that I should.

As the 1930s deepened, and anti-semitism swept through Central Europe, my father spent a great deal of time and money in getting not only his own family, but friends and acquaintances, out of Germany. At the same time, partly in response to my questions, partly to make his position clear, he insisted that to classify people as Jews had no basis in scientific fact, and that doing so was all but invariably the first step on the way to persecuting them: persecuting them, humiliating them, imprisoning them and – though I don't remember whether his foresight went as far as this – exterminating them. He held that to classify oneself as a Jew was just as vacuous, just as dangerous. He once recalled an incident in Berlin when, as a young man, he had asked a policeman the way, and the policeman had said: 'Why should I tell a Jewish dog like you?'

My father's first move was to Paris. This was in the very late 1890s. After a childish desire to be a woodcutter, and wear a green jacket with wooden buttons, he formed two ambitions: one to be a lawyer, the other to be a theatrical impresario, and, either through force of circumstance or through choice, he became an impresario, and to this he brought two qualities. He had great natural powers of discrimination – he loved, in no matter what area, to discern fine differences of quality – and he possessed a mind of a distinctly legal cast. In Paris he joined the Marinelli agency, and in 1900 came to England, perhaps to open, certainly to run, their London branch, and this he continued to do until 1911, when he opened an agency in his own name with an office in Charing Cross Road. On arriving in England, he went to live in Brixton, but, by the time the war broke out, he was living in the Adelphi, then one of the glories of London. He once described to me the rooms he occupied, with, over the fireplace, what he referred to as a Fragonard. One Sunday morning, years later, we were walking to the station, and he started to wonder what had happened to the Fragonard, as though he had not thought about it in the intervening decades. He was much like that about things that he had once owned, or thought he had. As he was dying, he started to think about a triangular plot of land high up on the slopes of Montmartre, which he had been given in partial payment of a debt, by his friend Lartigue, the owner of the Café des Ambassadeurs on the Champs-Elysées, who also had a share in the casino at Biarritz.

Around 1905 or 1906, with a recklessness of which I otherwise never saw a trace, he threw up his career, and went off to the South of France to attach himself to one of the most famous courtesans of the period, La Belle Otero. He was in his twenties, she was 11 years older, and I have no conception of their life together, how it began, what it was like, why or when it ended. Was he her lover, was he her homme d'affaires, was he the butler, did he merely stand outside the iron gates to catch a glimpse of the famous dancer as she strolled among the bougainvillea and the myrtle?

My father listed in *Who's Who in the Theatre* a number of artists he brought to England before the 1914–18 war, either as the deputy of Marinelli, or in his own person: they include Sarah Bernhardt, Madame Réjane, Karsavina, the Zancigs and Leo Fall, as well as the first production of Max Reinhardt's *Sumurun*. All this was interrupted when the war broke out. My father, who was by this time a naturalised subject, but had been declared medically unfit to serve, was not safe from the obloquy that fell on everything German. Dachshunds were kicked in the street, and my father, some time later, discovered that he had been reported to the police for signalling to enemy aircraft. Eventually he was asked to be the manager of a theatrical company that would tour the armed forces. It took him through the war, and it played a part in my coming to be.

My mother, Constance Mary Baker, was born on 9 March 1891 in

44 Gordon Square, the illegitimate daughter of William Henry Baker, who had a highly profitable career as a speculative builder of the vast rambling pubs that made late Victorian London a city of palaces, and Augusta Mary French. A few years after my mother was born, my grandfather moved his second establishment to a flat in a mansion block at 4 Cavendish Square, where he had a bath with a shower, a novelty which, according to my mother, he showed off to all the guests who came to dinner. This, and the careful way he arranged a rose in his buttonhole every morning, were the only specific memories she had of him. But she told me that he loved her to the point of idolatry: I know enough about a father's love for a daughter to believe that.

My grandfather's death in 1900 was a turning-point in the lives, certainly in the fortunes, of the second Baker family. Six months after his death Baker Brothers sued for bankruptcy. It was the end of the great period of affluence for the London pub and the London pub-owner. Family affairs further deteriorated through my grandmother's marriage to a man called Dr George Howell, who was a mining engineer and said to be involved in potentially lucrative oil explorations in the Caucasus. Outwardly the model of lower-middle-class respectability, a pillar of Welsh Nonconformity, who played the organ in chapel on Sunday, short, with a bowler hat, pince-nez, a worn dark suit covered in stains, watch-chain and fob, spats, a grey moustache full of spikes, and a constant clearing of the throat, Uncle Pops, as I was expected to call him, was a total rogue: a swindler, a pathological liar, most likely a bigamist who certainly managed to make off with whatever money my grandmother still had left. For the first 16 years of my life, Uncle Pops intermittently lived with my grandmother. It was bad when he left, probably worse when he returned.

In 1909, my mother had money enough left by her father to be sent to a finishing school in Paris, 24 Boulevard d'Inkermann, Neuilly, and it was there that she visited her last museum, and did her last reading. My mother would often say to me, 'I'm not a great reader,' and sometimes she would say: 'I'm not really an intellectual.' The facts that she was referring to were these: that, in Paris, she bought herself copies of Racine, Corneille and Molière. I still possess them, inscribed 'Connie Baker Paris 1909'. Most of the pages are uncut. After Paris in 1909 my mother, to the best of my knowledge, never read a word. She never opened a book, a newspaper, a woman's magazine, or anything I ever wrote.

On the completion of finishing school, a family council decided that my mother should become a milliner, and an opening was found for her in an establishment in Paris named Louise, which, rumours say, doubled as a high-class *maison de passe* patronised by the Prince of Wales. However, my mother was determined to go on the stage, and she returned to London, and entered the Academy of Dramatic Art, as it then was. She finished her course, she adopted the name Constance Luttrell, which reminded her of the West Country, where both her parents were born, and sometimes induced in her fantasies of noble birth, and she joined the Gaiety Theatre, not as a chorus girl, but as a showgirl, an all-important difference. The outward difference was that chorus girls moved, and showgirls did not; inwardly it was a difference in respectability. Gaiety girls of both sorts were much courted, and much taken out by what were called 'stage-door Johnnies', who spent large sums of money, first on bribing the doorman to deliver flowers and a note to the girl of their choice, then, if the note was lucky, on buying the supper that this precipitated. My mother found a supporter, protector, attenuated lover, in the powerful figure of C.B. Cochran, a schoolfriend of Aubrey Beardsley, who ruled the entertainment side of the London theatre for nearly fifty years. Late in life, she told me that she never 'went all the way' with Cochran, and asked me, 'Do you understand?' as though the secrets of sexuality were known exclusively to a generation that professed to have little use for them.

My mother, by this period, was inclined to turn herself into an actress proper, and her chance came in 1914 when the war broke out, and, through Cochran's intervention, she was invited to act in a theatrical company that would play to the troops. The arrangement lasted four years.

My parents were married at the beginning of 1920. My mother was a woman of great beauty with strong bones and deep-set eyes. My father was good-looking in the only way that I have really been able to think of men as good-looking: he was well-dressed. They spent their honeymoon at Gleneagles Hotel in Perthshire.

On the eve of her marriage, my mother was told by her uncle of her illegitimacy, and she went to my father, and was prepared to release him from his engagement vows: an idea that my father, who did not even understand her scruples, dismissed as ridiculous.

After my parents married, my father made two decisions. He decided that he and his family would live in suburban Surrey, and he decided that my mother should leave the stage. I believe it to be clear that both were bad decisions.

As to the decision that my mother should abandon the stage, there were several possible reasons for this. My father might have feared her failure, he might have feared her success, he might have wanted her at home. Years later, my mother openly resented the decision, and in retrospect it was easy to see that it meant two things for her: it meant that she had to think of new directions into which to channel the enormous energy with which she had been endowed, and it also meant that she had to think of a new way, or new ways, of getting praise. The discharge of energy and praise were the two overwhelming needs of her life, and her misfortune was that, after she left the stage, she was never able to find any means of satisfying them jointly. She devised some sort of solution for each: neither was adequate in itself, and they defied co-ordination. They pulled against one other.

For praise, my mother came to depend increasingly on herself. If sometimes the words came out of the lips of others, it was because she forced people to say what she made it so clear she wanted from them. 'You have to agree that . . .' she would begin, or 'You have to give it to me that . . .', and it would turn out to be her originality, or her courage, or her independence, or her sense of humour, that we were being asked not to overlook. As to a way of consuming her energy, my mother – and I do not know how early it was in her married life that she thought it up, or why – hit on something the ultimate appeal of which may very well have been that in itself it meant nothing to her: it was cleaning the house. She devised a system, which was no ordinary system, and it must be understood that, throughout the period when she put it into practice, there were always two or three servants in the house who could have done, or could have shared, the work. As things were, their presence did little except to endanger my mother's system, but that was not, from her point of view, so obviously a disadvantage.

At about nine o'clock in the morning, by which time my father, if he was in England, had left for London, my mother would put on an overall, she would tie a spotted scarf around her head, and she would start on her daily routine. She would begin with her own bedroom. The door would be shut, the readily moveable furniture would be put together somewhere in the middle of the room, and all the windows would be thrown open. Then, with a duster, she would brush the dust off all the tops and all the surfaces. When she was convinced that all the dust had been got out of its hiding places, and had settled on the floor, she would first use the sweeper, or the Ewbank, with its beautiful picture of a lion in a roundel, to remove the top layer. Then there was the dust that had sunk into the pile of the carpet, and for this she relied on the vacuum cleaner. Any residual dust, which had not fallen onto the floor, or had fallen onto the floor but had not been sucked up either by the sweeper or by the vacuum cleaner, would probably have floated out through the window. The room was now clean – cleaned and clean – and so my mother felt at liberty to open the bedroom door, and start on the next task, which was also the biggest, for it took in, first, the corridor that curved round past the lavatory and the airing cupboard to the bathroom, next, the stairs which descended to the hall, and finally the hall itself. From her point of view, all this formed a single, though not a simple, unit: it was not simple because of the twists and turns within it, but it was a unit because there was no internal door that could be shut, and thus seal off one part of it from the rest, with the consequence that there was no way of stopping the circulation of dust or germs. Accordingly, once my mother had persuaded herself of two things, one was that all the doors opening off the landing and the hall were shut, and there were ten in all that had to be checked, and the other was that all the windows were open, the same sequence of duster, sweeper and vacuum cleaner was applied without there being any natural break, or any way of storing what she had done.

And it was here that the system was vulnerable. So long as my mother was still at the stage of cleaning her bedroom, alternatively once she had got past the landing, stairs and hall, and was cleaning either the dining-room or the drawing-room, there was comparative immunity: nothing could go deeply wrong. But what could only too easily happen, and, if it did, would nullify everything that she had done up till that point, was that, while she was working on the large unit, someone in one of the first-floor rooms who hadn't noticed the stage she was at might unthinkingly open a door. And, when I say 'open a door', it was enough, on my mother's calculations, for it to be opened the merest crack for the dust, the germs, to be able to creep back, and for my mother to feel, no, for her to know, that her work was ruined. Within minutes, she had carried her three aids, the duster, the sweeper, the vacuum cleaner, right up to the very top of the house, to the small, linoleum-covered landing outside the boxroom and the maid's room, which, in the ordinary course of events, was not in her sphere, but was left to the maid to clean, but not when there had been a violation of the system, and what she was now called on to do was to set the process in motion from the very beginning, indeed from a point earlier than that at which it had started. By this means, my mother's day was set back by something between an hour and a half and two hours. The hairdresser in London, or a friend whom she had arranged to meet for tea, or my father who had booked a table at the Savoy Grill for lunch, had to be informed, and the day reorganised. This happened about once every two or three weeks, and was the cause of my mother's frequent latenesses.

My mother never felt called on to account for the routine in which she was so inflexible until one day there was a new arrival in the house who very much had her own idea of things. This was the new governess. She was French, she seemed to me of a very great age, she had grey hair in a bun, and eyes that did not focus, and her name was Mademoiselle de Saint-Germain. Before coming to us, she had worked, evidently for many years, as a governess in a Prussian family. I do not know how she was chosen. In opposition to my mother, and ultimately to my father, Mademoiselle believed that it was the out-of-doors, the air that came from the trees and the green things, the fresh air to which so much of my life had been sacrificed, that was the danger: it was the source of disease and ill-health. In consequence, when she cleaned the rooms that were her preserve, the nursery and the night nursery, she began by shutting the windows, and then she opened the door onto the corridor, even if my mother was in the course of cleaning it. When my mother objected, she formulated her opposition thus: 'Madame, you believe that the germs are inside, and must be swept out. I believe that the germs are outside, and must not be let in.' My mother loved these words, and she repeated them on every possible occasion, to me, on the telephone, at lunch to my father's friends, and she always put it as follows: 'Mademoiselle said: "You believe that the germs are inside, I believe the germs are outside."' My mother always quoted the words as Mademoiselle had used them, and she never adapted them grammatically to herself as a speaker. She never said: 'I believe the germs are inside, but she, Mademoiselle de Saint-Germain, believes that the germs are outside.'

To a child, whose head was filled with the idea of religious faith, my mother's insistence on the use of direct speech seemed momentous. What, according to my mother, was really at issue? Did she believe in the germs that she spent so much of her life trying to eradicate, or did she not? Did it, or did it not, matter in her eyes that someone disagreed with her? When someone disagreed with her, was it, or was it not, important for her to persuade this other person of the error of her ways? For me these were the issues, as simple as that, but my mother evaded them, just as she evaded the issue of religious faith itself, and she continued to put her trust in phrases like, 'I do what I do', 'That's what I'm like', 'You can't change what a person's like.' I do not know that I wanted to change what my mother was like, or at any rate not until many years later, by which time what I really wanted was to change her for someone else, but I wanted to know, because I needed to know, why it was that what my mother spent so much of her life doing was so important to her.

My father's work, as I can now see in retrospect, changed to a considerable degree over the years of my childhood, and this certainly influenced the background against which I grew up. When I was very young, or up to the age of six, my father was largely occupied with the Diaghilev ballet. I believe that he met Diaghilev before the war, for he is said to have taken him to see Adeline Genée dance in 1912. Whether the original meeting took place in Paris or Saint Petersburg or perhaps even in London I do not know, but from 1918 my father acted as the ballet's London manager, and also contributed to its survival in other places. He drew up the contracts, he made advance bookings with theatres, opera houses and music halls, and he endeavoured to raise money, to which end he acted as a go-between between Diaghilev and Lord Rothermere or the King of Spain. There was an almost daily exchange of lengthy telegrams. My father deeply admired Diaghilev, and he was, I feel, much drawn into his way of thinking and feeling. He was very sympathetic to the perfectionism, and I believe that he found the fury and the scenes of rage and jealousy very vital. At any rate in the moods that my father allowed himself to reveal, he was very different, and tended to fluctuate between amused calm and a very self-assured irritability, but this does not mean that he wanted the world to be so circumscribed: indeed he could himself on occasion give way to towering rage. My father was intrigued by Diaghilev's superstition and by his fear of water, and no small part of the special prerogatives with which he was credited came from the fact, magical in my father's eyes, that he was Russian. A journalist once asked my father in what way Diaghilev was so Russian, and my father, who had no great belief in national characteristics, said that to see this you had to watch the great man in a hurry, because, the more worried he was about time, the shorter and shorter steps he took, so that, in the end, he was at a standstill.

And yet I do not think that all this would have added up to so much if Diaghilev had not in the last resort conformed to my father's fundamental demands on life, which brought him so much in conflict with me. Certainly the Russian ballet represented for my father a lost Arcadia, a worldly Eden of which the capital was pre-Great War Monte Carlo, but Diaghilev's ultimate achievement was that he took hold of all this, and he wrenched it out of the realm of mere regret or nostalgia, with which my father had no sympathy, and he connected it with what people, some people, enough people, wanted to see. He turned it into what my father would have called, despite the debts with which it was encumbered, 'a paying proposition'.

My father set store by a few mementoes of Diaghilev: two photographs, one head and shoulders with the chinchilla streak carefully turned to the camera, and the other standing with Cocteau, both signed in French, which was the language Diaghilev and my father spoke together; a malacca cane, which a burglar stole; and a water-colour by Picasso, which Diaghilev bought from a scene-painter for the ballet in order to give to my father, and which I still possess. Years later, when the picture came into my possession, I learned that it was the handiwork of the scene-painter himself, called, I believe, Laforge.

After the death of Diaghilev, my father refused to have anything to do with the ballet. Throughout the 1930s, he concentrated on cabaret, and what had been his first attachment: music hall. He booked the cabaret for the Savoy and the Berkeley, and he became immersed in the daily life of the large hotel. He figured, he once told me, as a minor character, in Arnold Bennett's *Imperial Palace*. He still found singers for Covent Garden, and he brought over whatever he could extract from the dying life of Central Europe: the musical extra-vagances of Eric Charrell, *White Horse Inn*, *Waltzes from Vienna*, *Casanova*, Kurt Weill's *A Kingdom for a Cow*, the Ballets Joss.

Gradually Europe became a smaller and smaller pond in which my father could fish, and his whole way of life, of business, was imper-illed. In early 1933 he was staying in Berlin, at the Kaiserhof or the Adlon, and, as he got into the old-fashioned lift, found himself alone with Hitler, and very slowly they travelled up several floors together. From that moment onwards he was a terrified man. I recall him on a Saturday night, crouched over the large walnut cabinet in which the radio was housed, smoking cigarette after cigarette, as he listened to the marathon speeches of Hitler, the fanfare, the angry rhetoric, the long ovations, the endless Sieg Heils, and, when all seemed over, the return of the Führer to the podium. At the same time, my father was aware that the part of the theatre he was interested in was being taken over by people with whom he had nothing in common: they were English-born, they did not conduct business over long and large lunches, they smoked cigars to prove they were rich, they had bad haircuts. One of the new lot had once been an office-boy of my father's. Sometimes he could relent: he formed a more favourable opinion of George Black, who was already a tycoon, when he learned that he had read James Joyce.

In 1935 or 1936, in desperation my father, who thought that he owed it either to himself or to his family, decided to attempt to make his peace with the new regime in his native country, and he invited to England, and down to the house, the manager of a theatre in Munich. I remember the occasion vividly. I had just come in from a walk on which I had mistimed my visit to the lavatory, and had had what was called an 'accident'. I went upstairs, and changed hurriedly, determined not to miss the visitor. Herr Müller was a small, sandy-complexioned man, with wavy fair hair, which was thinning and brushed back without a parting, and a slightly effeminate manner. He wore a single-breasted brown suit, a cream-coloured silk shirt, a dark red tie with a large knot, and, in the lapel of his jacket, there was a diamond-shaped button with a black swastika on a white ground. As I shook hands, I stared, rudely perhaps, at the small button. My father did not pursue the arrangements with Herr Müller, who had already explained that he could not, for reasons of state outside his control, employ Jewish actors or artistes. He was one of the politest men I ever met.

The further decline in my father's fortunes lies outside the scope of my childhood.

15 April 2004

About Men
Mary-Kay Wilmers

I HAVE COMPLAINED a lot about men in my time. In fact, I do it more and more. But I have never been part of what used to be called the women's movement and those who have or who are, or who have never wanted to be, would probably consider me a retard of some kind. I didn't do consciousness-raising with my sisters in the late Sixties. I was married at the time and it seemed to me that if my consciousness were raised another millimetre I would go out of my mind. I used to think then that had I had the chance to marry Charles Darwin (or Einstein or Metternich) I might have been able to accept the arrangements that marriage entails a little more grace-fully. In the Eighties, long since divorced, I decided that marriage to Nelson Mandela (or Terry Waite) would have suited me fine.

When *The Female Eunuch* came out in 1970 the man I was married to bought me a copy (clearly *he* can't have been the cause of all my troubles). But it was the same with the book as it had been with the sisters – I couldn't get on with it. In the first place, I knew it all. Secondly, I couldn't bear to think about my condition any more than I already did – which was, roughly speaking, all the time that was left from thinking about what to wear, what to cook, and what colour to paint the downstairs lavatory. That's an exaggeration, of course, but not nearly as much of one as I would like it to be.

I am the same age as Germaine Greer and therefore in much the same relation to the subject of her new book, *The Change: Women, Ageing and the Menopause*, as I was to *The Female Eunuch*. It's my story. At least that's how I see it. ('Oh God,' my ex-husband said when I told him what I was writing about.) There are those – i.e. men – who say that a 'male menopause' deserves consideration, and it's true that even men get old and fat and die. But the admirable Greer has no time for their menopauses. 'This book will not devote any of its limited space to the "male menopause".' Later, and more bluntly, it's 'a phenomenon that doesn't exist'.

Would a more fair-minded woman have given the men a hearing? I don't see why, but then I wouldn't. 'Me, me, me,' the men shout and I hear them very clearly. 'Me, me, me,' I growl under my breath. Here I am, four paragraphs into my musings, or ravings, and beginning to doubt whether I will find anything to say about the menopause that isn't a way of saying something about men. I look out of the window and see a roly-poly middle-aged man about the same age as me walking along arm in arm with his eight-year-old daughter. His first wife, assuming he had one and she was the same sort of age, may now be a millionaire, she may own a chain of shops or be a top civil servant or the wife of a duke: but her womb, according to Greer, will be the size of an almond and one thing she won't have is an eight-year-old daughter. The menopause isn't some sort of metaphor and it doesn't make you believe in the even-handedness of God, or of human biology.

On the other hand, even I don't think it's the invention of a mean-minded Creator wanting to give women a bad time. Or do I? Other female animals, we learn from zoology, don't have a menopause; for better or worse, they carry on reproducing all their adult lives. Human animals take such a long time to get going, however, that they can't afford to have mothers who are reaching the end of the line. I remember wailing in the days of my marriage that if anyone could suggest one good reason why I should do it I wouldn't mind being the person who always washed up. Unfortunately I can't see myself zenning out on thoughts of the species when I next catch sight of that roly-poly man and his daughter. There we are, however. At some point between the ages of forty-five and fifty-five women dip out of the race while men carry on booming and fathering until the very brink of the grave.

An old man I used to know, a painter well into his eighties, was so confident and so predatory that at night you couldn't walk down the street with him unchaperoned. If it is part of the great scheme of things that men should go on contributing to the world's population (and the planet's decline) till they drop, then it follows that they will go on strutting and preening and considering themselves eligible for what Clive James used to call 'the grade A crumpet' until at last senility takes hold. (In James's phrase, Ford Madox Ford, himself neither young nor pretty, had the grade A crumpet 'coming at him like kami-kazes'.) Germaine Greer may say, uncontroversially, that 'many a man who was attractive and amusing at twenty is a pompous old bore at fifty,' and Melvyn Bragg got a lot of stick for the novel he wrote about an icky romance between a nice enough man in his fifties and an even nicer eighteen-year-old whose looks were out of this world, but women (for whatever reason) never seem to tire of telling stories about young ladies and older men and living happily ever after. It doesn't happen very much or very plausibly the other way round, not in life or in books. Even Colette, who pioneered the notion of the young man and the older woman, makes Léa give Chéri up for a biologically-appropriate wife.

'Men,' man-in-the-news Iron John Bly reports, 'are more lonesome in every generation.' In the last few days, as I've been getting more and more inflamed in my thoughts about the human (i.e. female, i.e. menopausal) condition, I've been hearing a lot about how hard it is being a man and having to stake your claim and prove your wonder-fulness at every turn. Robert Bly says men need a male mother, and that's fine by me. But I won't believe it isn't harder to be a woman until the day, should it ever come, when the balance of power is so drastically reversed that women can get into serious trouble, lose their jobs or be despatched to the gulag, for making jokes about men. However strongly I feel about the things I've been saying, I doubt whether anyone – i.e. any man – will find them upsetting. In fact, I wonder whether all my ironies aren't simply one more way of sucking up to the ruling class. Is it just me, or do men care what women say provided they don't look like Andrea Dworkin?

On the other hand, I can't say I think it's entirely men's fault that women live as if under their spell. Looking back at what I've written so far, it seems clear that I made a mistake in skipping those consciousness-raising sessions. The menopause isn't simply something that happens to women that doesn't happen to men. Nor is the big question the really big question why men, all men whatever they have or haven't got going for them, can always find a woman to sew on their buttons or proofread their books. What we need to know is whether women are going to go on for ever dreaming about men: dreaming of finding one if they haven't got one, of winning him back if he is slipping away, of killing themselves should he finally bolt. Greer, who, unlike almost every other woman in the world, has never seemed to share this obsessive interest in the opposite sex, is pretty clear: time to get out. 'I never have to think any more, oh a party,' she said in an interview in the *Independent on Sunday*, 'what clothes shall I wear, what men will be there, what am I going to do?' And even if, as I've heard suggested, she doesn't wholly mean it, it's good enough for me if she half-does.

'Unless you have a really decent guy, talking to him about menopause is like taking hemlock,' a (married) Californian woman remarks in this month's *Vanity Fair*. I don't know about hemlock, but I've always kept my cardy on through the most equatorial flushes for fear that some male bystander (or colleague) would understand what was happening and laugh. Greer, you could say, is vigorously alert to the ways in which women let themselves be enslaved by men – or rather the idea of a man:

The very notion of *remaining attractive* is replete with the contradictions that break women's hearts. A woman cannot make herself attractive; she can only be *found* attractive. She can only remain attractive if someone remains attracted to her. Do what she will she cannot influence that outcome. Her desperate attempts to do the impossible, to guide the whim of another, are the basis of a billion-dollar beauty industry. All their lives women have never felt attractive enough. They have struggled through their thirties and forties to remain attractively slim, firm-bodied, glossy-haired and bright-eyed. Now in the fifties 'remaining attractive' becomes a full-time job . . . Jane Fonda's body may look terrific, what there is of it, but has anyone looked at the strain taken up by her face and neck muscles? . . . Is a middle-aged woman supposed to have the buttocks of a twenty-year-old? Such buttocks are displayed on advertising hoardings all over town. The man who is still making love to the wife of his youth may be thinking of other breasts than his wife's. There is no lack of spectacular publications to furnish such imagery. The middle-aged woman who tries to compete with her husband's fantasy sex partners hasn't a hope.

She's the Norman Tebbit of feminism, a founder member of the on-yer-bike branch of the women's movement; and I don't imagine she'll be sorry to think that it's all over for her contemporaries; that for us what she memorably calls 'the white-slavery of attraction duty' is a thing of the past. 'To be unwanted,' she says in her introduction, 'is also to be free.' Which sounds good. But women, as men always say, are so unreliable; and no sooner has Greer got us off the hook than she's talking in a most un-Tebbit-like way about 'the older woman's love' being a 'feeling of tenderness so still and deep and warm that it gilds every grassblade and blesses every fly'.

So what do we do now, my ageing sisters and I? If we can't line up behind the new-order Greer, who do we take as our role model – Joan Collins or Alan Bennett's lady in the van? Or, to put it differently, do we or don't we put in a bid for hormone replacement therapy? (I don't want to get into difficulties here: Joan Collins swears she's never had it – she only looks as if she has.) There are reasons for taking it, and reasons for not taking it, and reasons for getting angry with your doctor either way, but if you do and it works, you feel better, you look better and you *are* better. (I speak from envy, not experience.) Then the question arises: what does 'better' mean? And is that sort of 'better' appropriate? Or, to quote Germaine Greer: 'We hear that Mrs Thatcher uses hormone replacement but do not know whether to be encouraged or disheartened by the result.'

Years and years ago I remember some poor woman being lambasted in the *Guardian* for liking a certain sort of maternity dress because in it she didn't look pregnant ('misses the point of *being* pregnant,' she was told). There are people on whom talk of hormone replacement therapy has a similar effect, as if it were to be blamed for overlooking or deferring the pleasure of being known and knowing yourself to be past it. No doubt in five or ten minutes' time it will be really chic to be menopausal. Perhaps thanks to Greer and others it's happened already. The only trouble is I'd rather go back on attraction duty than sit in my garden saying hello to the grass.

10 October 1991

Working Underground
Joe Kenyon

TRAMMING WAS ONE of the most painful and soul-destroying jobs in a pit. Only pits like the two in our village employed trammers. Other, better maintained pits in adjacent areas had high, wide roadways and used pit-ponies to pull the tubs from the coal-face to the haulage, but our pits used muscle and blood. A trammer had to be fit, strong, broad in the back and short, in his late teens or early twenties, and, I might add, weak in the head.

At the age of fifteen, I joined a Health and Strength Club – the subs were sixpence a week. The club was run by its members in an old chapel hall. I spent three hours a day during the week and three hours on Saturday and Sunday as well doing work-outs. I liked to wrestle and lift weights. I also punched the ball a bit. I developed a strong back and good muscles in my arms and legs. I was all of five feet four and, when I started tramming a few years later, in the mid-Thirties, it was a doddle.

A trammer's job was to push a 'tram' – an empty coal tub – up the gate and into the bank. The 'bank' was a short coal-face about ten yards wide and usually worked by two men, the filler and the trammer. The older, less agile man worked at the face all shift, filling the tubs; the young mate fetched the tubs into the bank, helped with the filling and then whizzed down the gate, taking the full tub into a main road, known as the 'level', from which it was hauled by winch into the pit bottom in loads of twenty tubs at a time.

The 'gate', as it was known, was a kind of tunnel leading up to the bank, or face. It was always just high enough and wide enough to allow a tub to scrape through. If a tub got fast – stuck between the roof and the floor – there was no way you could get past it to the front. If you wanted to get out, you had to crawl back up the gate, anything up to two or three hundred yards, into the bank, then crawl through the gob, the wasteland left after the coal had been got out, and into the next bank and down their gate.

A tub, or coal tub, is a miniature wagon made to hold an estimated eight cwt of coal. Some tubs were made of metal and others of wood. It was the wooden ones which mostly got stuck, because some were an inch higher than the metal ones. They were much heavier to push as well. Tubs measured two feet six inches wide, two feet six inches high and about three feet six inches long, and they only just scraped through. The slightest movement of the side, or roof or floor, and the tub got fast. Because the gates were so inadequate, ventilation was very poor: it was hot and steamy work. The coal-face was a yard and three inches high, which left twelve inches for the filler to manoeuvre his shovel-load of coal into the tub. You could make a bit more space by lifting the tub off the rail track at one end and onto the floor.

If everything went okay and there were no hold-ups because of tubs getting fast, we could fill about six tons of coal, six hard-gotten tons. We were paid two shillings and twopence per ton, with some time stoppages if the weighman thought the tub was on the heavy side and that a bit of stone had been added.

In addition to what we could earn by the ton, we were paid a graduated rate for tramming, depending on the distance. For the first 40 yards, we got nothing. For the next 25 yards we were paid a penny a tub, and then for every 30 yards an extra three halfpence. That meant that a trammer would have to fetch and push a tub for an average of

28 journeys a shift (14 times up and 14 times down) for eight shillings and one penny. There were other jobs, too: trimming, timbering, fetching materials and moving the rail track nearer to the face as we advanced. These helped to make up the wage a bit, but they were hard-fought gains which the boss begrudged paying for, and there was nothing extra for heaving your guts out on a tub that was fast. Dividing the total earnings at the end of a good day, a trammer and his mate could make up to about 12 shillings a shift. But good days were few and far between. Sometimes, when the going was rough and dangerous, we had to fall back on the 'mini', or minimum wage of eight shillings and elevenpence a shift. This was negotiated by the Union after much trouble and strife.

Sometimes it was the trammer who suffered most, towing his rop out, shredding his back when a lousy tub got fast and wouldn't move: nowt paid for this. When a tub got fast, stuck between the floor and the roof, it was reported to the deputy, a pit official in charge of the district. He reported it to the manager, who then gave orders to the nightshift deputy to send a dinter in. A dinter was usually an elderly man, on a low day-wage, who worked regular nights. He was usually past doing heavy work but useful for odd repair jobs that had been reported from the day-shift. One of these was to go into the bank gate where a tub was fast. His job was to lower the rail track an inch or two to allow the tub to go free. Pit-owners were very grudging about paying for this work. They would have the repair man skip jobs and make do. Spending time and money on this kind of work was costly.

The ground in a pit was always on the move. Sometimes the floor would lift, sometimes because of rising gas, sometimes because of the pressure of the roof pressing the sides and forcing it upwards. The dinter would crawl up the gate where a mark had been left, or where the tub was still fast. Using his pick, he would dig and scrape out the floor under the sleepers so as to lower the track. A makeshift solution, but the absolute maximum allowed by the boss, who wasn't given enough money to pay for a good and lasting job. It was always easier and less costly to let the trammer pay in sweat, blood and sometimes tears.

Coal seams are usually on the incline, a slight gradient of about one in twenty. Banks were organised to commence from the upside of a level. It was easier to push an empty tub up the incline than it would be to push a full tub. It was also easier to slide along the plates, holding onto the back of the full tub and let it go down the gate at its own speed. (The plates were the steel rails which came in six-foot or nine-foot lengths, and were nailed to wooden sleepers.) With the gates or roadways being so low, two feet six inches, the alternative was to crawl for about three hundred yards or more, which can be very tiresome, especially over rough ground.

As a trammer, I had to wear clogs to be able to 'slide' the plates. Beside the iron on the outer edge of the clog, there was also an inner iron. Inside the inner iron, I would nail a piece of tin which I had cut to size. Whenever I was taking a tub down the gate, I would grab hold of the handles – there were two at each end – give the tub a push-start onto the incline of the gate track, then quickly put my clogs on the plates, with one foot at an angle, so I could push my tin piece against the plate and keep some control over the speed of the tub as it hurtled down the gate. I kept my head well down below the level of the tub. A slight raising of the head in a moment of forgetfulness could result in a swift scalping. The easiest way to get an empty tub up the gate was to lean low into the back of it and push it with your head, resting your hands on the buffers. To protect my head and hair, I wore a bannicker – a small hat cut from an old trilby and fashioned to fit on top of the head without slipping. Some trammers just wore their day caps, but a bannicker was more comfortable and less sweaty.

The end of the shift was welcome, especially when your muscles and bones ached like hell. When I got home, I had my dinner and then before I started to drop off, I would go into the kitchen (a bath or a shower would have been heaven), strip off to my waist and wash my head, arms and chest from the kitchen sink. Then while I leant over the sink, my dear Ma would ever so gently and tenderly wash my back, using a flannel or a piece of lint, wiping around or gently swabbing the cuts and scabs down my spine. Sometimes, when I went to the pictures, I would forget myself and carelessly drop down onto the seat. I would curse and grunt as I felt the sudden pain of the sores on my back. There were times when, without thinking, I'd shuffle my back on a chair, especially if it was itching. Sometimes blood would trickle out as I opened up the sores. I'd then have to change my vest and shirt and have my back cleaned. If I didn't do it right away, they'd stick to my back and it would be much harder, and sometimes painful, getting them off without starting the bleeding again. When they did get stuck, the best way of getting the vest and shirt off was to dab over the cuts with a piece of lint soaked in warm water until they were softened, and then very slowly peel off the vest and shirt so as not to re-open the wounds. Even lying down in bed was painful.

One day my mate had a laker – a day off work. It was a Wednesday, and quite common for colliers to have a laker on Wednesday, especially if they'd been having a rough time of it for a shift or two. Normally a man wasn't allowed to work in a bank on his own, but the deputy allowed me to go in. I'd filled a couple of tubs, taken them down the gate and fetched up a couple of empties. I filled my third tub, went down the gate with it, speeding along for about a hundred yards, when – scrunch – the tub got fast. I shoved with my back to the tub, with my feet spragged against a sleeper, but it wouldn't shift. I tried pulling it back, shaking and cursing it, but it was stuck, and it was staying stuck.

There was nothing else for me to do but crawl back up the gate into the face, and fill another tub – I had a couple of spare ones – whip down the gate, letting the tub scurry down at its own speed, holding on by the handles, all tensed up waiting for the inevitable crunch as it hit the immovable tub. BANG! It stopped dead. I could feel my bones flying about the gate. Bells rang, lights flashed. I flopped down for some ten minutes, lying on the floor and cursing from here to eternity. Eventually I got up, and dragged at the second tub. Thankfully it wasn't stuck. I took it back the way I'd come and rammed it again against the fast tub with all my strength. Again, I pulled back the tub and rammed it again, but it would not budge. Pulled it back again and rammed again, and again. By now I was sobbing and bleeding and my back was badly cut.

I crawled my way back up the face. I had it in mind what I was going to do. I got into the face, took my hammer and then wildly and stupidly set about skittling the face timber out, pulling down a few rocks and stones from the roof. Filled a third, empty tub with it, then tugging and pushing, got it onto the gate track, gave it a massive push and shouted: Gerron! Knock the fucking hole in!

Having got that off my chest, I had a good swig of water, got dressed, took hold of my pick and shovel, then made my way through the gob and into the next bank.

'Hey up Jooer, what tha doing coming through there?'

'Going home,' I said. 'Can I put mi tackle on your tub?'

'Tha can tek this tub darn if tha likes, we've got a spare.'

I put my pick and shovel on the tub, making sure it was well below the level of the rib sides, and off I went.

I made my way to the pit bottom, and the onsetter, the bloke in charge of sending the chair up the shaft, said: 'Where's tha going?'

'Home,' I said.

'As tha got a note from't deputy?'

'No, I ent seen him.'

'Well I can't let thi up then.'

'Tha'd better,' I said, 'I'm badly. If tha dunt let me art, tha'll be in bother.'

I got out of the pit, walked across the pit yard, and without knocking, entered the manager's office and slung the pick and shovel onto the manager's desk. 'Go and get thi own fucking coal.' The manager was called Cookie by the lads. He jumped up, and yelled: 'What the hell's up wi thi, Jooer?'

'There's a couple a tubs fast in 428s' – the number of the bank where I was working – 'there's a couple a tubs fast, and they can fucking stop there for all I care. Tha'll not get me in that gate again for all the tea in China. I'm leaving and I want mi cards.'

On the Wednesday, the day I packed it in, I told my mother that I was finishing at the pit. 'I won't go back there at any price,' I said. Meantime, I was stripping to the waist and as I pulled my shirt off, she gasped: 'Good God, what have you done to your back? Come here, let me clean it for you.'

I'd been talking to our neighbour, Mr Roach. Their Brian had gone down south to Slough, near London, and he was doing well. Mr Roach told me there was a great new industrial estate being built and there were plenty of jobs.

'When are you going then?' Ma asked.

'Sunday morning,' I replied.

On Sunday morning, after breakfast, I stuffed a few things in the saddlebag on my bike, said goodbye to my family and off I went.

I arrived in Slough near about 11 o'clock that night. I looked in wonder at the dozens of multi-coloured neon lights surrounding the factories. Horlicks was the first one I spotted: I could see the lights before I got into Slough. Eventually I ended up in Farnham Road and recognised a few illuminated trade names – Aspro and Echo margarine, which stank something horrid when you passed the place; Fine Tubes and 4711, the perfume factory – that was an improvement. I finished up in a café crowded with lads and lasses, some in their early twenties, some a bit older. They were mostly on night shift waiting to start work at midnight at Weston's biscuit factory. One of them, a lad from Bolton, offered to take me to his digs. They had room for another lodger and they would take me in. I liked the house very much. It was one of the new semi-detached private houses being built at that time to accommodate the influx of workers from Scotland, Wales and the North of England.

Mrs Clatworthy, the landlady, a pleasant, good-looking woman of about thirty, told me that D.M. Davies, a furniture-makers, were 'setting on'. I went along, saw one of the foremen and asked for a job. He wanted to know if I had any tools. 'No,' I said, 'I've only just come down from Barnsley, but I'll pay for some if I can draw them from the stores.' Mrs Clatworthy had tipped me off about this. 'Okay, I'll set you on and you can start now,' the foreman said. 'I'll give you a note for some tools and you can pay for them out of your wages.'

I got a light hammer, two wood chisels, a tenon saw and a veneering knife. I was then shown to a bench, where a young chap from Maidenhead was working. We both had to trim and fix the base of Ultra wireless cases to the frame. We each had to do 200 cases a day, 100 in the morning and 100 in the afternoon. After I'd been on the job for a couple of weeks, I made some alterations to the jig in which we placed the bases for fixing to the case. After this adjustment I found that I could easily do 400 cases a day without any increase in effort. Without thinking about the consequences, I just went on happily banging out 400 a day. One day, three men in white coats walked past me a couple of times. 'They're coming to take me away,' I thought. One of them asked how I managed to get so many cases done at this pace. I showed them how I'd changed the jig, and in effect, doubled production. One of them remarked to the others that the modification meant they'd only need one chap at this bench. Oh dear, I thought, now I am creating unemployment, I'll never be forgiven!

Working at DMD's was a pleasure. All the scabs and sores on my back had gone. I worked at my own speed; I could do an extra hour in the evening and work Sunday morning. I also got a pay rise from 9d an hour to 11d. It was very handy working extra in the evening because I could do odd repair jobs as favours for the girls who worked in the polishing shop. Some of them would come to me in distress because they had botched up too many jobs that day and didn't want the foreman to know. I could have settled in Slough permanently, but somehow I never felt at home. In mid-August, the factory closed for a week's holiday. I packed a few things, got on my bike and went back to see the family, taking presents for my parents and the kids. I wanted to see my Dad as well: he had been discharged from the sanatorium after a bout of tuberculosis and returned home.

If you left Barnsley and got a job down in the South, you were regarded as doing very well. To me, it was a myth; life in Slough seemed unreal. If you said 'good morning' to strangers, you were looked at with great suspicion. It was thought that you were a bit touched. Mention the words 'trade union' at work and people backed off as though you had the plague. But now I was on holiday and I was at home. One evening in the Village Club, I was just about to order a pint when Old Cookie, the pit manager, hailed me, saying: 'I'll pay for that.' And then later those boring words: 'I hear you are doing well for yourself these days.' I said I'd much prefer to be in Barnsley.

'We've done away with tramming,' Cookie told me, 'we've got long-wall faces, 120 yards long, and the colliers – they're called fillers now – shovel the coal onto a conveyor belt running along the face. The money's not bad either. I've always like thi, in spite of thi cussedness.'

I decided to work as a filler. I went back to Slough on the Sunday by train – there were things I couldn't bring back on the bike. The charge-hand at DMD's tried to talk me out of leaving. Then he fetched the manager, who asked me if I wouldn't change my mind. He also offered me another threepence an hour on my wage. I apologised, told him I was needed at home, and went back to the pit.

Pit work is a dirty, dangerous job, a job you wanted to leave but wouldn't, or couldn't. Killings and accidents were common, part of a life you learned to live with. Every working day, two or more miners were killed, somewhere in the industry, and many more were maimed and crippled. Not counting those who went down and suffered because of pneumoconiosis and other lung diseases. Very few families were not touched by a death or serious accident at some time or other. Even our own village had its quota of men and young lads with broken backs, a leg or arm missing, hands crushed and useless. Fighting for compensation while you were off work was always a tough battle with the Compensation Doctor, who was also employed by the company.

When a chap was killed, not only his family, but his mates and, indeed, the whole village grieved for him, and for his widow and family. Out of respect for the man and his family, work stopped for the day. Every workman and boy had a shilling deducted from his wage, to be given to the grieving family. Collections were taken around the village. If the accident or death was caused by the negligence of the employer, the odds of winning compensation were stacked against you. The company used every ruse and dodge, even lying, or bribing witnesses to lie: anything to prevent the widow from getting compensation.

When I went back to the pit, and started work as a filler on a 'long-wall face', it was a damn sight easier and more pleasant than tramming. The coal-face had already been undercut by a coal-cutting machine which travelled along the face and cut a five-inch band of stone and coal to a depth of five feet. The coal-cutter was a clumsy chunk of steel about nine feet long, two feet wide and two feet high. It was a noisy, grinding hell of a machine and choked the cutting team with dust. After the coal was undercut, and the conveyor belt moved up, a shotfirer would insert explosives in the face. The blast, if he was good at his job, would be just sufficient to fracture the coal and make it easier for the filler to shovel it onto the belt. At the end of the face, the belt would go round a return drum (known as the 'gear-head') and then spill the coal into waiting coal tubs.

Like I said, filling coal onto a belt was a lot less painful than tramming, but it was still bloody hard graft. The height at the face was three feet, and when you'd slung 17 tons of coal at a mad pace on your knees all shift, you weren't fresh as a daisy. Indeed, there were times when it really got rough: the roof may have been fractured and unsafe, the cutter may not have done his job well, the borer might have drilled the holes at the wrong angle and the wrong depth, or too far apart, or the shotfirer mightn't have stemmed the shots well enough.

I'd been filling for a year when the pit explosion happened. It was 3 a.m. on the morning of 6 August 1936; 58 men were killed outright. Many were smashed almost beyond recognition. It all happened within a matter of seconds. The explosion (some accounts say there were two) was so fierce that its effects could be seen a long way from the spot at which it took place – nearly two miles along an underground roadway 1000 feet down. There was one survivor, an engine driver, and he was found bruised and battered, lying 1800 yards from the centre of the blast. He died later in hospital. The mutilated bodies lay in groups of three or four; some lay singly a few yards apart from each other. When SOS messages were sent out to neighbouring pits, hundreds of miners rushed to help. They stood in queues at the pithead, waiting to be called. Silent crowds of men, women and children stood around waiting. Four men had amazing luck. Half an hour before the explosion, they unexpectedly finished their work and left the pit. One of them returned as a member of a rescue team. 'It is impossible for anyone to escape,' he declared on his return to the surface.

All that day, and the days that followed, the crowds waited, and the rain fell ceaselessly. On their way from the pithead, the rescue workers walked grimly past the waiting crowd. Many were longing to call out for news, but no one did. One of the unbearable things about a pit disaster is the intensity of the waiting: more dread than patience – lest the question asked should bring an answer that snuffs out that last flicker of hope.

Doctor 'Jimmy' Henderson, the local village doctor, was among the rescue workers, and on emerging from the pit after five hours, said that it was hopeless. Most of the dead he had seen had been torn to pieces by the force of the blast; others were lying about in attitudes of suffocation brought about by carbon-monoxide poisoning. 'All along the roadways,' he reported, 'there were piles of rubble and stone where the roof had collapsed. Coal tubs had been hurled about and smashed, all this and the gas-filled air, made it impossible to get to the men.'

From the first day, ambulances stood by, but no bodies came up. The crowd of relatives and neighbours grew so large that the area had to be roped off to allow free passage for the rescue workers through the black mud to the pithead. And behind that rope, the crowd stood, hour by hour, day by day, until the waiting turned into grieving – no crying – as the rescuers began to bring the bodies up. The local school nearby was taken over and prepared to receive them. More than forty nurses were drafted in to help the doctors. Yet all this death and suffering was regarded by the law as an 'act of God' and no compensation was payable.

A year after the explosion, my Dad was killed on the pit top: the door of a wagon filled with rocks and stone burst open just as he was passing it. The stones, several tons of them, fell on my Dad, breaking his spine in two places. He died the next day. Because of the misleading evidence given by the pit bosses, my Dad's death was adjudged to be 'death by misadventure' rather than by accident. My mother was denied compensation. At the time, the *Sunday People* offered insurance cover to its regular readers. Death by accident warranted generous compensation, but even though we'd always taken the paper they refused to pay up because of the misadventure finding. After my Dad was killed, I spent three years studying mining science and, later, another year on a special study of the Coal Mines Acts and Regulations. After nationalisation, I won the right to become an accident-site observer. I had an eagle eye for anything that would support a claim for compensation. Many years later I discovered that one of the men who had testified at the inquiry into my Dad's case, and who died within a few months of giving evidence, had taken his own life.

27 November 1997

The Big One
Julian Barnes

I N MADRID THE other week a literary journalist told me the following joke. A man goes into a pet shop and sees three parrots side by side, priced at $1000, $2000 and $3000. 'Why does that parrot cost $1000?' he asks the owner. 'Because it can recite the whole of the Bible in Spanish,' comes the reply. 'And why does that one cost $2000?' 'Because it can recite the whole of the Bible in English *and* in Spanish.' 'And the one that costs $3000, what does he recite?' 'Oh, he doesn't say a word,' explains the pet shop owner: 'but the other two call him *Maestro*.'

This made me think, naturally enough, of E.M. Forster; and then of the fact that we were about to undergo the annual garrulity of the Booker Prize for Fiction. Would Forster have won the Booker? In 1905, when he published *Where angels fear to tread*, he would have been up against *Kipps*, not to mention more populist contenders like *The Scarlet Pimpernel* and Mrs Humphry Ward's *The Marriage of William Ashe*. In 1910 *Howards End* might have run into *Clayhanger*, and (Wells again) *The History of Mr Polly*; perhaps the Antipodean outsider Henry Handel Richardson would have scooped it with *The Getting of Wisdom*. In 1924 Forster's publishers might have thought they had a chance with his blockbuster, *A Passage to India*. For once, Wells wasn't dogging him: but there was Maurice Baring's *C*, Ford's *Some do not*, Masefield's *Sard Harker*, Mottram's *The Spanish Farm*, plus various dangerous floaters like *The Constant Nymph*, *The Inimitable Jeeves* and even (if it was to be a year for the booksellers) Mary Webb's *Precious Bane*.

Still, the mistake, then as now, is to look at the books themselves. When literary editors pen those overnight pieces on the Booker short-list and lament the omissions – where was McEwan? Where was Boyd? Where was Amis? And the other Amis? – they are examining the candidates (not all of whom they can possibly have read) rather than the judges. If I were Mr Ron Pollard of Ladbrokes (whose odds have got a great deal meaner since the days when some of us cleaned up on Salman Rushdie at 14–1), I would give only cursory attention to the books on the short-list: instead I would study the psychology and qualifications of the judges. And it does take all sorts. Three years ago, when I was short-listed for my novel *Flaubert's Parrot*, I was intro-duced after the ceremony to one of the judges, who said to me: 'I hadn't even heard of this fellow Flaubert before I read your book. But afterwards I sent out for all his novels in paperback.' This comment provoked mixed feelings. Still, perhaps there are judges of the Turner Prize who have never heard of – let alone seen a painting by – Ingres.

So how did the judges do this year? Well, let us begin by congratu-lating them: for having chosen a serious book by a serious novelist; for behaving, mostly, with propriety; and for having turned up to the dinner. These seem pale compliments? They aren't in Booker terms. Previously, some notably minor and incompetent novels have gained the prize; judges, inflated by their brief celebrity, have competed like kiss-and-tell memoirists to spill all to the radio and newspapers; while two years ago one of the judges didn't even make it to the judicial retiring-room. Joanna Lumley, already burdened with the annual 'non-reader' tag, understandably maintained her sense of priorities by playing a South Coast matinée rather than wrangle with literati over the competing merits of Iris Murdoch, Jan Morris and Keri Hulme.

This year the judges did make one interesting – and perhaps influential – early decision. Publishers have hitherto been allowed to nominate four books for the prize, but also submit a 'B' list which the judges can call in if tempted. This year the 'A'-list allowance was reduced from four to three, thus putting greater pressure on those publishers (not many, it has to be said) who issue more than three worthwhile novels a year. Some of these publishers – most notably Mr Tom Maschler of Cape – have for a few years legitimately exploited the two-list process by occasionally putting solidly established novelists on their 'B' list (knowing there was a high chance of such books being called in) while risking more left-field items in the 'A'. This year – to take one interpretation of events – the judges decided to call the publishers' bluff. No 'B'-list books at all were considered, and devious publishers were thus outwitted. There is, however, another interpretation: that the judges hoofed the ball into their own net. What they were in effect saying was this: we'll go along with what the publishers propose, we're sure they can judge a novel just as well if not better than us. So let's dutifully plough through these three bodice-rippers from Rudland and Stubbs, but call in Anita Brookner or Nadine Gordimer? No, no, we won't do that, even if they have won the prize before. More than an abnegation of responsibility, this displayed a singular lack of curiosity. And while the judges annually complain about the great burden of reading placed upon them, it must be the case that most of the hundred or so novels submitted can be discarded pretty quickly. I was going to say after twenty pages, until I remembered the case of a Booker judge a few years ago who was doing some early winnowing on a train and lofted one contender out into the passing prairie after no more than twenty pages. A couple of months later the judge wryly stuck to the doctrine of collective responsibility as the cow-fed fiction hoisted the big cheque.

The Booker, after 19 years, is beginning to drive people mad. It drives publishers mad with hope, booksellers mad with greed, judges mad with power, winners mad with pride, and losers (the unsuccessful short-listees plus every other novelist in the country) mad with envy and disappointment. The dinner itself is a painful experience for five out of the six writers, made worse by the fact that four weeks' expect-ation (during which no regular work can be done) usually produces some psychosomatic malady – a throbbing boil, a burning wire of neuralgia, the prod of gout. The only tip I can give future short-listed candidates is how to work out just in time that you haven't won. While the writers themselves never know the winner's identity in advance, various people in the hall do, including the TV technicians. You could ask them directly, of course (or bribe the judges' chauffeur, who is always a good source): but you will find out surely enough whether you have landed the big pot by following the movements of the hand-held camera on the Guildhall floor. Ten or fifteen seconds before the announcement is made it will head towards you – or, more probably, head towards someone else. This will give you time in which to prepare a generous smile, a quietly amused eyebrow or a scornful nostril.

How should novelists get the whole event in some sane perspec-tive? They cannot retreat into a grand carelessness until they are John le Carré or John Fowles. They might begin, however, by running through the list of previous winners and working out how many of the last 19 would feature in any 'true' list of Top 19 Novels 1969–87. They might observe that 'Booker' – a jaunty if hardly necessary shortening – is increasingly an affair of the book trade rather than a pointer to the state of fiction: thus a 'good' winner, in Booker parlance, is a novel that the bookshops can shift. They can further reflect that whereas in 1972 the three judges were Cyril Connolly, George Steiner and Elizabeth Bowen, in 1987 a television newscaster, by virtue of having written a biography of Viv Richards, was at least more 'literary' than one of the other judges. And then the novelists had better conclude that the only sensible attitude to the Booker is to treat it as posh bingo. It is El Gordo, the Fat One, the sudden jackpot that enriches some plodding Andalusian muleteer.

The Booker Prize is worthy in that it normally goes to a serious novel, seriously intended and seriously judged, and that the money helps a usually underfunded novelist. It's dubious because it now has an unwarranted influence on public perception of the novel; because if it continues to increase in power it may well end up Thatcherishly producing two nations of novelists; and because it distracts novelists from their novels (it's hard to realise, after the caravan has passed, that your book is just as good or just as bad as it was before it made the baggage-camel or not). At least so far, there's been no evidence of novelists 'Bookerising' their work to please the judges. Have there been certain items of fiction in recent years which seemed to have been using steroids? Yes indeed: but long before the Booker Prize existed writers were trying, as Ron Pickering has it, to pull out the big one.

In any case, pulling out the big one might not necessarily work. Sometimes the judges prefer you to pull out the small one. In France, on the other hand, prize novels are more likely to be successfully written to a formula. Over there, members of literary juries continue remorselessly in power until their ink dries; some judges double as literary advisers in publishing houses; and there exists an almost openly cynical attitude of 'Whose turn is it this year?' (the turn being the publisher's rather than the writer's). Nothing astonishes French journalists more than to be told that on the major British literary prizes the judges are replaced regularly, if not annually. *C'est le fair-play anglais*, they comment admiringly.

A year or so after missing out on El Gordo, I managed to land le *tiercé* in Paris: the Prix Médicis. The ceremony proves a little different from the affair at Guildhall. There is an announcement – at which the winner is not present; followed by a lunch – which the winner does not eat. Instead, you wait in a bar across the road from the

bulging Beaux-Arts building where the judges are assembled, and try
to pretend you don't already know you've won; a runner comes from
your publisher to break the 'news'; you cross the road into a swirl of
journalists who have heard the announcement you have missed; then
you search for your jury to thank them. My publisher and I tentatively
entered a large dining-room where a dozen literati were all well into
their lunch. *C'est Monsieur Barnes*, she announced, but not a single fork
paused on its way to a single mouth. Oh dear, I thought, I was obvi-
ously some terrible compromise candidate; I shall be the Keri Hulme
of the Prix Médicis. But no, we'd disturbed the jurors of the Prix
Fémina by mistake. So on to another dining-room, and another dozen
lunchers: *C'est Monsieur Barnes*. This time forks paused, and chairs
were scraped back: though not even a congratulatory glass of Badoit
came my way. A day or so later, the President of the jury asked how
I wanted my prize (humble by Booker standards – about £450). I took
his personal cheque. My bank refused it; I sent it back to them; again
they returned it; I sent it back to them again. Finally, they explained:
'Not only can we not honour this cheque, but we suspect that the
person who wrote it might be trying to evade exchange-control
regulations.'

The couple of weeks before this year's Booker announcement
contained some violent distractions for fretting short-listees: the
pseudo-Crash, which gave those uncharmed by the Tell-Sid society
some quiet *schadenfreude*; plus the far fiercer and more melancholy
events of the Hurricane. When a great storm ravaged Normandy in
1853, destroying gardens and greenhouses, Flaubert took stony
pleasure in this reminder that Nature was not there for our conveni-
ence: 'People believe a little too easily that the function of the sun is
to help the cabbages along.' But for us there was little comfort along
these lines: the nation was too busy roasting poor Mr Fish the weath-
erman (when did we believe him anyway?) to learn wider lessons; and
besides, the damage, as moral instruction, was way into overkill.

At least the Hurricane didn't have one of those cosy Christian names attached to it, as it would have done in the States. We were spared the notion of Hurricane Kevin or Hurricane Sabrina, with people first-naming disaster. 'Did you see what that Craig did to the back fence?' One thought it provoked rather adventitiously was about the Booker Prize. Perhaps, after getting down to the short-list, the organisers should admit the bingo aspect of the whole event and decide the winner on some random yet practical basis. This year, for instance, it might have been awarded to whoever suffered most in the Hurricane. Did Iris Murdoch lose some elms? Does Peter Ackroyd's cottage need re-thatching? The expatriate Brian Moore might not seem to qualify for Hurricane Relief: but he lives beside the San Andreas Fault, and might soon need underpinning. In the end, of course, the judges relied on the more established but just as frivolous system of polite compromise and Moore lost out to Penelope Lively. Trevor McDonald, writing in the next morning's *Independent*, revealed that 'what decided the issue in the end was the fact that their feeling against Moore was stronger than their views about Penelope Lively.' I'm thinking of calling my next novel *The Compromise*.

From Craig Raine

SIR: I was flattered when my friend Julian Barnes put forward my name for a natural phenomenon as subtle as a hurricane (LRB, 12 November). If I may, I'd like to thank him publicly.

On an entirely different matter, are readers of the LRB familiar with this passage in Primo Levi's *If This Is a Man*? 'Il y a Jules à attraper par les oreilles.' 'Jules' was the lavatory bucket, which every morning had to be taken by its handles, carried outside and emptied into the cess pool.' Heh, heh.

Craig Raine
Oxford

From Julian Barnes

SIR: Others before me have known the dubious privilege of being labelled 'my friend' by Craig Raine in the correspondence columns of LRB. I name a hurricane after him; he calls me a pisspot. If this is 'my friend' Craig Raine's grasp of proportionate response, then we should all be glad he hasn't yet acquired a driving licence. And what is to be done about our uprooted friendship now? I suppose I shall have to agree to edit *The Faber Book of Hurricanes*.

Julian Barnes

London NW5

12 November 1987

Three Scenes
Christopher Tayler

WHEN MY FATHER was diagnosed with colorectal cancer twenty months ago, the first thing his doctors decided to do was fit him with a stoma, which turned out to be a less dispiriting term for giving him a colostomy. He had private health insurance, so he was booked in at a small hospital outside Brighton with a view of the sea and, he was assured, a functioning wireless network. He bought a new laptop to take along – not for working on a book he'd always meant to write or even, primarily, for sending emails, but for playing Scrabble against opponents on the internet while convalescing. My brother and I visited him soon after the operation, and I remember thinking, on the way in, about the scene in *Blue Velvet* in which Kyle MacLachlan visits his father in hospital. As I remembered it, the father's horribly trussed up, with a respirator pumping and an oxygen mask on his face, as a result of his heart attack in the opening scene. My dad, post-surgery, looked healthier than Kyle's, but he did have a transparent oxygen mask on, and after I kissed him he indicated it and said: 'It's like *Blue Velvet*!' I think he meant Dennis Hopper's more memorable gas mask, and I admired him for joking about that then.

Without having really thought about it, I had a vague notion that having a terminal illness might lead one to experience moments of great clarity while listening to late Beethoven quartets. Maybe it does, but over the next few months I learned that it can also function like any other deadline, leading to much playing of online games and distracted reordering of MP3 files – in my dad's case, mostly operas by Rameau and Handel. My brother and I clubbed together and got him a new iPod (his fag packet-sized, early-adopted one was moribund), but in truth he was more interested in a touchscreen device made by Cowon for storing and playing films and music that he'd worked up enough desire for to order himself. The movie he downloaded to try it out with was an existentialist thriller by Jean-Pierre Melville, *Le Cercle rouge*, and not long after his 6oth birthday I watched it with him, having gone to my parents' house to look after him for the day (my mother had had to go and look after her mother). We managed to get it playing, in the middle of this strange scene, on the enormous flat screen TV that had sprouted on the dresser in my parents' bedroom. But my main memory is of us laughing – in his case a little breathlessly – at a later episode in which Yves Montand, playing a dipsomaniac sharpshooter, is menaced by psychedelically-rendered visions of lizards and tarantulas crawling over his bed.

My father died very suddenly the next day of a pulmonary embolism brought on by the drug treatment. My wife was pregnant with our second child, and one night, alarmed by signs of a possible miscarriage, we found ourselves back in the A&E department in which he'd been pronounced dead three days earlier. ('Died, eh?' the Polish scanner technician said when my wife tried to explain why I'd burst into tears so violently after we'd been told that all was well. 'Was it something serious?') So I wasn't paying much attention when Google Street View went live in the UK two days later – the culmination of months in which cars like this were to be seen around city centres, collecting data from people's wireless networks as well as pictures, it turns out. If I had noticed, I'd probably have thought that my dad would have been annoyed about not

getting to play with it: always a ready buyer when aerial photo-
graphers came by with snaps of the house and garden, he'd recently
ordered a wireless webcam for fitting to a bird feeder, with the idea
of keeping an eye on the local woodpeckers even when confined
to his bed. Arranging the return of this item, which arrived too
late in an urn-sized box, was one of the tasks I'd recently taken on.

My mother insisted that I should take the newish laptop, which
I'm writing this on, and last July – in the middle of moving somewhere
more pushchair-approachable – I used it to look my flat up on Google
Maps. After putting in my postcode and switching to Street View, the
first thing I saw was this:

And here I experienced a bodily reaction, a racing and tingling of
the blood: there's a figure on my now ex-balcony, between the trees.
I also began to feel like Harrison Ford in *Blade Runner*, using his voice-
operated 'Esper Machine' to pan and zoom around a photo in search
of clues. 'Track right,' as Harrison might say. 'Stop. Enhance. Centre
in. Stop. Enhance and stop.'

No prizes for guessing that that's my father, his features probably blurred by distance rather than Google's facial recognition software. Judging from the size of the child he's holding – my son – and the shagginess of the trees, it's July or August 2008, two or three months before his illness was diagnosed.

I'd like to be able to report that this ghostly image triggered a powerful epiphany in me. But I wasn't sure then, and I'm not sure now, what I felt about it beyond surprise and sadness, or even how much purchase my feelings have on it. As one of my dad's favourite novelists wrote about the telephone in 1920 or so, habit doesn't take long 'to divest of their mystery the sacred forces with which we are in contact', and the papers, too, have made short work of the potential for spookiness in 'Google Streak View'. One of my first responses was an internet-schooled one: who should I send a link to? I also remember feeling bad about not being someone like Milan Kundera, who'd have a better idea of what the picture was a metaphor for. But my experience is that high-tech toys and mourning don't work particularly well together: it's hard to invest much feeling in things when under the narcotic spell of consumer gadgetry, which was perhaps my dad's main use for it – and of course mine for our shared repertoire of movie references. All the same, I look up my old flat from time to time to see if he's still there. He is, though presumably another Google car will be along in a while.

16 June 2010

Between Worlds
Edward Said makes sense of his life

IN THE FIRST book I wrote, *Joseph Conrad and the Fiction of Autobiography*, published more than thirty years ago, and then in an essay called 'Reflections on Exile' that appeared in 1984, I used Conrad as an example of someone whose life and work seemed to typify the fate of the wanderer who becomes an accomplished writer in an acquired language, but can never shake off his sense of alienation from his new – that is, acquired – and, in Conrad's rather special case, admired home. His friends all said of Conrad that he was very contented with the idea of being English, even though he never lost his heavy Polish accent and his quite peculiar moodiness, which was thought to be very un-English. Yet the moment one enters his writing the aura of dislocation, instability and strangeness is unmistakable. No one could represent the fate of lostness and disorientation better than he did, and no one was more ironic about the effort of trying to replace that condition with new arrangements and accommodations – which invariably lured one into further traps, such as those Lord Jim encounters when he starts life again on his little island. Marlow enters the heart of darkness to discover that Kurtz was not only there before him but is also incapable of telling him the whole truth; so that, in narrating his own experiences, Marlow cannot be as exact as he would have liked, and ends up producing approximations and even falsehoods of which both he and his listeners seem quite aware.

Only well after his death did Conrad's critics try to reconstruct what has been called his Polish background, very little of which had found its way directly into his fiction. But the rather elusive meaning of his writing is not so easily supplied, for even if we find out a lot about his Polish experiences, friends and relatives, that information will not of itself settle the core of restlessness and unease that his work relentlessly circles. Eventually we realise that the work is actually constituted by the experience of exile or alienation that cannot ever be rectified. No matter how perfectly he is able to express something, the result always seems to him an approximation to what he had wanted to say, and to have been said too late, past the point where the saying of it might have been helpful. 'Amy Foster', the most desolate of his stories, is about a young man from Eastern Europe, shipwrecked off the English coast on his way to America, who ends up as the husband of the affectionate but inarticulate Amy Foster. The man remains a foreigner, never learns the language, and even after he and Amy have a child cannot become a part of the very family he has created with her. When he is near death and babbling deliriously in a strange language, Amy snatches their child from him, abandoning him to his final sorrow. Like so many of Conrad's fictions, the story is narrated by a sympathetic figure, a doctor who is acquainted with the pair, but even he cannot redeem the young man's isolation, although Conrad teasingly makes the reader feel that he might have been able to. It is difficult to read 'Amy Foster' without thinking that Conrad must have feared dying a similar death, inconsolable, alone, talking away in a language no one could understand.

The first thing to acknowledge is the loss of home and language in the new setting, a loss that Conrad has the severity to portray as

irredeemable, relentlessly anguished, raw, untreatable, always acute
– which is why I have found myself over the years reading and writing
about Conrad like a *cantus firmus*, a steady groundbass to much that
I have experienced. For years I seemed to be going over the same kind
of thing in the work I did, but always through the writings of other
people. It wasn't until the early fall of 1991 when an ugly medical
diagnosis suddenly revealed to me the mortality I should have known
about before that I found myself trying to make sense of my own life
as its end seemed alarmingly nearer. A few months later, still trying
to assimilate my new condition, I found myself composing a long
explanatory letter to my mother, who had already been dead for almost
two years, a letter that inaugurated a belated attempt to impose a
narrative on a life that I had left more or less to itself, disorganised,
scattered, uncentred. I had had a decent enough career in the
university, I had written a fair amount, I had acquired an unenviable
reputation (as the 'professor of terror') for my writing and speaking
and being active on Palestinian and generally Middle Eastern or
Islamic and anti-imperialist issues, but I had rarely paused to put the
whole jumble together. I was a compulsive worker, I disliked and
hardly ever took vacations, and I did what I did without worrying too
much (if at all) about such matters as writer's block, depression or
running dry.

All of a sudden, then, I found myself brought up short with some
though not a great deal of time available to survey a life whose
eccentricities I had accepted like so many facts of nature. Once again
I recognised that Conrad had been there before me – except that
Conrad was a European who left his native Poland and became an
Englishman, so the move for him was more or less within the same
world. I was born in Jerusalem and had spent most of my formative
years there and, after 1948, when my entire family became refugees,
in Egypt. All my early education had, however, been in élite colonial
schools, English public schools designed by the British to bring up

a generation of Arabs with natural ties to Britain. The last one I went to before I left the Middle East to go to the United States was Victoria College in Cairo, a school in effect created to educate those ruling-class Arabs and Levantines who were going to take over after the British left. My contemporaries and classmates included King Hussein of Jordan, several Jordanian, Egyptian, Syrian and Saudi boys who were to become ministers, prime ministers and leading businessmen, as well as such glamorous figures as Michel Shalhoub, head prefect of the school and chief tormentor when I was a relatively junior boy, whom everyone has seen on screen as Omar Sharif.

The moment one became a student at VC one was given the school handbook, a series of regulations governing every aspect of school life – the kind of uniform we were to wear, what equipment was needed for sports, the dates of school holidays, bus schedules and so on. But the school's first rule, emblazoned on the opening page of the handbook, read: 'English is the language of the school; students caught speaking any other language will be punished.' Yet there were no native English-speakers among the students. Whereas the masters were all British, we were a motley crew of Arabs of various kinds, Armenians, Greeks, Italians, Jews and Turks, each of whom had a native language that the school had explicitly outlawed. Yet all, or nearly all, of us spoke Arabic – many spoke Arabic and French – and so we were able to take refuge in a common language in defiance of what we perceived as an unjust colonial stricture. British imperial power was nearing its end immediately after World War Two, and this fact was not lost on us, although I cannot recall any student of my generation who would have been able to put anything as definite as that into words.

For me, there was an added complication, in that although both my parents were Palestinian – my mother from Nazareth, my father from Jerusalem – my father had acquired US citizenship during World War One, when he served in the AEF under Pershing in France. He had originally left Palestine, then an Ottoman province, in 1911, at the age of 16, to escape being drafted to fight in Bulgaria. Instead, he went to the US, studied and worked there for a few years, then returned to Palestine in 1919 to go into business with his cousin. Besides, with an unexceptionally Arab family name like Said connected to an improbably British first name (my mother very much admired the Prince of Wales in 1935, the year of my birth), I was an uncomfortably anomalous student all through my early years: a Palestinian going to school in Egypt, with an English first name, an American passport and no certain identity at all. To make matters worse, Arabic, my native language, and English, my school language, were inextricably mixed: I have never known which was my first language, and have felt fully at home in neither, although I dream in both. Every time I speak an English sentence, I find myself echoing it in Arabic, and vice versa.

All this went through my head in those months after my diagnosis revealed to me the necessity of thinking about final things. But I did so in what for me was a characteristic way. As the author of a book called *Beginnings*, I found myself drawn to my early days as a boy in Jerusalem, Cairo and Dhour el Shweir, the Lebanese mountain village which I loathed but where for years and years my father took us to spend our summers. I found myself reliving the narrative quandaries of my early years, my sense of doubt and of being out of place, of always feeling myself standing in the wrong corner, in a place that seemed to be slipping away from me just as I tried to define or describe it. Why, I remember asking myself, could I not have had a simple background, been all Egyptian, or all something else, and not have had to face the daily rigours of questions that led back to words that seemed to lack a stable origin? The worst part of my situation, which time has only exacerbated, has been the warring relationship between English and Arabic, something that Conrad had not had to deal with since his passage from Polish to English via French was effected entirely within Europe. My whole education was Anglocentric, so much so that I knew a great deal more about British and even Indian history and geography (required subjects) than I did about the history and geography of the Arab world. But although taught to believe and think like an English schoolboy, I was also trained to understand that I was an alien, a Non-European Other, educated by my betters to know my station and not to aspire to being British. The line separating Us from Them was linguistic, cultural, racial and ethnic. It did not make matters easier for me to have been born, baptised and confirmed in the Anglican Church, where the singing of bellicose hymns like 'Onward Christian Soldiers' and 'From Greenland's Icy Mountains' had me in effect playing the role at once of aggressor and aggressed against. To be at the same time a Wog and an Anglican was to be in a state of standing civil war.

In the spring of 1951 I was expelled from Victoria College, thrown out for being a troublemaker, which meant that I was more visible and more easily caught than the other boys in the daily skirmishes between Mr Griffith, Mr Hill, Mr Lowe, Mr Brown, Mr Maundrell, Mr Gatley and all the other British teachers, on the one hand, and us, the boys of the school, on the other. We were all subliminally aware, too, that the old Arab order was crumbling: Palestine had fallen, Egypt was tottering under the massive corruption of King Farouk and his court (the revolution that brought Gamal Abdel Nasser and his Free Officers to power was to occur in July 1952), Syria was undergoing a dizzying series of military coups, Iran, whose Shah was at the time married to Farouk's sister, had its first big crisis in 1951, and so on. The prospects for deracinated people like us were so uncertain that my father decided it would be best to send me as far away as possible – in effect, to an austere, puritanical school in the north-western corner of Massachusetts.

The day in early September 1951 when my mother and father deposited me at the gates of that school and then immediately left for the

Middle East was probably the most miserable of my life. Not only was the atmosphere of the school rigid and explicitly moralistic, but I seemed to be the only boy there who was not a native-born American, who did not speak with the required accent, and had not grown up with baseball, basketball and football. For the first time ever I was deprived of the linguistic environment I had depended on as an alternative to the hostile attentions of Anglo-Saxons whose language was not mine, and who made no bones about my belonging to an inferior, or somehow disapproved race. Anyone who has lived through the quotidian obstacles of colonial routine will know what I am talking about. One of the first things I did was to look up a teacher of Egyptian origin whose name had been given to me by a family friend in Cairo. 'Talk to Ned,' our friend said, 'and he'll instantly make you feel at home.' On a bright Saturday afternoon I trudged over to Ned's house, introduced myself to the wiry, dark man who was also the tennis coach, and told him that Freddie Maalouf in Cairo had asked me to look him up. 'Oh yes,' the tennis coach said rather frostily, 'Freddie.' I immediately switched to Arabic, but Ned put up his hand to interrupt me. 'No, brother, no Arabic here. I left all that behind when I came to America.' And that was the end of that.

Because I had been well-trained at Victoria College I did well enough in my Massachusetts boarding-school, achieving the rank of either first or second in a class of about a hundred and sixty. But I was also found to be morally wanting, as if there was something mysteriously not-quite-right about me. When I graduated, for instance, the rank of valedictorian or salutatorian was withheld from me on the grounds that I was not fit for the honour – a moral judgment which I have ever since found difficult either to understand or to forgive. Although I went back to the Middle East in the holidays (my family continued to live there, moving from Egypt to Lebanon in 1963), I found myself becoming an entirely Western person; both at college and in graduate school I studied literature, music and philosophy, but none of it had anything to do with my own tradition. In the Fifties and early Sixties students from the Arab world were almost invariably scientists, doctors and engineers, or specialists in the Middle East, getting degrees at places like Princeton and Harvard and then, for the most part, returning to their countries to become teachers in universities there. I had very little to do with them, for one reason or another, and this naturally increased my isolation from my own language and background. By the time I came to New York to teach at Columbia in the fall of 1963, I was considered to have an exotic, but somewhat irrelevant Arabic background – in fact I recall that it was easier for most of my friends and colleagues not to use the word 'Arab', and certainly not 'Palestinian', in deference to the much easier and vaguer 'Middle Eastern', a term that offended no one. A friend who was already teaching at Columbia later told me that when I was hired I had been described to the department as an Alexandrian Jew! I remember a sense of being accepted, even courted, by older colleagues at Columbia, who with one or two exceptions saw me as a promising, even very promising young scholar of 'our' culture. Since there was no political activity then which was centred on the Arab world, I found that my concerns in my teaching and research, which were canonical though slightly unorthodox, kept me within the pale.

The big change came with the Arab-Israeli war of 1967, which coincided with a period of intense political activism on campus over civil rights and the Vietnam War. I found myself naturally involved on both fronts, but, for me, there was the further difficulty of trying to draw attention to the Palestinian cause. After the Arab defeat there was a vigorous re-emergence of Palestinian nationalism, embodied in the resistance movement located mainly in Jordan and the newly occupied territories. Several friends and members of my family had joined the movement, and when I visited Jordan in 1968, '69 and '70, I found myself among a number of like-minded contemporaries. In the US, however, my politics were rejected – with a few notable exceptions – both by anti-war activists and by supporters of Martin Luther King. For the first time I felt genuinely divided between the newly assertive pressures of my background and language and the complicated demands of a situation in the US that scanted, in fact despised what I had to say about the quest for Palestinian justice – which was considered anti-semitic and Nazi-like.

In 1972 I had a sabbatical and took the opportunity of spending a year in Beirut, where most of my time was taken up with the study of Arabic philology and literature, something I had never done before, at least not at that level, out of a feeling that I had allowed the disparity between my acquired identity and the culture into which I was born, and from which I had been removed, to become too great. In other words, there was an existential as well as a felt political need to bring one self into harmony with the other, for as the debate about what had once been called 'the Middle East' metamorphosed into a debate between Israelis and Palestinians, I was drawn in, ironically enough, as much because of my capacity to speak as an American academic and intellectual as by the accident of my birth. By the mid-Seventies I was in the rich but unenviable position of speaking for two, diametrically opposed constituencies, one Western, the other Arab.

For as long as I can remember, I had allowed myself to stand outside the umbrella that shielded or accommodated my contemporaries. Whether this was because I was genuinely different, objectively an outsider, or because I was temperamentally a loner I cannot say, but the fact is that although I went along with all sorts of institutional routines because I felt I had to, something private in me resisted them. I don't know what it was that caused me to hold back, but even when I was most miserably solitary or out of synch with everyone else, I held onto this private aloofness very fiercely. I may have envied friends whose language was one or the other, or who had lived in the same place all their lives, or who had done well in accepted ways, or who truly belonged, but I do not recall ever thinking that any of that was possible for me. It wasn't that I considered myself special, but rather that I didn't fit the situations I found myself in and wasn't too displeased to accept this state of affairs. I have, besides, always been drawn to stubborn autodidacts, to various sorts of intellectual misfit. In part it was the heedlessness of their own peculiar angle of vision that attracted me to writers and artists like Conrad, Vico, Adorno, Swift, Adonis, Hopkins, Auerbach, Glenn Gould, whose style, or way of thinking, was highly individualistic and impossible to imitate, for whom the medium of expression, whether music or words, was eccentrically charged, very worked-over, self-conscious in the highest degree. What impressed me about them was not the mere fact of their self-invention but that the enterprise was deliberately and fastidiously located within a general history which they had excavated *ab origine*.

Having allowed myself gradually to assume the professional voice of an American academic as a way of submerging my difficult and unassimilable past, I began to think and write contrapuntally, using the disparate halves of my experience, as an Arab and as an American, to work with and also against each other. This tendency began to take shape after 1967, and though it was difficult, it was also exciting. What prompted the initial change in my sense of self, and of the language I was using, was the realisation that in accommodating to the exigencies of life in the US melting-pot, I had willy-nilly to accept the principle of annulment of which Adorno speaks so perceptively in *Minima Moralia*:

> The past life of émigrés is, as we know, annulled. Earlier it was the warrant of arrest, today it is intellectual experience, that is declared non-transferable and unnaturalisable. Anything that is not reified, cannot be counted and measured, ceases to exist. Not satisfied with this, however, reification spreads to its own opposite, the life that cannot be directly actualised; anything that lives on merely as thought

and recollection. For this a special rubric has been invented. It is called 'background' and appears on the questionnaire as an appendix, after sex, age and profession. To complete its violation, life is dragged along on the triumphal automobile of the united statisticians, and even the past is no longer safe from the present, whose remembrance of it consigns it a second time to oblivion.

For my family and for myself the catastrophe of 1948 (I was then 12) was lived unpolitically. For 20 years after their dispossession and expulsion from their homes and territory, most Palestinians had to live as refugees, coming to terms not with their past, which was lost, annulled, but with their present. I do not want to suggest that my life as a schoolboy, learning to speak and coin a language that let me live as a citizen of the United States, entailed anything like the suffering of that first generation of Palestinian refugees, scattered throughout the Arab world, where invidious laws made it impossible for them to become naturalised, unable to work, unable to travel, obliged to register and re-register each month with the police, many of them forced to live in appalling camps like Beirut's Sabra and Shatila, which were the sites of massacres 34 years later. What I experienced, however, was the suppression of a history as everyone around me celebrated Israel's victory, its terrible swift sword, as Barbara Tuchman grandly put it, at the expense of the original inhabitants of Palestine, who now found themselves forced over and over again to prove that they had once existed. 'There are no Palestinians,' said Golda Meir in 1969, and that set me, and many others, the slightly preposterous challenge of disproving her, of beginning to articulate a history of loss and dispossession that had to be extricated, minute by minute, word by word, inch by inch, from the very real history of Israel's establishment, existence and achievements. I was working in an almost entirely negative element, the non-existence, the non-history which I had somehow to make visible despite occlusions, misrepresentations and denials.

Inevitably, this led me to reconsider the notions of writing and language, which I had until then treated as animated by a given text or subject – the history of the novel, for instance, or the idea of narrative as a theme in prose fiction. What concerned me now was how a subject was constituted, how a language could be formed – writing as a construction of realities that served one or another purpose instrumentally. This was the world of power and representations, a world that came into being as a series of decisions made by writers, politicians, philosophers to suggest or adumbrate one reality and at the same time efface others. The first attempt I made at this kind of work was a short essay I wrote in 1968 entitled 'The Arab Portrayed', in which I described the image of the Arab that had been manipulated in journalism and some scholarly writing in such a way as to evade any discussion of history and experience as I and many other Arabs had lived them. I also wrote a longish study of Arabic prose fiction after 1948 in which I reported on the fragmentary, embattled quality of the narrative line.

During the Seventies I taught my courses in European and American literature at Columbia and elsewhere, and bit by bit entered the political and discursive worlds of Middle Eastern and international politics. It is worth mentioning here that for the 40 years that I have been teaching I have never taught anything other than the Western canon, and certainly nothing about the Middle East. I've long had the ambition of giving a course on modern Arabic literature, but I haven't got around to it, and for at least thirty years I've been planning a seminar on Vico and Ibn Khaldun, the great 14th-century historiographer and philosopher of history. But my sense of identity as a teacher of Western literature has excluded this other aspect of my activity so far as the classroom is concerned. Ironically, the fact that I continued to write and teach my subject gave sponsors and hosts at university functions to which I had been invited to lecture an excuse to ignore my embarrassing political activity by specifically asking me to lecture on a literary topic. And there were those who spoke of my efforts on behalf of 'my people', without ever mentioning the name of that people. 'Palestine' was still a word to be avoided.

Even in the Arab world Palestine earned me a great deal of opprobrium. When the Jewish Defence League called me a Nazi in 1985, my office at the university was set fire to and my family and I received innumerable death threats, but when Anwar Sadat and Yasser Arafat appointed me Palestinian representative to the peace talks (without ever consulting me) and I found it impossible to step outside my apartment, so great was the media rush around me, I became the object of extreme left-wing nationalist hostility because I was considered too liberal on the question of Palestine and the idea of co-existence between Israeli Jews and Palestinian Arabs. I've been consistent in my belief that no military option exists for either side, that only a process of peaceful reconciliation, and justice for what the Palestinians have had to endure by way of dispossession and military occupation, would work. I was also very critical of the use of slogan-clichés like 'armed struggle' and of the revolutionary adventurism that caused innocent deaths and did nothing to advance the Palestinian case politically. 'The predicament of private life today is shown by its arena,' Adorno wrote. 'Dwelling, in the proper sense, is now impossible. The traditional residences we grew up in have grown intolerable: each trait of comfort in them is paid for with a betrayal of knowledge, each vestige of shelter with the musty pact of family interests.' Even more unyieldingly, he continued:

> The house is past . . . The best mode of conduct, in the face of all this, still seems an uncommitted, suspended one: to lead a private life, as far as the social order and one's own needs will tolerate nothing else, but not to attach weight to it as something still socially substantial and individually appropriate. 'It is even part of my good fortune not to be a house-owner,' Nietzsche already wrote in the *Gay Science*. Today we should have to add: it is part of morality not to be at home in one's home.

For myself, I have been unable to live an uncommitted or suspended life: I have not hesitated to declare my affiliation with an extremely unpopular cause. On the other hand, I have always reserved the right to be critical, even when criticism conflicted with solidarity or with what others expected in the name of national loyalty. There is a definite, almost palpable discomfort to such a position, especially given the irreconcilability of the two constituencies, and the two lives they have required.

The net result in terms of my writing has been to attempt a greater transparency, to free myself from academic jargon, and not to hide behind euphemism and circumlocution where difficult issues have been concerned. I have given the name 'worldliness' to this voice, by which I do not mean the jaded savoir-faire of the man about town, but rather a knowing and unafraid attitude towards exploring the world we live in. Cognate words, derived from Vico and Auerbach, have been 'secular' and 'secularism' as applied to 'earthly' matters; in these words, which derive from the Italian materialist tradition that runs from Lucretius through to Gramsci and Lampedusa, I have found an important corrective to the German Idealist tradition of synthesising the antithetical, as we find it in Hegel, Marx, Lukács and Habermas. For not only did 'earthly' connote this historical world made by men and women rather than by God or 'the nation's genius', as Herder termed it, but it suggested a territorial grounding for my argument and language, which proceeded from an attempt to understand the imaginative geographies fashioned and then imposed by power on distant lands and people. In *Orientalism* and *Culture and Imperialism*, and then again in the five or six explicitly political books concerning Palestine and the Islamic world that I wrote around the same time, I felt that I had been fashioning a self who revealed for a Western audience things that had so far either been hidden or not discussed at all. Thus in talking about the Orient, hitherto believed to be a simple fact of nature, I tried to uncover the longstanding, very varied geographical obsession with a distant, often inaccessible world that helped Europe to define itself by being its opposite. Similarly, I believed that Palestine, a territory effaced in the process of building another society, could be restored as an act of political resistance to injustice and oblivion.

Occasionally, I'd notice that I had become a peculiar creature to many people, and even a few friends, who had assumed that being Palestinian was the equivalent of something mythological like a unicorn or a hopelessly odd variation of a human being. A Boston psychologist who specialised in conflict resolution, and whom I had met at several seminars involving Palestinians and Israelis, once rang me from Greenwich Village and asked if she could come uptown to pay me a visit. When she arrived, she walked in, looked incredulously at my piano – 'Ah, you actually play the piano,' she said, with a trace of disbelief in her voice – and then turned around and began to walk out. When I asked her whether she would have a cup of tea before leaving (after all, I said, you have come a long way for such a short visit) she said she didn't have time. 'I only came to see how you lived,' she said without a hint of irony. Another time a publisher in another city refused to sign my contract until I had lunch with him. When I asked his assistant what was so important about having a meal with me, I was told that the great man wanted to see how I handled myself at the table. Fortunately none of these experiences affected or detained me for very long: I was always in too much of a rush to meet a class or a deadline, and I quite deliberately avoided the self-questioning that would have landed me in a terminal depression. In any case the Palestinian intifada that erupted in December 1987 confirmed our peoplehood in as dramatic and compelling a way as anything I might have said. Before long, however, I found myself becoming a token figure, hauled in for a few hundred written words or a ten-second soundbite testifying to 'what the Palestinians are saying', and determined to escape that role, especially given my disagreements with the PLO leadership from the late Eighties.

I am not sure whether to call this perpetual self-invention or a constant restlessness. Either way, I've long learned to cherish it. Identity as such is about as boring a subject as one can imagine. Nothing seems less interesting than the narcissistic self-study that today passes in many places for identity politics, or ethnic studies, or affirmations of roots, cultural pride, drum-beating nationalism and so on. We have to defend peoples and identities threatened with extinction or subordinated because they are considered inferior, but that is very different from aggrandising a past invented for present reasons. Those of us who are American intellectuals owe it to our country to fight the coarse anti-intellectualism, bullying, injustice and provincialism that disfigure its career as the last superpower. It is far more challenging to try to transform oneself into something different than it is to keep insisting on the virtues of being American in the ideological sense. Having myself lost a country with no immediate hope of regaining it, I don't find much comfort in cultivating a new garden, or looking for some other association to join. I learned from Adorno that reconciliation under duress is both cowardly and inauthentic: better a lost cause than a triumphant one, more satisfying a sense of the provisional and contingent – a rented house, for example – than the proprietary solidity of permanent ownership. This is why strolling dandies like Oscar Wilde or Baudelaire seem to me intrinsically more interesting than extollers of settled virtue like Wordsworth or Carlyle.

For the past five years I have been writing two columns a month for the Arabic press; and despite my extremely anti-religious politics I am often glowingly described in the Islamic world as a defender of Islam, and considered by some of the Islamic parties to be one of their supporters. Nothing could be further from the truth, any more than it is true that I have been an apologist for terrorism. The prismatic quality of one's writing when one isn't entirely of any camp, or a total partisan of any cause, is difficult to handle, but there, too, I have accepted the irreconcilability of the various conflicting, or at least incompletely harmonised, aspects of what, cumulatively, I appear to have stood for. A phrase by Günter Grass describes the predicament well: that of the 'intellectual without mandate'. A complicated situation arose in late 1993 when, after seeming to be the approved voice of the Palestinian struggle, I wrote increasingly sharply of my disagreements with Arafat and his bunch. I was immediately branded 'anti-peace' because I had the lack of tact to describe the Oslo treaty as deeply flawed. Now that everything has ground to a halt, I am regularly asked what it is like to be proved right, but I was more surprised by that than anyone: prophecy is not part of my arsenal.

For the past three or four years I have been trying to write a memoir of my early – that is, pre-political – life, largely because I think it's a story worthy of rescue and commemoration, given that the three places I grew up in have ceased to exist. Palestine is now Israel, Lebanon, after twenty years of civil war, is hardly the stiflingly boring place it was when we spent our summers locked up in Dhour el Shweir, and colonial, monarchical Egypt disappeared in 1952. My memories of those days and places remain extremely vivid, full of little details that I seem to have preserved as if between the covers of a book, full also of unexpressed feelings generated out of situations and events that occurred decades ago but seem to have been waiting to be articulated now. Conrad says in *Nostromo* that a desire lurks in every heart to write down once and for all a true account of what happened, and this certainly is what moved me to write my memoir, just as I had found myself writing a letter to my dead mother out of a desire once again to communicate something terribly important to a primordial presence in my life. 'In his text,' Adorno says, the writer sets up house . . . For a man who no longer has a homeland, writing becomes a place to live . . . [Yet] the demand that one harden oneself against self-pity implies the technical necessity to counter any slackening of intellectual tension with the utmost alertness, and to eliminate anything that has begun to encrust the work or to drift along idly, which may at an earlier stage have served, as gossip, to generate the warm atmosphere conducive to growth, but is now left behind, flat and stale. In the end, the writer is not even allowed to live in his writing.

One achieves at most a provisional satisfaction, which is quickly ambushed by doubt, and a need to rewrite and redo that renders the text uninhabitable. Better *that*, however, than the sleep of self-satisfaction and the finality of death.

7 May 1998

V

Tony Harrison

My father still reads the dictionary every day.
He says your life depends on your power to master words.

Arthur Scargill
Sunday Times, 10 January 1982

Next millennium you'll have to search quite hard
to find my slab behind the family dead,
butcher, publican, and baker, now me, bard
adding poetry to their beef, beer and bread.

With Byron three graves on I'll not go short
of company, and Wordsworth's opposite.
That's two peers already, of a sort,
and we'll all be thrown together if the pit,

whose galleries once ran beneath this plot,
causes the distinguished dead to drop
into the rabblement of bone and rot,
shored slack, crushed shale, smashed prop.

Wordsworth built church organs, Byron tanned
luggage cowhide in the age of steam,

and knew their place of rest before the land
caves in on the lowest worked-out seam.

This graveyard on the brink of Beeston Hill's
the place I may well rest if there's a spot
under the rose roots and the daffodils
by which dad dignified the family plot.

If buried ashes saw then I'd survey
the places I learned Latin, and learned Greek,
and left, the ground where Leeds United play
but disappoint their fans week after week,

which makes them lose their sense of self-esteem
and taking a short cut home through these graves here
they reassert the glory of their team
by spraying words on tombstones, pissed on beer.

This graveyard stands above a worked-out pit.
Subsidence makes the obelisks all list.
One leaning left's marked FUCK, one right's marked SHIT
sprayed by some peeved supporter who was pissed.

Far-sighted for his family's future dead,
but for his wife, this banker's still alone
on his long obelisk, and doomed to head
a blackened dynasty of unclaimed stone,

now graffitied with a crude four-letter word.
His children and grandchildren went away
and never came back home to be interred,
so left a lot of space for skins to spray.

The language of this graveyard ranges from
a bit of Latin for a former Mayor

or those who laid their lives down at the Somme,
the hymnal fragments and the gilded prayer,

how people 'fell asleep in the Good Lord',
brief chisellable bits from the good book
and rhymes whatever length they could afford,
to CUNT, PISS, SHIT and (mostly) FUCK!

Or, more expansively, there's LEEDS v.
the opponent of last week, this week, or next,
and a repertoire of blunt four-letter curses
on the team or race that makes the sprayer vexed.

Then, pushed for time, or fleeing some observer,
dodging between tall family vaults and trees
like his team's best ever winger, dribbler, swerver,
fills every space he finds with versus Vs.

Vs sprayed on the run at such a lick,
the sprayer master of his flourished tool,
get short-armed on the left like that red tick
they never marked his work with much at school.

Half this skinhead's age but with approval
I helped whitewash a V on a brick wall.
No one clamoured in the press for its removal
or thought the sign, in wartime, rude at all.

These Vs are all the versuses of life
From LEEDS v. DERBY, Black/White
and (as I've known to my cost) man v. wife,
Communist v. Fascist, Left v. Right,

class v. class as bitter as before,
the unending violence of US and THEM,

personified in 1984
by Coal Board MacGregor and the NUM,

Hindu/Sikh, soul/body, heart v. mind,
East/West, male/female, and the ground
these fixtures are fought out on's Man, resigned
to hope from his future what his past never found.

The prospects for the present aren't too grand
when a swastika with NF (National Front)'s
sprayed on a grave, to which another hand
has added, in a reddish colour, CUNTS.

Which is, I grant, the word that springs to mind,
when going to clear the weeds and rubbish thrown
on the family plot by football fans, I find
UNITED graffitied on my parents' stone.

How many British graveyards now this May
are strewn with rubbish and choked up with weeds
since families and friends have gone away
for work or fuller lives, like me from Leeds?

When I first came here 40 years ago
with my dad to 'see my grandma' I was 7.
I helped dad with the flowers. He let me know
she'd gone to join my grandad up in Heaven.

My dad who came each week to bring fresh flowers
came home with clay stains on his trouser knees.
Since my parents' deaths I've spent 2 hours
made up of odd 10 minutes such as these.

Flying visits once or twice a year,
And though I'm horrified just who's to blame

that I find instead of flowers cans of beer
and more than one grave sprayed with some skin's name?

Where there were flower urns and troughs of water
And mesh receptacles for withered flowers
are the HARP tins of some skinhead Leeds supporter.
It isn't all his fault though. Much is ours.

5 kids, with one in goal, play 2-a-side.
When the ball bangs on the hawthorn that's one post
and petals fall they hum *Here Comes the Bride*
though not so loud they'd want to rouse a ghost.

They boot the ball on purpose at the trunk
and make the tree shed showers of shrivelled may.
I look at this word graffitied by some drunk
and I'm in half a mind to let it stay.

(Though honesty demands that I say *if*
I'd wanted to take the necessary pains
to scrub the skin's inscription off
I only had an hour between trains.

So the feelings that I had as I stood gazing
and the significance I saw could be a sham,
mere excuses for not patiently erasing
the word sprayed on the grave of dad and mam.)

This pen's all I have of magic wand.
I know this world's so torn but want no other
except for dad who'd hoped from 'the beyond'
a better life than this one, *with* my mother.

Though I don't believe in afterlife at all
and know it's cheating it's hard *not* to make

a sort of furtive prayer from this skin's scrawl,
his UNITED mean 'in Heaven' for their sake,

an accident of meaning to redeem
an act intended as mere desecration
and make the thoughtless spraying of his team
apply to higher things, and to the nation.

Some, where kids use aerosols, use giant signs
to let the people know who's forged their fetters
Like PRI CE O WALES above West Yorkshire mines
(no prizes for who nicked the missing letters!)

The big blue star for booze, tobacco ads,
the magnet's monogram, the royal crest,
insignia in neon dwarf the lads
who spray a few odd FUCKS when they're depressed.

Letters of transparent tubes and gas
in Düsseldorf are blue and flash out KRUPP.
Arms are hoisted for the British ruling class
and clandestine, genteel aggro keeps them up.

And there's HARRISON on some Leeds
    building sites
I've taken in fun as blazoning my name,
which I've also seen on books, in Broadway lights,
so why can't skins with spraycans do the same?

But why inscribe these *graves* with CUNT and SHIT?
Why choose neglected tombstones to disfigure?
This pitman's of last century daubed PAKI GIT,
this grocer Broadbent's aerosolled with NIGGER?

They're there to shock the living, not arouse
the dead from their deep peace to lend support
for the causes skinhead spraycans could espouse.
The dead would want their desecrators caught!

Jobless though they are how can these kids,
even though their team's lost one more game,
believe that the 'Pakis', 'Niggers', even 'Yids'
sprayed on the tombstones here should bear the blame?

What is it that these crude words are revealing?
What is it that this aggro act implies?
Giving the dead their xenophobic feeling
or just a *cri-de-coeur* because man dies?

So what's a cri-de-coeur, cunt? Can't you speak
the language that yer mam spoke. Think of 'er!
Can yer only get yer tongue round fucking Greek?
Go and fuck yourself with cri-de-coeur!

'She didn't talk like you do for a start!'
I shouted, turning where I thought the voice had been.
She didn't understand yer fucking 'art'!
She thought yer fucking poetry obscene!

I wish on this skin's words deep aspirations,
first the prayer for my parents I can't make,
then a call to Britain and to all nations
made in the name of love for peace's sake.

Aspirations, cunt! Folk on t'fucking dole
'ave got about as much scope to aspire
above the shit they're dumped in, cunt, as coal
aspires to be chucked on t'fucking fire.

OK, forget the aspirations. Look, I know
United's losing gets you fans incensed
and how far the HARP inside you makes you go
but all these Vs: against! against! against!

Ah'll tell yer then what really riles a bloke.
It's reading on their graves the jobs they did –
butcher, publican and baker. Me, I'll croak
doing t'same nowt ah do now as a kid.

'ard birth ah wor, mi mam says, almost killed 'er.
Death after life on t'dole won't seem as 'ard!
Look at this cunt, Wordsworth, organ builder,
this fucking 'aberdasher Appleyard!

If mi mam's up there, don't want to meet 'er
listening to me list mi dirty deeds,
and 'ave to pipe up to St fucking Peter
ah've been on t'dole all mi life in fucking Leeds!

Then t'Alleluias stick in t'angels' gobs.
When dole-wallahs fuck off to the void
what'll t'mason carve up for their jobs?
The cunts who lieth 'ere wor unemployed?

This lot worked at one job all life through.
Byron, 'Tanner', 'Lieth 'ere interred'.
They'll chisel fucking poet when they do you
and that, yer cunt, 's a crude four-letter word.

'Listen, cunt!' I said, 'before you start your jeering
the reason why I want this in a book
's to give ungrateful cunts like you a hearing!'
A book, yer stupid cunt, 's not worth a fuck!

'The only reason why I write this poem at all
on yobs like you who do the dirt on death
's to give some higher meaning to your scrawl.'
Don't fucking bother, cunt! Don't waste your breath!

'You piss-artist skinhead cunt, you wouldn't know
and it doesn't fucking matter if you do,
the skin and poet united fucking Rimbaud
but the *autre* that *je est* is fucking you.'

Ah've told yer, no more Greek . . . That's yer last warning!
Ah'll boot yer fucking balls to Kingdom Come.
They'll find yer cold on t'grave tomorrer morning.
So don't speak Greek. Don't treat me like I'm dumb.

'I've done my bits of mindless aggro too
not half a mile from where we're standing now.'
Yeah, ah bet yer wrote a poem, yer wanker you!
'No, shut yer gob a while. Ah'll tell yer 'ow . . .'

'Herman Darewski's band played operetta
with a wobbly soprano warbling. Just why
I made my mind up that I'd got to get her
with the fire hose I can't say, but I'll try.

It wasn't just the singing angered me.
At the same time half a crowd was jeering
as the smooth Hugh Gaitskill, our MP,
made promises the other half were cheering.

What I hated in those high soprano ranges
was uplift beyond all reason and control
and in a world where you say nothing changes
it seemed a sort of prick-tease of the soul.

I tell you when I heard high notes that rose
above Hugh Gaitskill's cool electioneering
straight from the warbling throat right up my nose
I had all your aggro in my jeering.

And I hit the fire extinguisher ON knob
and covered orchestra and audience with spray.
I could run as fast as you then. A good job!
They yelled 'damned vandal' after me that day . . .'

And then yer saw the light and up 'eavy!
And knew a man's not how much he can sup . . .
Yer reward for growing up's this super-bevvy,
a meths and champagne punch ini t'FA Cup.

Ah've 'eard all that from old farts past their prime.
'ow now yer live wi' all yer once detested . . .
Old farts with not much left'll give me time.
Fuckers like that get folk like me arrested.

Covet not thy neighbour's wife, thy neighbour's riches.
Vicar and cop who say, to save our souls,
Get thee beHind me, Satan, drop their breeches
and get the Devil's dick right up their 'oles!

It was more a *working* marriage that I'd meant,
a blend of masculine and feminine.
Ignoring me, he started looking, bent
on some more aerosolling, for his tin.

'It was more a *working* marriage that I mean!'
Fuck, and save mi soul, eh? That suits me.
Then as if I'd egged him on to be obscene
he added a middle slit to one daubed V.

Don't talk to me of fucking representing
the class yer were born into any more.
Yer going to get 'urt and start resenting
it's not poetry we need in this class war.

Yer've given yerself toffee, cunt. Who needs
yer fucking poufy words. Ah write mi own.
Ah've got mi work on show all ovver Leeds
like this UNITED 'ere on some sod's stone.

'OK!' (thinking I had him trapped) 'OK!'
'If you're so proud of it, then sign your name
when next you're full of HARP and armed with spray,
next time you take this short cut from the game.'

He took the can, contemptuous, unhurried
and cleared the nozzle and prepared to sign
the UNITED sprayed where mam and dad were buried.
He aerosolled his name. And it was mine.

The boy footballers bawl *Here Comes the Bride*
and drifting blossoms fall onto my head.
One half of me's alive but one half died
when the skin half sprayed my name among the dead.

Half versus half, the enemies within
the heart that can't be whole till they unite.
As I stoop to grab the crushed HARP lager tin
the day's already dusk, half dark, half light.

That UNITED that I'd wished onto the nation
or as reunion for dead parents soon recedes.
The word's once more a mindless desecration
by some HARPoholic yob supporting Leeds.

Almost the time for ghosts I'd better scram.
Though not given much to fears of spooky scaring
I don't fancy an encounter with mi mam
playing Hamlet with me for this swearing.

Though I've a train to catch my step is slow.
I walk on the grass and graves with wary tread
over these subsidences, these shifts below
the life of Leeds supported by the dead.

Further underneath's that cavernous hollow
that makes the gravestones lean towards the town.
A matter of mere time and it will swallow
this place of rest and all the resters down.

I tell myself I've got, say, 30 years.
At 75 this place will suit me fine.
I've never feared the grave but what I fear's
that great worked-out black hollow under mine.

Not train departure time, and not Town Hall
with the great white clock face I can see,
coal, that began, with no man here at all,
as 300 million-year-old plant debris.

5 kids still play at making blossoms fall
and humming as they do *Here Comes the Bride.*
They never seem to tire of their ball
though I hear a woman's voice call one inside.

2 larking boys play bawdy bride and groom.
3 boys in Leeds strip la-la *Lohengrin.*
I hear them as I go through growing gloom
still years away from being skald or skin.

The ground's carpeted with petals as I throw
the aerosol, the HARP can, the cleared weeds
on top of dad's dead daffodils, then go,
with not one glance behind, away from Leeds.

The bus to the station's still the No. 1
but goes by routes that I don't recognise.
I look out for known landmarks as the sun
reddens the swabs of cloud in darkening skies.

Home, home, home, to my woman as the red
darkens from a fresh blood to a dried.
Home, home to my woman, home to bed
where opposites seem sometimes unified.

A pensioner in turban taps his stick
along the pavement past the corner shop,
that sells samosas now, not beer on tick,
to the Kashmir Muslim Club that was the Co-op.

House after house FOR SALE where we'd played cricket
with white roses cut from flour-sacks on our caps,
with stumps chalked on the coal-grate for our wicket,
and every one bought now by 'coloured chaps',

dad's most liberal label as he felt
squeezed by the unfamiliar, and fear
of foreign food and faces, when he smelt
curry in the shop where he'd bought beer.

And growing frailer, 'wobbly on his pins',
the shops he felt familiar with withdrew
which meant much longer tiring treks for tins
that had a label on them that he knew.

And as the shops that stocked his favourites receded
whereas he'd fancied beans and popped next door,
he found that four long treks a week were needed
till he wondered what he bothered eating for.

The supermarket made him feel embarrassed.
Where people bought whole lambs for family freezers
he bought baked beans from check-out girls too harassed
to smile or swap a joke with sad old geezers.

But when he bought his cigs he'd have a chat,
his week's one conversation, truth to tell,
but time also came and put a stop to that
when old Wattsy got bought out by M. Patel.

And there, 'Time like an ever rolling stream''s
What I once trilled behind that boarded front.
A 1000 ages made coal-bearing seams
and even more the hand that sprayed this CUNT

on both Methodist and C of E billboards
once divided in their fight for local souls.
Whichever house more truly was the Lord's
both's pews are filled with cut-price toilet rolls.

Home, home to my woman, never to return
till sexton or survivor has to cram
the bits of clinker scooped out of my urn
down through the rose-roots to my dad and mam.

Home, home to my woman, where the fire's lit
these still chilly mid-May evenings, home to you,
and perished vegetation from the pit
escaping insubstantial up the flue.

Listening to *Lulu*, in our hearth we burn,
As we hear the high Cs rise in stereo,
what was lush swamp club-moss and tree-fern
at least 300 million years ago.

Shilbottle cobbles, Alban Berg high D
lifted from a source that bears your name,
the one we hear decay, the one we see,
the fern from the foetid forest, as brief flame.

This world, with far too many people in,
starts on the TV logo as a taw,
then ping-pong, tennis, football; then one spin
to show us all, then shots of the Gulf War.

As the coal with reddish dust cools in the grate
on the late-night national news we see
police v. pickets at a coke-plant grate,
old violence and old disunity.

The map that's colour-coded Ulster/Eire's
flashed on again as almost every night.
Behind a tiny coffin with two bearers
men in masks with arms show off their might.

The day's last images recede to first a glow
and then a ball that shrinks back to a blank screen.
Turning to love, and sleep's oblivion, I know
what the UNITED that the skin sprayed *has* to mean.

Hanging my clothes up, from my parka hood
may and apple petals, browned and creased,
fall onto the carpet and bring back the flood
of feelings their first falling had released.

I hear like ghosts from all Leeds matches humming
with one concerted voice the bride, the bride
I feel united to, *my* bride is coming
into the bedroom, naked, to my side.

The ones we choose to love become our anchor
when the hawser of the blood-tie's hacked, or frays.
But a voice that scorns chorales is yelling: *Wanker!*
It's the aerosolling skin I met today's.

My *alter ego* wouldn't want to know it,
His aerosol vocab would baulk at LOVE,
the skin's UNITED underwrites the poet,
the measures carved below the ones above.

I doubt if 30 years of bleak Leeds weather
and 30 falls of apple and of may
will erode the UNITED binding us together.
And now it's your decision: does it stay?

Next millennium you'll have to search quite hard
to find out where I'm buried but I'm near
the grave of haberdasher Appleyard,
the pile of HARPs, or some new neonned beer.

Find Byron, Wordsworth, or turn left between
one grave marked Broadbent, one marked Richardson.
Bring some solution with you that can clean
whatever new crude words have been sprayed on.

If love of art, or love, gives you affront
that the grave I'm in's graffitied then, maybe,
erase the more offensive FUCK and CUNT
but leave, with the worn UNITED, one small v.

Victory? For vast, slow, coal-creating forces
that hew the body's seams to get the soul.
Will earth run out of her 'diurnal courses'
before repeating her creation of black coal?

If, having come this far, somebody reads
these verses, and he/she wants to understand,
face this grave on Beeston Hill, your back to Leeds,
and read the chiselled epitaph I've planned:

Beneath your feet's a poet, then a pit.
Poetry supporter, if you're here to find
How poems can grow from (beat you to it!) SHIT
find the beef, the beer, the bread, then look behind.

24 January 1985

'Author Loses Leg in Lagoon'
R.W. Johnson

I N EARLY MARCH, while staying at our holiday cottage in Trafalgar on the KwaZulu-Natal south coast, I went swimming, as has been my habit for many years, in the idyllic Mpenjati lagoon. The lagoon looks pretty much the way it did when Vasco da Gama first saw it; the lower south coast and Trafalgar in particular are unspoiled – we frequently get duikers as well as monkeys in our garden.

As I neared the shore I hit my foot painfully on a submerged rock; a quick inspection showed that several toes were bleeding. I waded ashore, got home quickly and showered. The bleeding soon stopped but the next day my whole foot was sore. I tried to ignore it but matters rapidly got worse and soon I was running a fever and felt so ill I was giddy and unsteady on my feet. Eventually I decided I had to see a doctor, but things were so bad that I fell repeatedly while trying to get to the car and had to half-crawl across the garage to get in. How I managed to drive the 12 kilometres to Port Edward remains a mystery – I was lurching all over the road. Arriving at the offices of Dr Chetty, whose board advertises him as a *dokotela* (Zulu for 'doctor') trained in Mysore, I found several other patients ahead of me but stumbled over to the receptionist's desk and explained that I was seriously ill.

Dr Chetty was wonderful. He immediately laid me on a table, gave me a drip, and in no time at all an ambulance had been arranged to take me to Margate Hospital. It turned out later – a great stroke of luck – that Dr Chetty had once before seen a patient suffering from what I had: necrotising fasciitis, caused by flesh-eating bacteria which rapidly invade and poison the body (the other man had died, as is normal with this disease). Almost certainly the reason the lagoon was polluted with such a deadly organism was to do with the dumping of raw sewage by communities living upriver.

Only months later was I able to Google necrotising fasciitis and find a long list of famous people who died from the disease, usually within 24 or 48 hours of contracting it. The medics at Margate muttered something about amputation but I was too far gone to say more than 'whatever it takes.' My conscious memory stops there – I was too ill and too sedated to participate in the drama that followed.

My wife, Irina, was teaching at Moscow's new School of Economics when she heard the news and straight away flew back to Durban. She rang Margate from the airport and asked whether I was still alive. 'He is critical,' they said. She explained that it would take her 90 minutes to drive to the hospital: would I still be alive then? 'He may – or may not be. He's very, very critical.' They had amputated the toes on my left foot and then, when the leg continued to swell, amputated my leg at the knee. But the poison had already invaded other parts of my body and all my systems – kidneys, lungs, heart etc – began to switch off. Multiple organ failure: that is, I began to die – that's what dying is. I came close to fulfilling one of Woody Allen's ambitions: 'I don't mind dying,' he once said, 'I just don't want to be there when it happens.'

My blood pressure kept shrinking to levels where it was thought I must die at any moment. To counter the septicaemia I was shot full of antibiotics and to prevent my blood pressure falling too far I was given adrenalin. When Irina arrived my chances of survival were less than 30 per cent. I rallied twice, only for crises to follow each time. My brother and children flew in and there were anguished discussions about where I should be buried.

My surgeon, Dr Otto, and his colleagues at Margate undoubtedly saved my life. Yet I needed not only a ventilator and a dialysis machine, but also a hyperbaric chamber, which Margate didn't have, so Irina decided to move me to St Augustine's Hospital in Durban. I deteriorated further, and my left leg was amputated above the knee. To make things worse, the overdose of adrenalin, though it had saved my heart, had badly damaged the fingers of both hands – on my left hand three fingertips are blackened with dry gangrene and have lost all feeling – and the toes of my right foot. I also had bedsores on my head and bottom. Doctor friends warned Irina not to get her hopes up – the odds against my survival were still daunting.

I drifted in and out of consciousness a number of times but my first memory is of waking up in St Augustine's intensive care unit in the first week of April with tubes controlling all my functions, unable to talk, and learning for the first time that I was missing a leg. Irina tells me that when it was explained to me that my leg had gone, I cried, but I have no memory of that. The regular morphine injections gave me the most terrifying and sophisticated nightmares I have ever experienced. Irina, my daughter and brother were all there and I communicated by tracing a spidery scrawl on a pad – my muscles had atrophied so much that I lacked the strength to write a sentence or lift an arm over my head.

Irina was at my bedside all hours of the day and night. I could never have recovered without her. Gradually things got a little better and some of the tubes came out, and then, one wonderful day, the dialysis was over. Better still, I moved out of the ICU – but then had to return because of persistent nausea and vomiting. Happily, this didn't last long. I began to do more and more physio and exercise to rebuild my muscles; I followed the news and was able to learn about the progress of the book I had just published. Despite or possibly because of my complete inability to do any of the usual promotional work, the book was selling well and there were many nice reviews. That made a real difference.

After two more months in hospital I was basically evicted by my insurance company, Discovery Health, which refused to continue to pay for me to be there, though I was far from ready to leave. It was a gloomy business realising how threadbare my care policy was, as huge medical bills poured in of which they paid only a fraction. Discovery wanted me to go to a 'step-down facility' (which no one at the hospital had ever heard of) in a high-crime area. We decided that if we were thrown out it would be better to go back to the beach cottage at Trafalgar and take our chances.

In the meantime it was sobering to read of the ANC's proposed new National Health Insurance scheme, which would forcibly conflate the public and private health sectors. Under ANC management the public sector has deteriorated very nearly to the point of collapse, with incompetent political placemen appointed as hospital managers, shortages of everything and, often, appallingly high mortality rates – all of it aggravated by a tidal wave of Aids victims that has pushed most other things aside. Doctors' organisations have warned that the NHI scheme would be unworkable, that it would end access to First World healthcare for everybody and would lead to a huge new emigration of medical personnel. I am hardly an unqualified fan of the way private health works here, but I need no reminding that without access to First World hospital care I would have died. Should the NHI plan go ahead not only would most doctors emigrate but so too would many of the seven million South Africans of all races who currently depend on private health insurance as patients. What would be left of the economy if these seven million go is a subject worthy of a morphine nightmare.

So now I'm back at Trafalgar, paying for a private nurse and physio, exercising like crazy and getting steadily stronger. Some people make nice remarks about my positive attitude but actually I owe everything to Irina. For the rest I feel like Theseus, sent to fight the Minotaur in the labyrinth. That is, I'm in an intolerable situation and the only way out – learning how to walk with a prosthesis, to drive and be self-sufficient again – is to keep a tight hold on Ariadne's thread and follow where it leads. That means working meticulously at the physio and teaching myself to do things like type this article with my gangrenous fingers.

I look out from my bed at the Indian Ocean, which is the purest blue and pullulates with whale spouts, dolphins and the approaching signs of the annual sardine run, when shoals 30 or 40 kilometres long, billions upon billions of fish, move up the coast, allowing every imaginable predator a feast day. Everyone celebrates the sardine run as a sort of popular carnival, but of course like so many great natural events it's built on the deaths of millions of creatures. Sometimes, as I gaze at the sea, I think about dying and how I nearly managed it, several times over. It seems incongruous given the gorgeous sunshine, the surf and the tropical vegetation – until you realise that it was in exactly these conditions that I cut my foot in the first place. I survived by a fluke; there's no merit to it, though doctor friends try to make me feel good by telling me how strong I am and what a fight I put up. 'Author Loses Leg in Lagoon': my children saved the newspaper hoarding for me, its sheer banality a warning too. But mainly as I look at the waves I feel, 'so far, so good.' I spend no time at all regretting my left leg. It's just so good to be alive.

6 August 2009

Saving Masud Khan
Wynne Godley

T HIS IS THE story of a disastrous encounter with psycho-analysis which severely blemished my middle years.

    I was about thirty years old when I found myself to be in a state of terrible distress. It was the paralysis of my will, rather than the pain itself, which enabled me to infer, using my head, that I needed help different in kind from the support of friends. A knowledgeable acquaintance suggested that I consult D.W. Winnicott, without telling me that he was pre-eminent among British psycho-analysts.

I don't think that living through an artificial self, which is what had got me into such an awful mess, is all that uncommon. The condition is difficult to recognise because it is concealed from the world, and from the subject, with ruthless ingenuity. It does not feature in the standard catalogue of neurotic symptoms such as hysteria, obsession, phobia, depression or impotence; and it is not inconsistent with worldly success or the formation of deep and lasting friendships. The disjointed components of the artificial self are not individually artificial.

What is it like to live in a state of dissociation? In a real sense, the subject is never corporeally present at all but goes about the world in a waking dream. Behaviour is managed by an auto-pilot. Responses are neither direct nor spontaneous. Every event is re-enacted after it has taken place and processed in an internal theatre. On the one hand, the subject may be bafflingly insensitive but this goes with extreme vulnerability, for the whole apparatus can only function within a framework of familiar and trusted responses. He or she is defenceless against random, unexpected or malicious events. Evil cannot be countered because it cannot be identified.

The short personal story which follows is so familiar in its outline that it may seem stale, but I cannot explain how I allowed such strange things to happen to me unless I tell it.

My parents separated from one another, with great and protracted bitterness, at about the time I was born, in 1926, and I hardly ever saw them together. In infancy I was looked after, in various country houses in Sussex and Kent, by nannies and governesses as well as by a fierce maiden aunt who shook me violently when I cried. My mother, though frequently in bed with what she called 'my pain', was a poet, playwright, pianist, composer and actress, and these activities took her away from home for long and irregular periods of time. When she rematerialised, we had long goodnights during which, as she sang to me, I undid her hair so that it fell over her shoulders. She used to parade naked in front of me, and would tell me (for instance) of the intense pleasure she got from sexual intercourse, of the protracted agony and humiliation she had suffered when giving birth to my much older half-sister, Ann, who grew up retarded and violent (screamed, spat, bit, kicked, threw), and of her disappointment when my father was impotent, particularly on their honeymoon. The intimacies we shared made me love her 'over the biggest number in the world'.

My father was shadowy to begin with; he was an elderly man – always approaching sixty. I first perceived him as an invalid – disturbingly unlike other children's fathers. But he had great personal authority, distinction and charm, which I could identify in the responses of other people to him. Occasionally he gave me superlative presents – a toy launch which got up its own steam, a flying model of a biplane.

Neither of my parents had a social circle. No one came to stay. There were no children next door to play with.

As a young child I believed myself to be special, endowed with supernatural, even divine, powers which would one day astonish the world. I also knew that I was worthless, with no gifts or rights, and that I looked fat, dull and unmanly. The achievements of others, particularly those of my older brother John, stood in for anything that I might achieve myself, and afterwards a series of distinguished men were to step into John's shoes. I acquired a spectacular ability to not see, identify or shrewdly evaluate people or situations. Although passive and sickly, I enjoyed secret fantasies of violence. When asked what I was going to be when I grew up, I replied that I was going to be 'a boy actress'.

When I was six, an abscess developed in my inner ear which eventually, in a climax of torture, burst through my eardrum. For years afterwards I often had to wear a bandage round the whole of my head to contain the discharge. I became 90 per cent deaf in one ear; I also started to get short-sighted and wear spectacles.

When just seven years old I was sent to a boarding school, for eight solid months of each year, without the elementary social or other skills that were needed. I could hardly read and had never dressed myself, so that doing up my back braces was painful and nearly impossible; it never occurred to me that I could slip them off my shoulders. The little boys were often beaten and kicked by the masters and I found this extremely frightening; one child was severely caned in front of the whole school. Lessons were an impenetrable bore. Occasionally I had severe panic attacks associated with strange fantasies – for instance, that I would soon die and be reincarnated as a rabbit in a hutch, unable to communicate with my parents or siblings.

When I was ten, my father, having inherited a peerage and a great deal of money, remarried and recovered a family estate of unsurpassable loveliness in a remote part of Southern Ireland. My stepmother,

Nora, created a luxurious and beautiful home, full of light and flowers, in a mansion house which overlooked two large lakes with woods running down to them. With John and my sister Katharine I was cocooned, during the school holidays, in total complaisance by a full complement of servants, gardeners, handymen and farm hands, of whose irony I was never conscious. On the morning of my 11th birthday my father walked into my bedroom, still wearing his pyjamas, with a 20-bore shotgun under his arm. I learned to shoot snipe and play tennis.

Around this time, my mother revealed that for years and years my father had been 'the most terrible drunkard'. In response to my anxious inquiry she emphasised that he drank 'until he became completely fuddled'. Meanwhile she had taken as a lover an ebullient young man, 15 years younger than herself, who emanated genius. This was William Glock, later to become the most versatile and influential musician of his generation. It was through his ears that I first heard and loved music and therefore started to learn the oboe. He soon fell in love with Katharine, and, sort of, with me (now aged 14) and we three drank a lot of rum and lime, with enormous hilarity.

When I was about fifteen, while John was fighting a gallant war over the Atlantic, my father started to drink again.

Heavy drinking is often associated with boisterous behaviour in a social context. My father never drank publicly at all and, drunk or sober, was never boisterous. He saw himself as a nobleman; and his style was that of a distinguished barrister, which is what he really was. But having suffered previously from delirium tremens, one or two shots caused him to collapse into bestial incoherence. He had convinced himself that if he was alone when he put the bottle to his lips no one would notice what was going on. I colluded with him in this, never referring to his drinking in any way. His drunkenness, when it occurred, was conspicuous and desperately embarrassing, whether he was in residence as a grandee in the Irish countryside or asleep in the Chamber of the House of Lords or visiting me at school. When he was not drinking, he recovered his authority completely. He was a fine violinist and during his abstinent periods, with Katharine at the piano, we played the great Bach double concertos together.

As my father started to deteriorate in earnest he became violently anti-semitic and, just as the war was ending, he used to say: 'Would it really have been so bad if the Germans had come here?' My step-mother confided to me, as my mother had done, that my father had generally been impotent and that she had a lover in Dublin.

For all the confidences I had received, for all my precocity and sense of having been through more than my contemporaries, I did not know, at the age of 17, that the vagina existed, supposing that childbirth was painful because it took place through the urethra. Nor did I know that men ejaculated.

I spent four supremely happy years at Oxford and owe my higher education entirely to Isaiah Berlin, who taught me philosophy, tête-à-tête, through 1946–47. I designed my first essay for him with a conscious intent to please but he was not to be seduced; he interrupted me at once and tore my work to pieces. A week later I adapted my first philosophical position to one which, so far as I could infer, must be closer to his, but he left me in shreds again. In response to his seemingly inconsistent criticisms, I invented ever more complicated structures which must, I supposed, be getting me closer to what he really thought. One day he asked me to repeat a passage and when I did so he burst into merry laughter exclaiming: 'How gloriously artificial!' I was deeply hurt but impelled thereafter to make the stupendous effort which, over a period of 15 months, was to transform my intellect.

All my old people faded away very sadly. Nora shot herself in the head with a shotgun; my father, his entire fortune squandered, died alone in a hospital where the nurses were unkind to him; my half-sister was committed to a high security mental institution at Epsom; my mother had a bad stroke and lived out her last six years hemiplegic and helpless, her mind altered. She told her nurses that they were 'lower-class scum' and complained that I was 'marrying the daughter of a New York yid'. This yid was Jacob Epstein.

Soon after my mother died I had a dream. I saw her in a bathtub in which there was no water. She was paralysed from the waist down and instead of the pubic hair I had seen as a young child there was a large open wound. Through the upper part of the room there was a system of ropes, pulleys and hooks. Although the lower part of her body was inert, she could operate the ropes skilfully with her hands and arms in a way which enabled her to get her body to move, with extreme agility, about the bathroom. She was confined to the room because the whole contraption was slung from the ceiling and attached to the walls. Her lower half sometimes got left behind or forced into strange shapes against the walls or over the edge of the tub as she moved around.

Winnicott's elegant white suit was crumpled; so was his handsome face. He reminded me of a very frail Spencer Tracy. His sentences were not always coherent but I experienced them as direct communications to an incredibly primitive part of myself; I want to say that we spoke to one another baby to baby. The crumpled face was a tabula rasa, impassive but receptive.

I described my impasse to Winnicott, adding that 'my tears were tightly locked into their ducts.' After desultory responses he asked me whether I had any 'cot' recollections. 'Yes,' I replied, scouring my mind and recollecting myself in a pram in a place where it could not, in reality, have stood – in the middle of a main road.

'Was there an object with you?' he asked.

'Yes,' I replied, 'there was a kaleidoscope.'

'What a hard thing,' was Winnicott's comment.

Winnicott next asked me if I would have any objection to seeing a

Pakistani analyst. As I left he said, very kindly, 'You have been very frank with me,' adding: 'I think you were a lonely child.'

I arranged an appointment with Masud Khan from my office in the Treasury, where I was now an economic adviser, and he met me at the foot of the stairs leading to his attic apartment in Harley Street. He was in his mid-thirties, a tall, erect and substantially built man with beautiful Oriental features. He had abundant black hair swept back over his ears and was slightly overdressed in the style of an English gentleman.

I repeated to Khan the story of my impasse and in the course of telling it mentioned that I read a lot of newspapers. He looked up and asked me whether, if I read all these papers, I hadn't read something about him. When I said that I hadn't he assumed an expression of mock disbelief. A little later he broke into my narrative and asked irrelevantly: 'Haven't you got some connection with Epstein?' At this I checked, expressing concern about the confidentiality of what I was telling him, since his question implied that he already knew something about me and perhaps that we had social friends in common. Khan did not answer directly. He grunted and tried to look impassive.

Khan next explained that he was going to get married to Svetlana Beriosova, the loveliest of the Royal Ballet's ballerinas, in about ten days' time; this was why I might have read about him in the press. At the end of the interview, he drove me slowly part of the way home in his Armstrong Siddeley. In the car he produced a book of poems by James Joyce from the pouch in the door and told me that he read them when he was stuck in traffic jams. He asked, 'Did you never think of killing yourself?' but answered the question himself: 'You would not know whom to kill.'

It is astonishing to me, with the knowledge I now have, that Khan so intruded himself into that first interview, which should have held out the promise of a safe, private and neutral space in which a dialogue with its own dynamic could take place. Yet within minutes of our first meeting, as I can now clearly see, the therapeutic relationship had been totally subverted. He needed my endorsement, as will become increasingly clear; he also needed to intrude on me. I had no way of registering that there was something amiss in his expecting me to know about his forthcoming marriage (which implied that he would be leaving me for his honeymoon almost as soon as we had begun work) or in his showing me that he was a literary man who drove a smart car. But I did know that there was something completely wrong about the Epstein question; it had given me a sense of contamination, which I suppressed in a sickeningly familiar way.

Khan now distanced himself. I referred the following day to his 'girl' and he corrected me, 'my future wife', adding: 'You thought you were going to cuddle up with me, didn't you?' I did not, by a very long way, have the understanding or presence of mind to reply that this was an expectation which he himself had created; and I felt that it was, indeed, I who had intruded.

During the next few days my artificial self came, in stages, completely to pieces although my adult mind continued to function in a completely normal way; for instance, I continued to work in the Treasury without a break. The meltdown, which took the form of a series of quasi-hallucinations accompanied by storms of emotion, all took place at home, although I reported them to Khan. These waking dreams came to a climax after about three days. I 'saw' a blanket inside my skull which was very tightly wrapped around my brain. And it began to loosen! First intermittently, then decisively, the blanket came right away like a huge scab and I reached, as it seemed, an extraordinary new insight. My father had hated me! By appearing at my school when obviously drunk, he had maliciously used my love for him as a weapon against me! And he had cruelly separated me from my sister by sending me away to school. These 'perceptions' generated an outburst of infantile rage. While in this strange condition I saw, as in a vision, a sentence which was lit up, flickering and suspended in the air. The words were:

UNLESS HE JUSTIFIES HIMSELF I MUST SAVE HIM

The meaning I attributed, with partial understanding, to this sentence was that unless the parent is perceived by the infant as strong and self-sufficient, the caring process will go into reverse with the force of the ocean bursting through a dam.

No one, as I now know, has written with more penetration about the genesis of the artificial self than Winnicott. The birthright of every child is to receive, starting from the primal union, a uniquely empathetic response which nurtures its growth and establishes its identity. If this does not happen, the infant may come under an overpowering compulsion, as a condition for its very survival, to provide whatever it is the parent needs from the relationship. An incredibly destructive but deeply concealed reversal of roles then takes place.

My cathartic explosion was perfectly sincere and real. A fantastic distortion of my character that had governed my life up to that point, a bizarre mushroom growth, had been clearly revealed to me and I experienced a feelingfulness which had been blockaded for as long as I could remember.

By the time Khan returned from his honeymoon in Monte Carlo, I was having dreams about cars slipping backwards down icy pathways in the darkness. But I clung to the firm belief that another emotional breakthrough would soon occur.

It never did. What followed was a long and fruitless battle culminating in a spiral of degradation.

A crucial component of the analytic process resides in the patient's ability to articulate thoughts, fantasies or images as they occur to him or her, especially any hostile thoughts he or she may have towards the analyst. Unless this happens, the primitive reversal of roles can never be undone. But it is extremely difficult, requiring great concentration, courage and trust, to express murderous thoughts and insults to their object. The way such insults are negotiated is one of the keenest measures of an analyst's skill, character and fitness to practise; the artificial self knows all too well how to make others bleed.

As I come to describe Khan's failure to pass this elementary test, I realise that I am in danger of making him seem a mere figure of fun. There was indeed something wholly ridiculous about him – as there was about Adolf Hitler. But he had a formidable and quick-acting intelligence, astonishing powers of observation and an unrivalled ability straightaway to see deeply below the surface. He was impossible to worst. He knew how to exploit and defy the conventions which govern social intercourse in England, taking full advantage of the fact that the English saw him instinctively as inferior – as 'a native' – and tried to patronise him.

When I asked Khan why he wore a riding jacket which had a silly slit in the middle of his behind, he replied stiffly: 'Ask the man who tailored it.' When I said his flat was furnished like a hotel he referred reproachfully to 'my wife's superb style', which I had failed to recognise, turning the flat, in my mind, into a 'a shabby hotel'. I didn't have the presence of mind to tell him that what I objected to was that his flat was like a *smart* hotel. Khan told me that he 'wanted to give me a good start' and went on to explain how the infant eats the breast but that the breast also eats the infant. Summoning up my courage (for I was also afraid of hurting him) I said: 'This silly buffoon is talking drivel.' To this Khan replied that, unlike some of his colleagues, he believed in paying back aggression from his patients in kind. And I was presuming to look for help 'from the man whom in your mind you call a buffoon' in a clipped, whispered and venomous tone, adding that I lived 'like a pig' in my own home. He wasn't going to pretend, so he said, that things were other than they were; he had been sadistic towards me and for days and months afterwards he referred to this as 'the sadistic session'.

Beriosova was often featured, scantily dressed, in press photographs. I wanted to know which bit of her was grabbed by her partner when he held her on top of a single outstretched arm, as well as other more intimate things. Khan told me that I was 'using the analytic situation as a licence to articulate [my] intrusive fantasies'. And he soon became enraged. 'You say that to me to annoy me,' he said and then, after a pause: 'Which it does.' He then went into a tirade about my crude assault ('You Englishman!') on a being so precious to him. 'I do know how to protect my wife,' he said as though I had attacked her. At the least slight it was Khan's invariable response to deliver a righteous speech, often finishing up with some withering coda such as 'And to think you people ruled the world!' Only now can I see how easy it was to bait him.

We hardly ever spoke of my childhood. Khan preferred, he said, to 'work out of' the material which was thrown up by contemporary experiences. Everything of significance that had happened in the past could be reinterpreted in terms of what was happening now. This gave him a licence to interfere actively, judgmentally and with extraordinary cruelty in every aspect of my daily life.

We entered a long period of painful stasis. 'When is something going to happen?' I would ask and he would reply: 'I wonder too when something is going to happen. I have exhausted' – these were his exact words – 'every manoeuvre that I know. You are a tiresome and disappointing man.'

How did I account to myself for what was happening? I thought that everything unkind Khan said to me was justified and that I was learning to accept home truths; that this was extraordinarily painful but the essence of what a good and true analysis should be. We weren't having one of those soppy analyses that the ignorant public imagines, where a pathetic neurotic talks about himself and is passively listened to, and endlessly comforted. The characteristic sensation I experienced was a smouldering rage which carried me from session to session. I felt like a kettle that had been left on the flame long after the water had boiled away.

Khan liked it when I moved up through the Treasury ranks, greatly overestimating the importance and significance of the positions which I held. Meanwhile he began increasingly to fill the sessions with tales about his own social life in London or, occasionally, New York. The stories were not good ones. Many were obscene and many were flat, but there was one feature common to every one of them: Khan had got the better of someone. He had rescued Mike Nichols from a man with a fierce dog in New York. He had fought physically with Peter O'Toole, using a broken bottle. He had got the overflow from his lavatory to pour a jet of water onto the head of a woman who was making her car hoot in the street below. Often it would be nothing more than an ugly exchange at a drinking party for which he needed my approval and endorsement. The following characteristic tale, being brief, must stand in for a limitless number of other stories that I can immediately recall.

A man comes up to Khan at a party and says: 'Every night I go to bed with two beautiful women. I make love to one of them and then, if I feel like it, I turn over and make love to the other. Sometimes I make love to both of them at once.' 'Yes,' Khan says, 'but by the laws of topology there must always be one orifice which remains vacant.'

Very occasionally he appealed to me for sympathy. Princess Margaret had tripped him up over the way he had pronounced something. Lord Denning (it was Profumo time) had not replied to his invitation to come to dinner.

Khan always answered telephone calls during sessions. When Winnicott rang up I could clearly hear both sides of the conversation, so presumably he angled the phone towards me. Winnicott spoke respectfully to Khan, for instance about a paper which he had recently published. 'I learned a great deal from it,' Winnicott said deferentially. This particular conversation ended with a giggly joke about homosexual fellatio – the final two words of the conversation – accompanied by loud laughter.

A gynaecologist rang up during one of my sessions to enquire about a patient of Khan's whom I shall call Marian and who was expecting a baby. Khan spoke harshly about her to the gynaecologist, closing the conversation with the advice: 'And charge her a good fee.' Khan kept me in touch with the progress of Marian's pregnancy. She was not married, and as her confinement approached he referred to it bitingly as 'the virgin birth'.

After the child was born, Khan started speaking of Marian as a suitable partner for me – although I was happily married and although, as I much later discovered, he had secretly invited my wife Kitty to an interview with him. Marian and I were 'handmade for one another'. Khan induced me to take her out to lunch. 'If she's not really beautifully dressed, but really beautifully dressed, give her hell.' I took her to Overton's in Victoria where we ate seafood and had an amiable conversation without there being any spark between us.

We now started meeting à trois, Marian, Khan and myself. On one occasion we went to a literary group in Battersea where Khan gave a talk on 'Neurosis and Creativity'. On another, Marian watched from the gallery while I trounced Khan at squash, breaking his nose with my racquet in the process; immediately following which Khan, bloody nose and all, insisted on playing, because he could win, a game of ping-pong. And the three of us spent a whole evening playing poker for matchsticks. Khan cheated; he grabbed half my growing pile of matchsticks when I wasn't looking, although I didn't allow myself to realise it at the time. He chortled that with the power he possessed over each of us he could 'orchestrate the conversation at any level he chose'. At my next session he told me that this had been the happiest evening he had ever spent in his life.

At my next session! I was still seeing the man five times a week and paying him large fees. And I went on doing so until the end, although it is inconceivable that any therapy was taking place; for a long time now I was the one who was looking after him. Paying fees was part of keeping up the absurd fiction that a great patient was having a great analysis with a great analyst. 'I have the virtues which are the counterpart of my defects,' he was fond of saying. He had saved my life, the story went – and no one else could have done it. About this time Khan began to shower me with presents. He gave me a silver pen, a complete *Encyclopaedia Britannica*, a signed lithograph of sunflowers by Léger, an Indian bedspread, a Nonesuch Bible in three volumes, and several books, including *The Naked Lunch*.

Sometimes Beriosova was the hostess. Her physical movements were light and regal though she smoked heavily and drank a great deal of gin. On one occasion there were other analysands besides me present. Beriosova drank more gin than usual, retired to the Khan bedroom and screeched: 'Get them out of here, get them out of here.'

One evening I found myself alone with Khan and Beriosova in their flat. Both of them were drunk. They left the room separately so that I was alone for some minutes. I heard a faint moan which was repeated more loudly; the moan turned into my own name – an inarticulate appeal for assistance from someone helpless and in severe pain. Going into the hall, I saw Khan, lying full length and motionless on the ground. In agony he whispered: 'My wife has kicked me in the balls.' As he slowly recovered his wind I supported him back to the drawing-room. Re-entering the hall I found Beriosova lying full length on the floor exactly where Khan had been. I tried to lift her up. (It must be easy to pick up dancers – they have no weight – I somehow thought.) But Beriosova was a substantial woman, inert and apparently insensible. I left the hall and on my return a few moments later she had disappeared. At the next session I observed to Khan that I might, at some stage, have to say that things had got so far out of hand that I would have to break off the analysis. His reply was that if it got that far, *he* would break off the analysis 'one day' before I did. So he won that trick too.

Eventually Khan irrupted into my home. He rang up announcing that he and Beriosova were going to call on us within the next few minutes. Khan fidgeted about the house and made a lot of suggestions as to how we should manage our minor affairs (I should mow the lawn diagonally, for example, or set the lamp which hung low over the dining-room table upside down). He teased Kitty's younger daughter, then a patient of Winnicott's, by doing a ludicrous imitation of her. For this he 'got a tremendous rocket from Winnicott' he later recounted with loud laughter.

We now started to meet quite frequently, and go to parties, as two married couples. It is part of the story that we often met celebrities and that I found myself in conversation with, say, Rudolf Nureyev and François Truffaut.

As a prelude to the final tale, I must record that Kitty, having had a miscarriage a year or two before, had reached the third month of an exceptionally difficult pregnancy in the course of which all hope of saving the child had been given up more than once. We had not yet had a child.

We went out to dinner à quatre to a Chinese restaurant in Knightsbridge. Khan outdid himself in a tour de force of meaningless aggression. The only precise things I can remember are that he bullied and insulted the Chinese waiters, for instance by openly 'imitating' them. (I use inverted commas because it was not a genuine imitation, but a high-pitched whine appropriate to a schoolboy joke.) Although I was incapable of any vital response, Khan's behaviour was so extreme and unremitting, and there was so little space in which to move, that I began at last to feel something curdling deep within myself.

The next day Kitty came into the room and told me that Khan had rung her up and torn into her. She had a sharp pain in her womb.

The perception that, at the level of reality, Khan had made an attempt on the life of our unborn only child was painful beyond anything I can convey. I believe that one of the Nazi medical experiments was to inject ammonia into victims' veins. I felt that the living, if deformed, armature inside myself was corroding.

I rang up Winnicott and said, 'Khan is mad,' to which he said emphatically, 'Yes,' adding: 'All this social stuff. . .' He didn't finish the sentence but he came round to our house immediately, saying that he had told Khan not to communicate with me again. As he said this, the telephone rang and it was, indeed, Khan wanting not only to speak to me but to see me, which I refused to do.

And that was the end of my 'analysis'.

Ten years after the Chinese meal, having had an operation for cancer of the throat, Khan made a direct appeal to me, in a hoarse whisper, to visit him. When I arrived at his flat in Bayswater, a small Filipino servant pointed towards his drawing-room door saying: 'The prince is in there.' Khan had entirely changed his style; he had lost his beauty and now wore a black tunic and a necklace with a heavy ornament hanging from it. He was very drunk and insisted on talking pidgin French, which was completely incomprehensible. His companions were sycophants but there was one beautiful and elegant woman among them. From time to time he pointed to me and said: 'He and I the same. Aristocrats.'

I hear that Khan slept at will with his female patients, became an even more serious drunkard and shortly before he died was struck off. And that Beriosova appeared drunk on the stage at Covent Garden, faded away and died, first separated then divorced from Khan. I have also discovered, to my astonishment, that throughout the whole time that I was seeing Khan, *he was himself in analysis with Winnicott*. And this has led me to reinterpret some letters which I sent to Winnicott at Khan's instance, and the replies I received from him, as an aggressive flirtation between the two of them, using my body as unwitting intermediary.

It is now perfectly clear to me that, after seeing Khan daily for several years, and after untold expense and travail, no therapy whatever had taken place. What a trap! He had reproduced and re-enacted every major traumatic component of my childhood and adolescence. The primal union had been ruptured. The confidences which he reposed in me had made me special, just as my mother's had; he had the same need as she to perform and be performed for. And the same destructive gymnastics that I had once had to negotiate, given the deep attachment I had to my deteriorating father, were played out all over again. For the second time, I was overcome by a compulsion to attempt the transformation of a drunken, anti-semitic, collapsing wreckage into a living armature on which to build myself.

HE COULD NOT JUSTIFY HIMSELF SO I WAS COMPELLED TO SAVE HIM

What I have written is not an attack on psychoanalysis, for which, as a discipline, I have the utmost respect. I could not have gained the insight to write this piece, nor could I have recovered from the experiences I have described, if they had not at last been undone at the hands of a skilful, patient and selfless American analyst beside whom the conceited antics of Khan and, indeed, Winnicott seem grotesque beyond words.

But what recommendation could I now make to someone in need of help? One answer might be: 'Ask the president of the British Psychoanalytic Society.' But this, it turns out, is precisely what I did, without realising it. And Khan himself was training analysts for years after my break with him. Yet his personal defects were so severe that he should never under any circumstances have been allowed to practise psychoanalysis. I understand that his disbarment, when after twenty odd more years it came, was the consequence not of psychoanalytic malpractice, but of his outspoken anti-semitism. This, it seems, was more important than the deep, irreparable and wanton damage he wrought, from a position of exceptional privilege and against every canon of professional and moral obligation, on distressed and vulnerable people who came to him for help and paid him large sums of money to get it.

22 February 2001

The Old Devil and His Wife

Lorna Sage recalls her childhood

G RANDFATHER'S SKIRTS WOULD flap in the wind along the churchyard path, and I would hang on. He often found things to do in the vestry, excuses for getting out of the vicarage (kicking the swollen door, cursing) and so long as he took me he couldn't get up to much. I was a sort of hobble; he was my minder and I was his. He'd have liked to get further away, but petrol was rationed. The church was at least safe. My grandmother never went near it – except feet first in her coffin, but that was years later, when she was buried in the same grave with him. Rotting together for eternity, one flesh at the last after a lifetime's mutual loathing. In life, though, she never invaded his patch; once inside the church-yard gate he was on his own ground, in his element. He was good at funerals, being gaunt and lined, marked with mortality. He had a scar down his hollow cheek too, which grandma had done with the carving knife one of the many times when he came home pissed and incapable.

That, though, was when they were still 'speaking', before my time. Now they mostly monologued and swore at each other's backs, and he (and I) would slam out of the house and go off between the graves, past the yew tree with a hollow where the cat had her litters, and the various vaults that were supposed to account for the smell in the vicarage cellars in wet weather. On our right was the church; off to our left the graves stretched away, bisected by a grander, gravel path leading down from the church porch to a bit of green with a war memorial, then – across the road – the mere. The church was popular for weddings because of this impressive approach, but he wasn't at all keen on the marriage ceremony, naturally enough. Burials he relished, perhaps because he saw himself as buried alive.

One day we stopped to watch the gravedigger, who unearthed a skull – it was an old churchyard, on its second or third time around – and grandfather dusted off the soil, and declaimed: 'Alas, poor Yorick, I knew him well . . .' I thought he was making it up as he went along. When I grew up a bit and saw *Hamlet*, and found him out, I wondered what had been going through his mind as he mystified me and the gravedigger, our jaws doubtless dropped to match Yorick's. I suppose the scene struck him as an image of his condition – exiled to a remote, illiterate rural parish, his talents wasted, and so on. On the other hand, his position afforded him a lot of opportunities for indulging secret, bitter jokes, hamming up the act and cherishing his ironies, so in a way he was enjoying himself. Back then, I thought that was what a vicar was, simply. Someone bony and eloquent and smelly (tobacco, candle grease, sour claret), who talked into space. His disappointments were just part of the act for me, along with his dog collar and cassock. He occupied the whole foreground. I was like a baby goose imprinted by the first mother-figure it sees – he was my black marker.

It was certainly easy to spot him at a distance too. But this was a village where it seemed everybody *was* their vocation. They didn't just 'know their place', it was as though the place occupied them, so that they all knew what they were going to be from the beginning. People's names conspired to colour in this picture. The gravedigger was actually called Mr Downward. The blacksmith who lived by the mere was called Bywater. Even more decisively, the family who owned the village were called Hanmer, and so was the village. The Hanmers had come over with the Conqueror, got as far as the Welsh border, and stayed ever since in this little rounded isthmus of North Wales sticking out into England, the detached portion of Flintshire (Flintshire Maelor) as it was called then, surrounded by Shropshire, Cheshire and – on the Welsh side – Denbighshire. There was no town in the Maelor district, only villages and hamlets: Flintshire proper was some way off; and (then) industrial, which made it in practice a world away from these pastoral parishes, which had become resigned to being handed a Labour MP at every election. People in Hanmer well understood, in almost a prideful way, that we weren't part of all that. The kind of choice represented by voting didn't figure large on the local map, and you only really counted places you could get to on foot or by bike.

The war had changed this to some extent, but not as much as it might have because farming was a reserved occupation, and sons hadn't been called up unless there were a lot of them, or their families were smallholders with little land. So Hanmer in the Forties in many ways resembled Hanmer in the Twenties, or even the late 1800s, except that it was more depressed, less populous, and more out of step – more and more islanded in time as the years had gone by. We didn't speak Welsh either, so that there was little national feeling, rather a sense of stubbornly being *where you were*, and that was that. Also very un-Welsh was the fact that Hanmer had no chapel to rival grandfather's church: the Hanmers would never lease land to Nonconformists, and there was no tradition of Dissent, except in the form of not going to church at all. Many people did attend, though, partly because he was locally famous for his sermons, and because he was High Church and went in for dressing up and altar boys and frequent communions. Not frequent enough to explain the amount of wine he got through, however. Eventually the Church stopped his supply, and after that communicants got watered-down Sanatogen, from Boots the chemist in Whitchurch, over the Shropshire border.

The delinquencies that had denied him preferment seemed to do him little harm with his parishioners. Perhaps the vicar was expected to be an expert in sin. At all events, he was 'a character'. To my childish eyes people in Hanmer were divided between characters and the rest, the ones and the many. Higher up the social scale there was only one of you: one vicar, one solicitor, each farmer identified by the name of his farm, and so *sui generis*. True, there were two doctors, but they were brothers and shared the practice. Then there was one policeman, one publican, one district nurse, one butcher, one baker . . . Smallholders and farm labourers were the many, and often had large families too. They were irretrievably plural, and supposed to be inter-changeable (feckless all), nameable only as tribes. The virtues and vices of the singular people turned into characteristics. They were picturesque. They had no common denominator and you never judged them in relation to a norm. Coming to consciousness in Hanmer was oddly blissful, at the beginning: the grown-ups all played their parts to the manner born. You knew where you were.

Which was in a hole, according to grandma. A dead-alive dump. A muck heap. She'd shake a trembling fist at the people going past the vicarage to church each Sunday, though they probably couldn't see her from behind the bars and dirty glass. She didn't upset my version of pastoral. She lived in a different dimension, she said as much herself. In her world there were streets with pavements, shop-windows, trams, trains, teashops and cinemas. She never went out except to visit this paradise lost, by taxi to the station in Whitchurch, then by train to Shrewsbury or Chester. This was *life*. Scented soap and chocolates would stand in for it the rest of the time – most of the time in fact, since there was never any money. She'd evolved a way of living that resolutely defied her lot. He might play the vicar, she wouldn't be the vicar's wife. Their rooms were at opposite ends of the house, and she spent much of the day in bed. She had asthma, and even the smell of him and his tobacco made her sick. She'd stay up late in the evening, alone, reading about scandals and murders in the *News of the World* by lamplight among the mice and the silverfish in the kitchen (she'd hoard coal for the fire up in her room, and sticks to relight it if necessary). She never answered the door, never saw anyone, did no housework. She cared only for her sister and her girl-hood friends back in South Wales and – perhaps – for me, since I had blue eyes and blonde hair and was a girl, so just possibly belonged to her family line. She thought men and women belonged to different races, and any getting together was worse than folly. The 'old devil' my grandfather had talked her into marriage, and the agony of bearing two children, and he should never be forgiven for it. She would quiver with rage whenever she remembered her fall. She was short (about four foot ten) and as fat and soft-fleshed as he was thin and leathery, so her theory of separate races looked quite plausible. The rhyme about Jack Sprat ('Jack Sprat would eat no fat,/His wife would eat no lean./And so between the two of them/They kept the platter clean') struck me when I learned it as somehow about them. Looking back, I can see that she must have been a factor – along with the booze (and the womanising) – in keeping him back in the Church. She got her revenge, but at the cost of living in the muck-heap herself.

Between the two of them my grandparents created an atmosphere in the vicarage so pungent and all-pervading that they accounted for everything. In fact, it wasn't so. My mother, their daughter, was there. I only remember her, though, at the beginning, as a shy, slender wraith kneeling on the stair with a brush and dust-pan, or washing things in the scullery. They'd made her into a domestic drudge after her marriage – my father was away in the Army and she had no separate life. It was she who answered the door and tried to keep up appearances, a battle long lost. She wore her fair hair in a victory roll, and she was pretty but didn't like to smile. Her front teeth were false

– crowned, a bit clumsily – because in her teens, running to intervene in one of their murderous rows, she'd fallen down the stairs and snapped off her own. During these years she probably didn't feel much like smiling anyway. She doesn't come into the picture properly yet, nor does my father. My only early memory of him is being picked up by a man in uniform, and being sick down his back. He wasn't popular in the vicarage, though it must have been his army pay that eked out grandfather's exiguous stipend.

The grandparents weren't grateful. They both felt so cheated by life, they had their histories of grievance so well worked-out, that they were *owed* service, handouts, anything that was going. My mother and her brother they'd used as hostages in their wars, and otherwise neglected, being too absorbed in each other, in their way, to spare much feeling. With me it was different: since they no longer really fought they had time on their hands, and I got the best of them. Did they love me? The question is beside the point, somehow. Certainly they each spoiled me, mainly by giving me the false impression that I was entitled to attention nearly all the time. They played. They were like children, if you consider that one of the things about being a child is that you are a parasite of sorts and have to self-righteously brazen it out. I want. They were good at wanting, and I shared much more common ground with them than with my mother when I was three or four years old. Also, they measured up to the magical monsters in the story-books. Grandma's idea of expressing affection to small children was to smack her lips and say, 'You're so sweet, I'm going to eat you all up!' It was not difficult to believe her, either, given her passion for sugar. Or at least I believed her enough to experience a pleasant thrill of fear. She liked to pinch too, and she sometimes spat with hatred when she ran out of words.

Domestic life in the vicarage had a Gothic flavour at odds with the house, which was a modest 18th-century building of mellowed brick, with low ceilings, and attics and back stairs for help we didn't have.

At the front it looked on to a small square traversed only by visitors and churchgoers. The barred kitchen window faced this way, but in no friendly fashion, and the parlour on the other side of the front door was empty and unused, so that the house was turned in on itself, against its nature. A knock at the door produced a flurry of hiding-and-tidying (my grandmother must be given time to retreat, if she was up, and I'd have my face scrubbed with a wash-cloth) in case the visitor was someone who'd have to be invited in, and shown to the sitting-room at the back which – though a bit damp and neglected – was always 'kept nice in case'. If the caller was on strictly Church business, he'd be shown upstairs to grandfather's study, lined with bookcases in which the books all had the authors' names and titles on their spines blacked out as a precaution against would-be borrowers who'd suddenly take a fancy to Dickens or Marie Corelli. His bedroom led off his study, and was dark, under the yew tree's shadow, and smelt like him. Across the landing was my mother's room, where I slept too when I was small, and round a turn to the right my grandmother's, with coal and sticks piled under the bed, redolent of Ponds face cream, powder, scent, smelling salts and her town clothes in mothballs, along with a litter of underwear and stockings. On this floor, too, was a stately lavatory, wallpapered in a perching peacock design, all intertwined feathers and branches you could contemplate for hours – which I did, legs dangling from the high wooden seat. When the chain was pulled, the water tanks on the attic floor gurgled and sang. In the other attics there were apples laid out on newspaper on the floors, gently mummifying. It just wasn't a spooky house, despite the suggestive cellars, and despite the fact that we relied on lamps and candles. All of Hanmer did that, in any case, except for farmers who had their own generators. In the kitchen the teapot sat on the hob all day, and everyone ate at different times.

There was a word that belonged to the house: 'dilapidations'. It was one of the first long words I knew, for it was repeated like a mantra. The Church charged incumbents a kind of levy for propping up its crumbling real estate and those five syllables were the key. If only grandfather could cut down on The Dilapidations there'd be a new dawn of amenity and comfort, and possibly some change left over. Leaks, dry rot, broken panes and crazy hinges (of which we had plenty) were, looked at rightly, a potential source of income. Whether he ever succeeded, I don't know. Since the word went on and on, he can't have got more than a small rebate, and no one ever plugged the leaks. What's certain is that we were frequently penniless, and there were always embarrassments about credit. Food rationing and clothes coupons must have been a godsend since they provided a cover for our indigence. As long as austerity lasted, the vicarage could maintain its shaky claims to gentility. There was virtue in shabbiness. Grandfather had his rusty cassock, grandmother her mothballed wardrobe, and my mother had one or two prewar outfits that just about served. Underwear was yellowed and full of holes, minus elastic. Indoors our top layers were ragged too: matted jumpers, socks and stockings laddered and in wrinkles round the ankles, safety pins galore. Outside we could pass muster, even if my overcoat was at first too big (I would grow into it), then all at once too small, without ever for a moment being the right size.

Grandpa and I must have pottered about in church almost every day, and the echoing spaces, the stained glass and the smell of Brasso, chrysanthemums, damp pew-oak and iron mould from the choir's surplices were heady compensations for isolation. He'd tell me stories and read to me, too. It was his regular task to read me to sleep at night, when he'd often drop off first, stretched out on the couch, mouth open, snoring, his beaky profile lit up by the candle. In fact, he got so impatient with my favourite books (which both he and I knew by heart) that one momentous day, before I was four, he taught me to read, in self-defence. This confirmed me as his creature.

I knew my name came out of one of the blacked-out books – Lorna from *Lorna Doone* – and that he'd chosen it. Now he'd given me a special key to his world, it seemed. We were even closer allies afterwards, so that when he took me with him in the rattling Singer to Whitchurch, and into the bar of the Fox and Goose down Green End, it never occurred to me to tell on him. There were several expeditions like that. He was well-known in drinking circles, and was looked on as something of a speciality act, a cynical and colourful talker, always with his dog-collar to set him apart. I was the perfect alibi, since neither my mother nor my grandmother had any idea that there were pubs so low and lawless that they would turn a blind eye to children. Few were willing to, however; and there were other times when I found myself sitting outside on the steps of one of his favourite haunts, an unfriendly place with a revolving door called the Lord Hill, in the company of streetwise kids a lot more scary than the Duckets. Perhaps I did tell about that, or perhaps someone spotted me: at any rate, the pub-outings came to an end.

Not the collusion, though. I'd kneel on the threadbare rug in his study while he worked on his sermon, or talked to the odd visitor, pulling out the books and puzzling over big words. Sometimes he'd show off my reading to strangers, but for the most part I was meant (this was the point of it, after all) to be quiet. When he was in very good moods he would draw pictures for me, starting mysteriously from the vanishing point and drawing out the rest into perspective. I learned that trick too, never very well, but well enough to disconcert people. Our mutual 'minding' turned by untidy stages into a sort of education. Since he was a man of many wasted talents, not only with words and images, but also music, I might have had a full set of pre-school 'accomplishments' except that I was tone-deaf. Despite that, I was made a member of the choir as soon as I could sit still long enough – under strict instructions to open and shut my mouth in silence, along with the words. I was quite useful, in fact: I could be shifted across from the girls' bench to the boys' (my pigtails bundled up into my cap) depending on where there were the most gaps. Watching grandpa dress up in the vestry, processing behind him, listening to him intone the liturgy and preach, I basked in his reflected glory.

7 October 1993

A Spy in the Archives
Sheila Fitzpatrick

T HEY GATHERED US in a dark-panelled windowless basement in the Foreign Office for a briefing. The year was 1966, and the group was made up of 20 or so British students selected to go to the Soviet Union for ten months under the auspices of the British Council. Plus one Australian, myself, who had managed to get on the British exchange because Australia didn't have one. Our nameless briefer, who we assumed to be from MI6, told us that everybody we met in the Soviet Union would be a spy. It would be impossible to make friends with Russians because, in the first place, they were all spies, and, in the second, they would make the same assumption about us. As students, we would be particularly vulnerable to Soviet attempts to compromise us because, unlike other foreigners resident in Moscow and Leningrad, we would actually live side by side with Russians instead of in a foreigners' compound. We should be particularly careful not to be lured into sexual liaisons which would result in blackmail (from the Soviet side) and swift forcible repatriation (from the British). If any untoward approach was made to us, or if we knew of such an approach being made to someone else in the group, we should immediately inform the embassy. This was not a normal country we were going to. It was a Cold War zone.

I ended up spending a total of a year and a half in Cold War Moscow, between autumn 1966 and spring 1970. I travelled under a false identity, or that's what it felt like: the nationality on my passport was British, not Australian; the surname was Bruce, which was my husband's name but not mine; and, to top it off, I had decided to use my middle name, Mary, on the grounds that it could be shortened to Masha and would be easier for Russians. (Nothing came of this: I could not believe in Mary as my name, and in any case it turned out that all educated Russians knew the name Sheila – which had an easy diminutive, Shaylochka – because they had read C.P. Snow.)

It was impossible to live in the Soviet Union as a foreigner and not become obsessed with spying. (If anyone doubts this, read Michael Frayn's wonderful novel *The Russian Interpreter*, published the year I first went to Moscow.) 'Do you think X is a spy?' we were always asking each other about new Russian acquaintances, and sometimes about each other. It was a question that went the other way, too. 'Are you a spy?' '*Ty shpionka?*' I was asked by an ingenuous schoolgirl in Volgograd. I said no, of course, but it wasn't an answer I was 100 per cent sure about. What exactly was a spy, anyway? One could view it as a narrow professional designation, but the Soviets often used it to refer to any foreigner who tried to find out things they wanted to hide (which were many, and not always predictable). We students had been through an official government briefing, would perhaps be debriefed at the end, and were expected to write a detailed final report to the British Council. Could one be a spy without knowing it? Or a spy by virtue of involuntary association with spies and ex-spies (this was a particular worry for me, since there seemed to be so many of the latter at St Antony's, my Oxford college)? We thought anxiously about the case of Gerald Brooke, a British teacher sentenced to five years' imprisonment for 'subversive anti-Soviet activity' the previous year, hoping he had been a real spy and not someone like us.

I wondered later if our London briefer knew how wrong he was about the impossibility of making Soviet friends. In fact, almost everyone in our group made friends, close ones, but perhaps we were all too prudent (I certainly was) to mention this in our final reports. You made only a few friends, as the Soviets themselves did: too wide a circle was seen as dangerous and promiscuity in friendship strongly discouraged. But the friends you had were friends for real, like family (if one had been lucky enough to have had that kind of family), offering unlimited practical as well as spiritual support. The warmth of Russian friendship was a source of perpetual wonder to us, something beyond our experience as well as our expectations.

There were various ways of acquiring Russian friends. Some foreign students acquired their Soviet family by having a love affair (these were common, despite the briefer's warnings), and, as a result, being adopted by the lover's family. That 'as a result' was another odd thing: Soviet families were close, and the adolescent's challenge to his or her parents' values was something that seemed to have passed them by, so it was natural that a lover would become part of the family (also, as the lovers usually had nowhere to go but the family apartment, pragmatically necessary).

I acquired my family through my research. My topic was Anatoly Lunacharsky, the Bolshevik intellectual who was the first Commissar of Enlightenment after the Revolution. Lunacharsky, I knew, had a daughter (she had edited some of his work), and I asked my adviser if it would be possible to meet her. We all had these advisers, some of whom were cautiously helpful and others merely watchdogs. Mine, a literary scholar who had reputedly made his name unmasking Jewish scholars with Russian names in the 'anti-cosmopolitanism' campaign of the late Stalin period, seemed to be the watchdog type, but since I had no other way of finding Lunacharsky's daughter (there were no telephone directories), I asked him anyway. His response was surprising. Abruptly shifting from his official register of right-thinking clichés, he launched into a stream of malicious gossip about the Lunacharsky family. Lunacharsky's young second wife, a Jewish actress, had caused all sorts of trouble and embarrassment. Her brother, Igor Sats, had been the only person present when Lunacharsky died in Menton in 1933, and could well have murdered him (I wondered at the time if I had understood him correctly, but later heard the same unfounded rumour circulating in the Russian diaspora in California). The daughter of the second marriage, Irina, was not Lunacharsky's natural daughter, for all her devotion to him, but the product of the second wife's first youthful marriage to a Jew who died fighting in the Civil War – probably, my adviser said, on the wrong side. He was willing to give me Irina's telephone number if, in return, I would try to get access to her father's diaries, which she was said to have in her possession but (understandably, I thought) wouldn't let my adviser see. Then, presumably, I was to hand them over to him. Or perhaps, as now occurs to me, just tell him I had seen them, so that he could pass on to the authorities that Irina Lunacharskaya had shown secret Soviet documents to a foreign spy. I had no intention of telling him anything, but that didn't stop me producing some (I hope) ambiguous formula of agreement and getting the telephone number.

Irina was formidable: small, bristling with energy, worldly, notably elegant in the general drabness of Moscow, a fluent conversationalist and relentless interrogator. She was a science journalist by profession, but her avocation was restoring Lunacharsky's reputation from the trough into which it had sunk since the Stalin period. To this end, she exercised vigilant control and, where possible, personal censorship over the work of Lunacharsky scholars, teasing them with her possession of the diaries, which she never allowed anyone to copy or even look at for more than a minute. A great coup in her Lunacharsky crusade had been getting his former apartment declared a museum, and acquiring for herself, in compensation, an apartment on the best street in Moscow. Khrushchev's son-in-law Alexei Adzhubei, a good friend of hers who no doubt had some hand in this, lived in the same building. Irina's apartment was huge – eight rooms, if I remember rightly, at a time when a family of four would have been grateful for two – and included a wonderful little hexagonal room, used as her office, filled with what seemed to be genuine 18th-century furniture and paintings. This was the room she ushered me into on my first visit, but I was too raw at the time to understand how extraordinary it was in a Soviet context. Later, on more informal occasions, we would either sit and talk in the kitchen, or, when too many family members were present to fit in the kitchen, eat meals prepared by an old retainer in the elegant dining-room. (Irina was the first person I ever knew who had a live-in servant.) On that first visit, however, it was not clear that I would be allowed to return. Irina was suspicious of me, not just as a Westerner but also as someone sent by a man who, as she wasted no time telling me, was universally known to be a scoundrel. She decided to send me along to her uncle Igor for further vetting. This was the same Igor slanderously mentioned by my adviser. Irina described him as a wise man who knew the world, which I understood to mean that if I were a spy, he would see through me.

I turned up on Igor Sats's doorstep, nervous and rather cold in my unsuitable coat, dark green wool with gold buttons, bought at Fenwick's and made for a British winter rather than a Russian one. The door was opened by a man in his sixties with a big nose (one could see why he was cast as First Jewish Murderer), bright white hair flopping over his forehead, and an expression that was at once wily, charming and benign. 'A British girl wearing the uniform of the tsarist Ministry of Railways!' he exclaimed as he ushered me in. 'What a nice thing to see. But why have you no proper winter coat? We have to find you one.' We never found the coat: Igor, as I later discovered, was an old socialist who was indifferent to material possessions, a point of contrast between him and Irina. But Igor had found another stray to adopt, and I had found my Soviet family.

When I later asked Igor how he knew I wasn't a spy, he just laughed. He was an old spy himself, he used to say (using the neutral term *razvedchik*, rather than the pejorative *shpion*), having commanded a unit of army field spies during the Second World War. He maintained a benevolent interest in his former subordinates ('my spies') and still drank with them occasionally. He was also an Old Bolshevik, who as a schoolboy and aspiring pianist had run away from his prosperous bourgeois family to fight for the Reds in the Civil War; when the KGB wanted to ask him about me, they summoned him as a token of respect to the Party Central Committee building on Old Square instead of the Lubyanka. But according to him, it amounted to the same thing. As he told me (it was outrageous, in Soviet terms, to tell a foreigner any of this, but Igor liked being outrageous), they instructed him to maintain Party vigilance in his dealings with me and let them know of anything untoward. If I turned out to be a spy, he would be held to blame for faulty surveillance. He agreed to this. To be on the safe side, he said to me afterwards, I had better let him know about any new acquaintances so that he could check up on them (he didn't say how). I did that on several occasions, and it was thumbs down every time. After a while I wondered whether what Igor had against these new acquaintances was that they were young men. I felt bad about one of them: in addition to cooking me an excellent whole fish in his apartment (hard to come by in Moscow), he told me that his father was in the KGB and that he would understand if, under the circumstances, I decided not to see him anymore. It seemed unkind to reward his honesty with a brush-off. But of course a clever KGB man – and there were clever as well as stupid ones – might have worked out that this was a double bluff I would fall for, so perhaps Igor was right.

As a young man, Igor had been Lunacharsky's secretary as well as his brother-in-law, so he was an incredible primary source for my dissertation: he remembered everything, knew everybody in the Party elite, admired very few of them, and skewered each one with a deft characterisation. Perhaps this free-ranging disrespect was the secret of his survival through the Great Purges and the postwar anti-semitic campaigns, since, with a less critical view of Trotsky's arrogance, Zinoviev's stupidity and Bukharin's naivety, he might have joined one of the opposition groups of the 1920s and thus sealed his fate under Stalin. In his milieu, survival more or less unscathed was not the norm: his stories of the past were full of friends who had perished, and he had a host of orphaned children to keep an eye on. When I asked him how he had managed to survive, he said it was a matter of luck, helped by his lack of ambition for high office. Igor never had a high opinion of the Soviet security services: many of his funniest stories were about absurd mistakes or incompetence, and once he was infuriated to receive a letter that had not only been clumsily opened but had had its address partly defaced; in my presence, he mailed off the damaged envelope, together with a sharp protest, to the post office. The best option in time of purges, according to Igor, was simply to vanish without telling anyone where you were going, like the friend who went south, got himself arrested for stealing chickens and sat out the Great Purges safely in jail. But Igor himself had sat them out in Moscow, keeping his head down. It was a great relief when the Second World War came and he could volunteer for active service, hoping (as I gathered) to be killed.

The war turned out to be a great time for Igor: full of excitement, adventure and human interest; dangerous, but free of the psychological pressures of peacetime on someone who, despite everything, remained a Communist. He lost all his teeth in a hard winter on the Smolensk front, but otherwise came through without significant injuries. That was in contrast to the Civil War, during which he nearly died of the wounds that kept him in hospital for several years in his early twenties and left bullets lodged in his spine. He talked more about the Second World War than the earlier one; in fact, he talked about it so much that I became almost an expert on the various fronts and multiple armies and commanders. But in the end, in 1979, it was the after-effects of the Civil War wounds that killed him.

When I met Igor, he lived on Smolensk Square on the Arbat, in a two-room apartment that had been built in the early 1930s in a spirit of communalism, with shared bathrooms and lavatories on the corridor. That turned out to be a tremendous problem for Igor's wife, Raisa, on whom surgeons had performed a colostomy, although no colostomy bags were then available in the Soviet Union. (I was to become a skilled smuggler of colostomy bags through Soviet customs.) Raisa, who was very ill when I first met the family, lived in an L-shaped room which also contained a grand piano and, somehow, Sasha, their pianist son, when he was home. The rest of the apartment consisted of a tiny kitchen in the entrance hall (the original design must have had communal kitchens, too) and Igor's small room off to the right. Since there was space only for a desk, a bed and a bookcase, I would sit on the wooden desk chair and Igor on the bed, a Soviet divan that rose up alarmingly in the middle and looked extremely uncomfortable. After a few years, Irina decided that this flat was impossibly difficult for Raisa, and found them another one nearby with two bigger rooms plus kitchen and bathroom. It was almost opposite the American Embassy; according to Igor, the roof of the building was used for bugging and surveillance. Only Irina would have been able to procure such a treasure as this new apartment (which Igor, ungratefully, regarded as soulless), calling in who knows how many IOUs from her well-placed friends. Privately, she said to me that if Igor had a fault (apart from womanising and drinking), it was his absurd refusal to do the things necessary in Soviet life to maintain a decent standard of living, like cultivating connections.

His stubbornness in this respect was all the more notable in that he was a member of the Union of Soviet Writers, whose members were accustomed to make heavy use of its perks and slush funds.

Igor disliked writing, despite or because of being such a gifted racon-
teur, and did it rarely and unwillingly. His chosen profession was
editor – he called himself 'the nanny of Soviet literature' – and before
the war he had worked with Lukács at the journal *Literaturnyi kritik*.
In the years I knew him Igor ran the criticism section of *Novyi mir*,
famous in the 1960s as the centre of reform thinking and 'loyal oppo-
sition' – that is, criticism of Soviet society, culture and government
from a Communist standpoint; it was the first publisher of
Solzhenitsyn's *One Day in the Life of Ivan Denisovich*. *Novyi mir* was often
hailed in the West as a dissident publication, the assumption being
that its stance of critical Communist loyalty was just a tactic; this
drove the *Novyi mir* people mad, not just because it was untrue but
also because it was so damaging. They were always in danger of
having an article pulled at the last minute, the print run reduced, an
editor dropped from the board, or even losing their chief editor, the
charismatic people's poet Aleksandr Tvardovsky, famous among
the troops in the Second World War for his saga of the Svejk-like
Vasily Terkin. From their standpoint, the worst that could happen
was to be seen as an internal ally of 'anti-Soviet forces' abroad.

Tvardovsky liked Igor, respected him as a true intellectual and
enjoyed his company as a drinking partner; others (including
Solzhenitsyn) saw him as a sinister behind-the-scenes manipulator.
(There was an anti-semitic tinge to this.) Igor revered Tvardovsky, as
he had done Lukács; he was the only person Igor never made jokes
about. *Novyi mir* was always engaged in some battle with the authori-
ties, of which I would be given blow-by-blow descriptions (some of
Igor's colleagues were not happy about this, but Igor never listened
to hints: he would just stick out his bottom lip and go his own way).
One of these battles was at a particularly dramatic stage just when I
had to go back to Britain, and Igor promised to let me know the
outcome by letter, using a simple code to confuse the postal censors:
he would refer to Brezhnev as 'Nikolai Pavlovich', the name and

patronymic of a provincial writer who was one of the *Novyi mir* crowd. The letter came, and it did indeed contain news of Nikolai Pavlovich – the real one, reported to be complaining of a shortage of sausage in Voronezh. Igor had forgotten about his code.

I spent my whole time in Moscow sitting on hard wooden chairs. When I wasn't on Igor's chair, I was at the Lenin Library or, after the first three months, the archives, where I was pursuing my own mission, which was to find out the real story of Soviet educational and cultural policy in the 1920s. Getting into the archives was an idée fixe of mine because I thought that was what a historian had to do; I was too naive to know that for a Western historian of the Soviet period this was next to impossible. Getting permission to do anything was a big problem in the Soviet Union, involving endless visits to bureaucrats who demanded ever more documents and would make you wait for hours outside their little windows and then, when you finally got to the front of the queue, slam down their shutters triumphantly (*Closed for lunch! Closed for the day! Closed for repairs! Closed for ever!*). But archival permissions were the worst, except perhaps for permission to marry. Not long before, the central archive administration had actually been part of the security ministry, and the contents of state archives were still considered state secrets, which foreigners wanted to get hold of in order to slander the Soviet state. Not knowing how hopeless my quest was, for months I tramped round Moscow asserting in bad Russian my rights (the very word must have made them laugh) as an exchange student and scholar to various unresponsive officials. I remember going to the Central Party Archives, whose location I was not supposed even to know, and putting this argument. I received a swift and effective rebuff: 'What right have you to see Party documents? Are you a member of the Communist Party?'

The state archives were a little more accessible, since foreigners working on pre-revolutionary history had been let in for the past few years, and finally I got permission to work there. How this happened I don't know: I had asked my adviser to intercede for me (perhaps rashly, since I never procured Lunacharsky's diary for him and was close-mouthed about my friendship with Irina and Igor), but all he did was tell them not to admit me, or so I was told later by a friendly archivist. There was a special reading room for foreigners, most of them from 'fraternal' (socialist bloc) countries, not capitalists like me. The entrance was on a different street from the entrance for the Soviet reading room, and the fragile-looking cloakroom attendants, barely capable of lifting briefcases and heavy coats, were said to be Gulag returnees. I was told this by a savvy fraternal foreigner from Poland, working on the 17th century because who in their right mind would try to work on the 20th. We weren't allowed to go to the snackbar or cafeteria because that would have meant wandering unsupervised around the building; instead, kind-hearted supervisors (*dezhurnye*, always women) made tea for us and allowed us to eat sandwiches at our desks, dropping crumbs on the state secrets. Even foreigners had to be allowed to go to the lavatory, however, and that was how I scored my big break. As my fraternal friend informed me, the director's (unmarked) office was on the way to the lavatory. So when the archivists told me after a few weeks that I had exhausted all available materials, I burst into his office unannounced and put my case. He listened for a minute or so and said flatly 'No,' at which, to my great chagrin, I burst into tears. This was the best thing I ever did in my quest for archives. 'Grown-ups don't cry,' the director said patronisingly. Then, with a look of infinite self-satisfaction – the occasional arbitrary granting of bureaucratic favours being even more fun than the usual surly refusal – he picked up the phone and laconically instructed someone to 'give her some more.'

They never did give me (or any of the capitalist foreigners) the catalogues which would have allowed us to find out for ourselves what materials the archives contained; instead, everything had to be selected and ordered by an archivist on the basis of conversations with the scholar about what he or she needed. This made for a wonderful guessing game: might the institution you were interested in have kept stenographic reports? Protocols? Protocols with documentary attachments? If you got the term right, you might get the material, or not as the case might be. And exactly which bureaucratic institution was it that would have stored the information you wanted? As a crash course in bureaucratic organisation, there was nothing better than working in the Soviet archives. And, after a while, if they thought you were a hard worker and therefore a real scholar (not a spy), the archivists would cautiously begin to help you. Once, out of the blue, when at the postdoctoral stage I was working on Soviet industry, they delivered a file I hadn't requested on the industrial use of convict labour, a topic completely off limits for foreigners. I thought it was a mistake – the file's label was innocuous – but years later, during perestroika, I met the archivist in charge of this section (too senior for me ever to have come across in the old days) and she said: 'Weren't you astonished when you got that file? It was my little present to you, you were such a good worker and so conscientious!'

That word 'conscientious' (*dobrosovestna*) meant that her intuition told her I was harmless, a real scholar, not a muck-raker or a spy. In other words, her private classification of me was not 'bourgeois falsifier' but perhaps something milder, like 'so-called-objective bourgeois historian'. Most Western historians were categorised as 'bourgeois falsifiers', the most notorious being the American scholar Richard Pipes, known for his anti-Soviet politics (he was later national security adviser on Soviet and East European affairs under Reagan), who got a whole book to himself (*Mister Paips falsifitsiruet istoriiu*). I was quite critical of American Sovietology myself, though when it came to falsification, the Soviets had the edge. There was a deadening predictability about both American and Soviet writing on Soviet history, the one seemingly a mirror image of the other. On any given topic, the Soviet historians would say that the Communist Party, free of internal doubts or dissent, had planned every detail of the 'progressive' policy, which turned out to be a smashing success. American scholars, agreeing that the Party planned every detail, would call the policy misguided and ideological, and judge it a disaster. I always thought there must be some more interesting way of interpreting the Soviet Union than simply reversing the value signs in its propaganda. And the thing that first struck me – that should have struck anybody working in the archives of the Soviet bureaucracy – was that the Soviet leaders didn't know what was happening half the time, were good at throwing hammers at problems but not at solving them, and spent an enormous amount of time fighting about things that often had little to do with ideology and much to do with institutional interests.

Soviet analyses ignored institutional interest because they had no concept for it; American social scientists, who had a concept for it in democratic contexts, rejected it in the Soviet case because they defined that state as 'totalitarian'. I was pleased by my discovery, and at the same time amused by the thought that scholars develop institutional interests as well: if you give a scholar just one bureaucratic archive (education, in my case), they will tend to see things from the perspective of that institution, even to take its side. One of my fantasies – along with importing a branch of Marks and Spencer and a Penguin bookshop to Moscow – was that one day the Soviets would realise this and give Western scholars access to the most taboo of Soviet archives, the NKVD's, so that the scholars would stop slandering this fine institution and see things from its perspective: the Central Committee cadres department reassigning any Gulag officers who showed signs of competence and sending the Gulag administration nothing but duds, the difficulties in setting up native-language kindergartens for Chechen deportees to Kazakhstan, and so on.

You couldn't get into NKVD archives (you still can't: it's one institution that didn't lose control of its archives come regime change). Nor could you find out much about topics like the Great Purges by consulting the public catalogues in Soviet libraries. Still, there were treasures even in those catalogues, providing ecstatic moments of serendipitous discovery. Once, trawling through the catalogue of the social sciences library under the heading of 'Communist Party of the Soviet Union, Congresses', I came across something with the bland title 'Material'. When I ordered it, it turned out to be a numbered copy of a transcript from the OGPU (the predecessor of the NKVD) of its interrogations of 'bourgeois wreckers' in 1930. It was marked 'Top Secret. For Congress delegates only', so I suppose a delegate had deposited it in the Communist Academy library, which after the academy's dissolution served as the foundation of the social sciences library. On another occasion, I found prewar telephone directories, listed by title, in the catalogue of the Lenin Library. They used to publish such things every couple of years before the war (though not after), and it occurred to me that one way of estimating numbers of Great Purge victims – a topic of great speculation and few hard data at the time – might be to compare the lists of Moscow telephone subscribers for 1937 and 1939. I did not, of course, order only these years ('1937' on a library slip always rang alarm bells), but finally the volumes I really wanted arrived, and I set about painstakingly copying out every tenth name for a random sample. I think they saw what I was doing: for the next decade, whenever I tried to order telephone directories, I was told they were unavailable, lost or had never existed. But by this time, I had learned patience and the wisdom of Soviet citizens that nothing is for ever. When perestroika came, I got my telephone books back.

All this affected my formation as a historian: I became addicted to the thrill of the chase, the excitement of the game of matching your wits and will against that of Soviet officialdom. How boring it must be, I thought, to work on British history, where you just went to the PRO, and polite, helpful people gave you catalogues and then brought you the documents you wanted. What would be the fun of it? Knowledge, I decided, had to be fought for, achieved by ingenuity and persistence, even – like pleasure, in Marvell's words – snatched 'through the iron gates of life'. I thought of myself as different from the general run of British and American scholars, with their Cold War agenda (as I saw it) of discrediting the Soviet Union rather than understanding it. But that didn't stop me getting my own kicks as a scholar from finding out what the Soviets didn't want me to know. Best of all was to find out something the Soviets didn't want me to know *and* Western Cold Warriors didn't want to hear because it complicated the simple anti-Soviet story.

After each of my returns from the Soviet Union, in 1967, 1968 and 1970, I wrote a careful final report for the British that described my archival and other researches at length, gave an unflattering characterisation of my dissertation adviser, said something about conditions of student life in the dormitory and Soviet interactions with foreign students, and omitted the part of my Soviet life connected with Igor Sats and *Novyi mir*. Some time later, after I had finished the dissertation and got a postdoc in London, the director of my institute, a (former?) intelligence man, invited me to lunch, an unprecedented gesture, and asked me in great detail about Igor Sats and *Novyi mir*. I was not sure how he knew I knew them, but perhaps British intelligence, as well as the Soviet postal censors, were reading Igor's letters. I regarded it as a debriefing and resented it. If it was a choice between *Novyi mir* and British intelligence, I was on *Novyi mir*'s side.

But the Soviets were having none of me: I had already been outed. The denunciation was published in the Soviet daily *Sovetskaia Rossiia* at the end of my first year in the Soviet Union, although I didn't know about it until I got back to Oxford. 'He who is obliged to hide the truth' was the heading, and the story below it attacked me and a couple of other Western scholars as bourgeois falsifiers. The offending article – my first and only scholarly publication at that time – was about Lunacharsky, noting his occasional divergences from Soviet orthodoxy. According to the story's author, my article was an example of 'bourgeois so-called research' whose sole purpose was to tarnish the Soviet Union and discredit socialism. 'The ploys of such ideological diversionaries,' he concluded ominously, 'are hard to distinguish from those of bourgeois spies.'

The author was 'V. Golant, PhD in history'. Somebody later told me that Golant, while writing for the most reactionary and anti-Western paper in Moscow, was actually a quasi-dissident who subsequently emigrated to Israel. For all I know, he may privately have liked my article, or perhaps even thought it insufficiently anti-Soviet. In any case, it didn't matter. The article was signed S. Fitzpatrick, and Golant assumed that Fitzpatrick was a man. But the person whom the British Council had sent to the Soviet Union was not a man called S. Fitzpatrick but a woman called (in Cyrillic spelling) Sh. M. Brius (Bruce). To be sure, these two people were both British scholars who seemed to be working on the same topic. But nobody made the connection between Bruce and Fitzpatrick – a typical screw-up. My cover held. The spy in the archive remained unnoticed.

2 December 2010

Online Dating
Emily Witt

I AM NOT usually comfortable in a bar by myself, but I had been in San Francisco for a week and the apartment I sublet had no chairs in it, just a bed and a couch. My friends in town were married or worked nights. One Tuesday I had lentil soup for supper standing up at the kitchen counter. After I finished, I moved to the couch in the empty living room and sat under the flat overhead light refreshing feeds on my laptop. This was not a way to live. A man would go to a bar alone, I told myself. So I went to a bar alone.

I sat on a stool at the centre of the bar, ordered a beer, and refreshed the feeds on my mobile. I waited for something to happen. A basketball game played on several monitors at once. The bar had red fake leather booths, Christmas lights and a female bartender. A lesbian couple cuddled at one end of it. At the other end, around the corner from where I sat, a bespectacled man my age watched the game. As the only man and the only woman alone at the bar, we looked at each other. Then I pretended to watch the game on a monitor that allowed me to look the other way. He turned his back to me to watch the monitor over the pool tables, where the pool players now applauded some exploit.

I waited to be approached. A few stools down, two men broke into laughter. One came over to show me why they were laughing. He handed me his mobile and pointed to a Facebook post. I read the post and smiled obligingly. The man returned to his seat. I drank my beer.

I allowed myself a moment's longing for my living room and its couch. The couch had a woollen blanket woven in a Navajo-inspired pattern, exemplary of a trend in San Francisco that a friend of mine calls 'White People Gone Wild'. When I moved in, the receipt for the blanket was on the mantelpiece. It had cost $228. There was a cast-iron gas stove in the fireplace. I had fiddled with the knobs and the gas, but couldn't figure out how to ignite it. At night the room had the temperature and pallor of a corpse. There was no television.

I returned to my mobile and opened OK Cupid, the free internet dating service. I refreshed the feed that indicated whether other people in the neighbourhood were sitting alone in bars. This service is called OK Cupid Locals. An OK Cupid Locals invitation has to start with the word 'Let's':

Let's smoke a joint and hang out ☺

Let's grab a brunch, lunch, beer or some such for some friendly Saturday revelry.

Let's get a drink after *Koyaanisqatsi* at the Castro.

Let's meet and tickle.

Let's enjoy a cookie.

Let's become friends and explore somewhere.

'Let's go now you and I' always comes into my mind, but I've never broadcast an OK Cupid chat signal, I just respond. That night I scrolled until I found a handsome man who had written a benign invitation: 'Let's get a drink.' I looked at his profile. He was Brazilian. I speak Portuguese. He played the drums. 'Tattoos are a big part of my friends' and family's life,' he wrote. Every era has its own utopian possibilities: ours is the chance to make our lives more bearable through technology.

The man generally held responsible for internet dating as we know it today is a native of Illinois called Gary Kremen, but Kremen was out of the internet dating business altogether by 1997, just around the time people were signing up for the internet en masse. Today he runs a solar energy financing company, is an elected official in Los Altos Hills, California and is better known for his protracted legal battle over the ownership of the pornography website sex.com than he is for inventing internet dating. Like many visionary entrepreneurs, Kremen doesn't have very good management skills. His life has passed through periods of grave disarray. When I met him, at a conference on the internet dating industry in Miami last January, he asked where I was from. 'Ah, Minnesota,' he said: 'Have you ever been to the Zumbro River?' The Zumbro flows south of Minneapolis past Rochester, home of the Mayo Clinic. It turned out that Kremen had once driven, or been driven, into the river. He used to be addicted to speed.

In Miami Kremen recounted the genesis of his ideas about internet dating to a room full of matchmakers. In 1992, he was a 29-year-old computer scientist and one of the many graduates of Stanford Business School running software companies in the Bay Area. One afternoon a routine email with a purchase order attached to it arrived in his inbox. But it wasn't routine: the email was from a woman. At the time, emails from women in his line of work were exceedingly rare. He stared at it. He showed the email to his colleagues. He tried to imagine the woman behind it. 'I wonder if she would date me?' Then he had another idea: what if he had a database of all the single women in the world? If he could create such a database and charge a fee to access it, he would most probably turn a profit.

In 1992, that couldn't be done – modems transmitted information too slowly. Then there was the scarcity of women with online access. Because in its early days the internet was prevalent in worlds that had historically excluded women – the military, finance, mathematics and engineering – women were not online in big numbers. As late as 1996 America Online estimated that of its five million users, 79 per cent were men. In more administrative fields, however, a growing number of women had email.

So Kremen started with email. He left his job, hired some programmers with his credit card, and created an email-based dating service. Subscribers were given anonymous addresses from which to send out their profiles with a photo attached. The photos arrived as hard copy, and Kremen and his employees scanned them in by hand. Interested single people who did not yet have email could participate by fax. By 1994 modems had got faster, so Kremen moved to take his company online. He and four male partners formed Electric Classifieds Inc, a business premised on the idea of re-creating online the classifieds section of newspapers, beginning with the personals. They rented an office in a basement in San Francisco and registered the domain match.com.

'ROMANCE – LOVE – SEX – MARRIAGE AND RELATIONSHIPS' read the headline on an early business plan Electric Classifieds presented to potential investors. 'American business has long understood that people knock the doors down for dignified and effective services that fulfil these most powerful human needs.' Kremen eventually removed 'sex' from his list of needs, but many of the basic parts of most online dating sites were laid out in this early document. Subscribers completed a questionnaire, indicating the kind of relationship they wanted – 'marriage partner, steady date, golf partner or travel companion'. Users posted photos: 'A customer could choose to show himself in various favourite activities and clothing to give the viewing customer a stronger sense of personality and physical character.'

The business plan cited a market forecast that suggested 50 per cent of the adult population would be single by 2000 (a 2008 poll found 48 per cent of American adults were single, compared to 28 per cent in 1960). At the time, single people, particularly those over the age of 30, were still seen as a stigmatised group with which few wanted to associate. But the age at which Americans marry was rising steadily and the divorce rate was high. A more mobile workforce meant that single people often lived in cities they didn't know and the chummy days when a father might set his daughter up with a junior colleague were over. Since Kremen started his company little has changed in the industry. Niche dating sites have proliferated, new technology has made new ways of meeting people possible and new gimmicks hit the market every day, but as I knew from my own experience, the fundamental characteristics of the online dating profile have remained static.

At the same time big cities have a way of shrinking. In her essay about leaving New York Joan Didion tells a man she'll take him to a party where he might meet some 'new faces', and he laughs at her. 'It seemed that the last time he had gone to a party where he had been promised "new faces", there had been 15 people in the room, and he had already slept with five of the women and owed money to all but two of the men.' Didion doesn't say, but I've always assumed her friend went to the party anyway.

I joined OK Cupid at the age of 30, in late November 2011, with the pseudonym 'viewfromspace'. When the time came to write the 'About' section of my profile, I quoted Didion's passage, then added: 'But now we have internet dating. New faces!' The Didion bit sounded unpleasant, so I replaced it with a more optimistic statement, about internet dating restoring the city's possibilities to a life that had become stagnant between work, subway and apartment. Then that sounded depressing, so I finally wrote: 'I like watching nature documentaries and eating pastries.' From then on I was flooded with suggestions of YouTube videos of endangered species and recommendations for pain au chocolat.

OK Cupid was founded in 2004 by four maths majors from Harvard who were good at giving away things people were used to paying for (study guides, music). In 2011 they sold the company for $50 million to IAC, the corporation that now owns Match. Like Match, OK Cupid has its users fill out a questionnaire. The service then calculates a user's 'match percentage' in relation to other users by collecting three values: the user's answer to a question, how she would like someone else to answer the same question, and the importance of the question to her. These questions ranged from 'Does smoking disgust you?' to 'How often do you masturbate?' Many questions are specifically intended to gauge one's interest in casual sex: 'Regardless of future plans, what's more interesting to you right now, sex or true love?' 'Would you consider sleeping with someone on the first date?' 'Say you've started seeing someone you really like. As far as you're concerned, how long will it take before you have sex?' I found these algorithms put me in the same area – social class and level of education – as the people I went on dates with, but otherwise did very little to predict whom I would like. One occurrence in both online and real-life dating was an inexplicable talent on my part for attracting vegetarians. I am not a vegetarian.

I should note that I answered all the questions indicating an interest in casual sex in the negative, but that's fairly common for women. The more an internet-dating site leads with the traditional signifiers of (male) sexual desire – pictures of women in their knickers, open hints about casual sex – the less likely women are to sign up for it. At a 51/49 male to female ratio, OK Cupid has a near parity many sites would envy. It's not that women are averse to the possibility of a casual encounter (I would have been very happy had the right guy appeared), but they need some sort of alibi before they go looking. Kremen had also noticed this, and set up Match to look neutral and bland, with a heart-shaped logo.

I wanted a boyfriend. I was also badly hung up on someone and wanted to stop thinking about him. People cheerily list their favourite movies and hope for the best, but darkness simmers beneath the chirpy surface. An extensive accrual of regrets lurks behind even the most well-adjusted profile. I read 19th-century novels to remind myself that sunny equanimity in the aftermath of heartbreak was not always the order of the day. On the other hand, online dating sites are the only places I've been where there's no ambiguity of intention. A gradation of subtlety, sure: from the basic 'You're cute,' to the off-putting 'Hi there, would you like to come over, smoke a joint and let me take nude photos of you in my living room?'

The largest free dating site in America is another algorithm-based service, Plenty of Fish, but in New York everyone I know uses OK Cupid, so that's where I signed up. I also signed up to Match, but OK Cupid was the one I favoured, mostly because I got such constant and overwhelming attention from men there. The square-jawed bankers who reigned over Match, with their pictures of scuba diving in Bali and skiing in Aspen, paid me so little attention it made me feel sorry for myself. The low point came when I sent a digital wink to a man whose profile read, 'I have a dimple on my chin,' and included photos of him playing rugby and standing bare-chested on a deep-sea fishing vessel holding a mahi-mahi the size of a tricycle. He didn't respond to my wink.

I went to a lecture by the novelist Ned Beauman who compared the OK Cupid experience to Carl Sagan pondering the limits of our ability even to imagine non-carbon-based extraterrestrial life, let alone perceive when it was beaming signals to us. We troll on OK Cupid for what we think we want, but what if we are incapable of seeing the signals being sent to us, let alone interpreting them?

OK Cupid gave the almost awe-inspiring impression of Kremen's dream database: unlimited choice. There are drawbacks to this. As the sociologist Eva Illouz writes in Cold Intimacies, 'the experience of romantic love is related to an economy of scarcity, which in turn enables novelty and excitement.' In contrast, 'the spirit presiding over the internet is that of an economy of abundance, where the self must choose and maximise its options and is forced to use techniques of cost-benefit and efficiency.' At first it was exciting but after a couple of months the cracks began to show. What Beauman says about our inability to gauge what might be attractive turned out to be true. Consider the following.

I went on a date with a classical composer who invited me to a John Cage concert at Juilliard. After the concert we looked for the bust of Béla Bartók on 57th Street. We couldn't find it, but he told me how Bartók had died there of leukaemia. I wanted to like this man, who was excellent on paper, but I didn't. I gave it another go. We went out for a second time to eat ramen in the East Village. I ended the night early. He next invited me to a concert at Columbia and then to dinner at his house. I said yes but I cancelled at the last minute, claiming illness and adding that I thought our dating had run its course. I was in fact sick, but he was angry with me. My cancellation, he wrote, had cost him a 'ton of time shopping, cleaning and cooking that I didn't really have to spare in the first place a few days before a deadline . . .' He punctuated almost exclusively with Pynchonian ellipses.

I apologised, then stopped responding. In the months that followed he continued to write, long emails with updates of his life, and I continued not responding until it came to seem as if he was lobbing his sadness into a black hole, where I absorbed it into my own sadness.

I went on a date with a furniture craftsman. We met at a coffee shop. It was a sunny afternoon in late February, but a strange snowfall began after we arrived, the flakes sparkling in the sun. The coffee shop was below ground, and we sat at a table by a window that put us just below two chihuahuas tied to a bench on the sidewalk outside. They shivered uncontrollably despite their fitted jackets. They looked down at us through the window, chewing on their leashes. The woodworker bought me a coffee and drank tea in a pint glass.

Our conversation was strained. He seemed bored. His blue eyes shifted restlessly and he had a moustache. He had gone to a school for graphic design in Arizona. He showed me photos of furniture he made. He had calloused hands and was tall. He was attractive but dour and I wondered why: was it me, or a generalised posture against the world? We discovered we had been born in the same hospital, Allentown Hospital in Allentown, Pennsylvania, except that I was seven months older. In another era, the era when marriage was dictated by religion, family and the village, we might have had several children by now. Instead my parents had moved halfway across the country when I was three years old, he had stayed in Allentown until adulthood and now we both lived in bleak Bedford-Stuyvesant and were thirty. He thought of himself as defiant, and loved being a craftsman only as much as he had hated working in an office. After drinking his tea, he went to the bathroom, came back and wordlessly put on his coat. I stood up and did the same. We walked up the stairs into the February wind. We said goodbye.

I went on a date with a man who turned out to be a hairstylist who had attracted me with his Texas charm: 'A nod and a bow, Ms Space,' he had written. He arrived late to our date in Alphabet City, having accommodated some last-minute clients who wanted unscheduled blow-drys for their own dates. On either side of his neck he had tattoos of crossed scimitars. I asked him what the tattoos meant. He said they meant nothing. They were mistakes. He pushed up his sleeves and revealed more mistakes. As a teenager in Dallas he had let his friends use him as a training canvas. To call the tattoos mistakes seemed to be different from regretting them. He didn't regret them. He said it was just that his sixteen-year-old self was giving him the finger. 'You think you've changed,' the sixteen-year-old version of him was saying through the tattoos: 'Fuck you, I'm still here.'

OK Cupid had another unintended effect, which was that in posting my profile, however pseudonymously, I had adorned myself with the equivalent of a 'For Sale' sign. Those who saw me on OK Cupid whom I knew in real life and who recognised my photo would often contact me: 'I saw you on OK Cupid and I thought I would write.' I went for Colombian food in Greenpoint with one of these. When I arrived my date was reading some documents that the National Security Agency had recently declassified to do with John Nash, the schizophrenic genius portrayed in *A Beautiful Mind*. We ordered arepas and beers. I liked this man. He had a job he loved at a blue-chip art gallery and lived in a spacious, high-ceiling apartment overlooking a tree-filled park with benches that formed a serpentine pattern. We talked about Cascadian black metal bands and the idea of resisting capitalism through unlistenable music and sustainable agriculture. We walked from Cafecito Bogotá back to his impeccable apartment, where he played ambient records and I petted his two cats. We decided to conduct an OK Cupid Locals experiment: he broadcast 'Let's lkjdlfjlsjd-fijsflsjlj.' I sat next to him on the couch. I refreshed my phone to see if his broadcast came up. It did. We looked at each other. He walked me to the train.

Around this time I met someone in the real world. It didn't work out, but it was a vivid enough reminder of what it feels like to want to sleep with someone and not even know what their favourite books are to make internet dating all but impossible for a while. The boredom returned, the ex-boyfriend resumed his place in the halls of memory. I went west and the walls of the all but unfurnished apartment in San Francisco loomed over me.

Like most people I had started internet dating out of loneliness. I soon discovered, as most do, that it can only speed up the rate and increase the number of encounters with other single people, where each encounter is still a chance encounter. Internet dating destroyed my sense of myself as someone I both know and understand and can also put into words. It had a similarly harmful effect on my sense that other people can accurately know and describe themselves. It left me irritated with the whole field of psychology. I began responding only to people with very short profiles, then began forgoing the profiles altogether, using them only to see that people on OK Cupid Locals had a moderate grasp of the English language and didn't profess rabidly right-wing politics.

Internet dating alerted me to the fact that our notions of human behaviour and achievement, expressed in the agglomerative text of hundreds of internet dating profiles, are all much the same and therefore boring and not a good way to attract other people. The body, I also learned, is not a secondary entity. The mind contains very few truths that the body withholds. There is little of import in an encounter between two bodies that would fail to be revealed rather quickly. Until the bodies are introduced, seduction is only provisional.

In the depths of loneliness, however, internet dating provided me with a lot of opportunities to go to a bar and have a drink with a stranger on nights that would otherwise have been spent unhappy and alone. I met all kinds of people: an X-ray technician, a green tech entrepreneur, a Polish computer programmer with whom I enjoyed a sort of chaste fondness over the course of several weeks. We were both shy and my feelings were tepid (as, I gathered, were his), but we went to the beach, he told me all about mushroom foraging in Poland, he ordered his vegetarian burritos in Spanish, and we shared many mutual dislikes.

As for that night in San Francisco, I responded to an online beacon, and I went for a drink with a stranger. We kissed, he showed me his special collection of marijuana plants, and we talked about Brazil. Then I went home and never spoke to him again.

25 October 2012

In Pyongyang
Tariq Ali

F ORTY-TWO YEARS AGO, I was mysteriously invited to visit
North Korea. Pakistan's military dictatorship had been toppled
after a three-month struggle and in March 1970 the country
was in the throes of its first ever general election campaign. I was
travelling to every major town and many smaller ones, interviewing
opposition politicians and those who'd taken part in the uprising for
a book. I was still there in May, my work unfinished, when the
invitation arrived. North Korea was even then a country set apart.

The letter came via a local Communist known as Rahim
'Koreawallah', secretary of the Pak-Korea Friendship Society. Short,
paunchy, loquacious and full of beer, he was out of breath as he
handed me the letter from Pyongyang. I had to leave straightaway,
he said. Why? Because the North Koreans were convinced that the
US was preparing to invade and needed global solidarity. In January
1968 the Koreans had captured the USS *Pueblo*, a naval intelligence
vessel, and arrested its crew. Relations between the two countries
remained poor. Could I leave next week, Koreawallah asked? I laughed
and said no.

I was on my way to what was then East Pakistan. North Korea was
a distraction. Koreawallah was both angry and insistent, but his argu-
ment was weak. There was no evidence that Washington was preparing
for war. I had experience to back me up. A few years earlier I had

spent six weeks in North Vietnam and, as well as crouching in air-raid shelters during US bombing raids on Hanoi, I sat through several military briefings by senior Vietnamese officers who made it clear that they would eventually win the war. For the Americans, already overstretched in Indochina, a new war in Korea would be suicidal.

I had other reasons not to go. I thought Kim Il-sung a ridiculous and abhorrent leader, his regime a parody of Stalinist Russia. I turned down the offer again, this time more forcefully. But my parents, both of them Communists, thought I should take advantage of the opportunity to see the country (they had never been). And Koreawallah would not be deterred. With a sly smile, he let drop that I could go via China, taking a train from Beijing to Pyongyang. That decided the matter. I was desperate to visit Beijing and this seemed my only chance. I just said I couldn't go until mid-June.

When I returned to Dhaka after two gruelling weeks in the countryside, a problem had arisen. The East Pakistan trade unions had called a one-day general strike – a show of strength against General Yahya Khan's transitional regime in Islamabad – on the day I was due to get an early morning flight from Dhaka to Canton. I took it personally. Friends asked the Communist leaders of the taxi and rickshaw drivers' unions for a 30-minute exemption so I could get to the airport. Their pleas were rightly rejected. When the local student leaders stepped in, the unions relented. There could be no motorised traffic on the streets, but I could travel by cycle rickshaw.

My suitcase and I were too much for the emaciated driver. After ten minutes of huffing and puffing we'd got nowhere. Worried I might miss the flight, I asked him to get in the back and pedalled like crazy for the five or so miles to the airport. Apart from stray animals, there was nothing else on the road. When we got to the airport the rickshaw-wallah, seeing me bathed in sweat, grinned broadly and refused to accept my money. I stuffed it down his dry vest and ran to the plane. Soon after it took off, the strike committees closed down the airport.

I had predicted that Pakistan was about to break up but I didn't think as I watched the morning sun rise over the paddy fields that it would be my last glimpse of East Pakistan.

In Beijing posters decorated the streets, loud music blared from speakers and groups of children bowed before portraits of the Great Helmsman. A stream of bicycles flowed along unpolluted thoroughfares. How lucky they were, I thought, not to fetishise the car. I wandered away from the hotel, managed to find Tiananmen Square, discovered a cheap and good restaurant, then headed back to the hotel, where two Korean Embassy officials were waiting to take me on a low-key tour of the Forbidden City. We appeared to be the only foreign visitors.

Later that afternoon, I packed for the two-day train journey to Pyongyang and we set off for the station. There was no phrasebook in the hotel. The only Chinese I knew was 'Mao Chushi Wansui' – 'Mao Zedong will live ten thousand years' – which wasn't much help in ordering a meal or finding the lavatory. Mercifully a Sikh courier from the Indian Embassy came into my compartment before the train left the station. By chance, I think. After we had exchanged greetings in Punjabi he told me he was fluent in Mandarin and, much more important, that his wife had cooked food for the journey and he hoped I would share it.

Just before the train began to move, two PLA officers also entered the compartment. No, they laughed, they were not going to Pyongyang. My efforts to draw out their thoughts on the Cultural Revolution failed, but they were eager to discuss Pakistan and surprised to hear my criticism of its military dictators: Chinese propaganda portrayed them as 'anti-imperialist allies'. They hadn't heard about the recent uprising. The jollier of the two warned me about the 'personality cult' in Korea and my Sikh friend roared: he never stayed more than a night at the embassy in Pyongyang. The PLA men got off at Beidaihe, a seaside resort east of Beijing. Once frequented by emperors, their wives and concubines, it had become a favourite spot for Communist Party leaders. 'If these two are holidaying here,' my fellow traveller muttered, 'they must be important or related to someone who is, just like in our part of the world.' Unlike me, he found this thought reassuring.

At Sinuiju, I was welcomed onto the sacred soil of the DPRK with a bunch of flowers. Standing in front of a life-size statue of Kim Il-sung, my host told me that he was a bit disturbed by the scale of the personality cult in China. In Pyongyang a Young Pioneer gave me another bouquet of flowers. I was shocked at what I saw as we drove through the city: we could have been in Eastern Europe after the Second World War. Then I remembered that what General Curtis LeMay had threatened to do to North Vietnam had already been done to North Korea: it had been bombed into the Stone Age. There were no protests in the West against the heavy bombing of Pyongyang at only 15 minutes' notice: 697 tons of bombs were dropped on the city, 10,000 litres of napalm; 62,000 rounds were used for 'strafing at low level'.

Three years earlier in Phnom Penh the Australian journalist Wilfred Burchett had told me that what I had seen in Vietnam was 'nothing compared to what they did to Korea. I was there. There were only two buildings left standing in Pyongyang.' It was alleged that the US had used germ warfare, and although the US dismissed these claims as 'outrageous', on 9 August 1970 the *New York Times* reported that chemical weapons had been considered after 'American ground forces in Korea were overwhelmed by Chinese Communist human wave attacks near the Yalu River'. Pentagon policymakers wanted to 'find a way to stop mass infantry attacks', so 'the army dug into captured Nazi chemical warfare documents describing sarin, a nerve gas so lethal that a few pounds could kill thousands of people in minutes if the deadly material were disbursed effectively.' Was it used in Korea? Probably not, though germ warfare tests were conducted in US cities.

In one test 'harmless' bacteria were introduced into the Pentagon's air-conditioning system.

I asked to see the foreign minister to discuss the tensions with the United States, but, to my minders' surprise, I didn't ask to meet Kim Il-sung. My first few days in Pyongyang were spent visiting museums with my excellent interpreter and a minder – 'the chief of protocol'. They both accompanied me everywhere. At the war museum I asked why there was no sign of the Chinese 'volunteers' without whom the war would have been lost. No reply. Finally the guide went upstairs and returned with the museum director. I repeated my question. 'We did have the display but those rooms have been closed for repairs and painting. The photographs have been removed to safe places.' I asked to see where they had been, but the men's embarrassment was so painful I gave up. We moved on to the museum of art. After seeing four rooms filled with bad paintings of Kim Il-sung, his mother and other relatives, I lost my cool and asked to see something from earlier centuries. After a hurried consultation with my minder, the director asked us to follow him, making it clear that he was doing me a huge favour.

Locked away in the underground vaults were the most stunning tomb paintings I have ever seen. Some dated back 2000 years, others were from the 11th and 12th centuries. They depicted soldiers, hunters, scenes of wealth, exquisitely beautiful women. I thanked the director profusely and said I hoped that Koreans would one day be able to see these treasures. He smiled and shrugged. He was the only person I met there who didn't mention Kim Il-sung once, let alone refer to him as the 'great and beloved leader' – GBL – of 40 million Korean people. One day I was driven to Mangyongdae, where I was promised a real treat. It turned out to be Kim's birthplace and virtually the whole city was a shrine to him, with all the same stories I had heard dozens of times about his heroism repeated yet again.

Back at the hotel I saw a very pregnant Kathleen Cleaver in the

lobby with Maceo, her son with the Black Panther leader Eldridge
Cleaver. We spoke briefly before she was whisked away and I never
caught sight of her again. Later I discovered that her husband had
met Kim Il-sung and pledged the support of the Black Panther Party.
That no money changed hands in return for this is inconceivable.
American friends told me afterwards that Kathleen had been kept in
her room in Pyongyang for four months, a punishment her husband
had decreed after discovering that the baby wasn't his. Kim had
obliged his new friend. Useful to know, I thought.

It was still early evening. There was no bar in the hotel so I went
to the billiard room to bash balls. Three tall men I hadn't seen before
were at the table. Two of them spoke English. They were students
from the University of Havana, in Pyongyang on a three-year course
in exchange for the hundreds of Korean students who were sent to
Cuba to train as doctors. Why them? They laughed. Protocol demanded
that someone be sent. They thought I would get on with the Cuban
ambassador and so we left in the embassy car for tamarind juice and
mojitos followed by a very good meal. The ambassador was a veteran
of the revolution. Sending him to Korea had not been a friendly act:
'I'd got a bit critical of Fidel and the way things were being done in
Cuba. I talked to many others about this and Fidel got angry. I would
have preferred prison but they sent me here instead. It's worked.
Havana's a paradise and Fidel is God. Just get me out of here. I'll
never open my mouth again.' It was the most enjoyable evening I
spent in the DPRK.

The next week was spent in trains and cars. The car would often
stop in the middle of nowhere. We would get out and I would be
shown a site where 'GBL Comrade Kim Il-sung gave on-the-spot
guidance to peasants on the wheat harvest.' At one point, in the
middle of nowhere, I asked them to stop. My bladder was full. As I
got out of the car I said: 'I'm just going to give on-the-spot guidance
to that tree.' The interpreter and minder convulsed with laughter. It

was the most reassuring sight of my trip. Nothing was said when I returned to the car, but we never stopped again.

At Panmunjom on the 38th parallel the loudspeakers were blaring out cliché-ridden propaganda. American soldiers were lounging around, occasionally pointing at the speakers and laughing. I asked the Koreans if I could use a loudhailer. When they finally agreed, I asked the Americans why they were hanging around in Asia given that their own country was on fire. They woke up a bit. I gave an account of the Kent State shootings – the Ohio National Guard had fired on and killed four students for protesting against Nixon's invasion of Cambodia – which had taken place only a few weeks before. Four million US students had gone on strike. I asked the soldiers to join me in a minute's silence in memory of the dead students, at which point a senior officer came and shepherded them all back to barracks. The Koreans were amazed. I resisted the temptation to point out that my 'on-the-spot guidance' had been more effective than GBL's propaganda.

Back in Pyongyang I was granted my appointment with the foreign minister, who gave me the official Korean position on the world. I listened politely. As I was about to leave he said: 'We appreciated your talk at Panmunjom, but there is one thing you don't seem to understand about our country. You do not appreciate the role that Comrade Kim Il-sung played in liberating and creating the DPRK.' I couldn't deny this. He gave me an odd smile.

Two years later I was asked back, to give a speech at a conference on the 'role of US imperialism in Asia'. I was reluctant but the Vietnamese persuaded me. They hadn't been invited and wanted their position on the subject defended. This time the journey took even longer. We were flown first to Prague, where the Russian military plane that was to transport us to Pyongyang was five days late. When it finally arrived it was filthy and rank; in the middle of the night it stopped to refuel at Omsk in below freezing conditions, and a few of us rushed out to breathe some fresh air. In Pyongyang, each delegate was assigned a chauffeur-driven Mercedes. I'd been hoping to be assigned the same interpreter, but my luck was out. He'd asked me for an English dictionary: I gave the one I'd brought to the new team and asked them to pass it on to him. They said he'd been transferred to a small town. At the hotel a senior party apparatchik was meeting with each delegate or delegation separately. The subject of the conference had been changed, he told me. It was GBL's 60th birthday and they thought we should discuss 'Comrade Kim Il-sung's contribution to Marxism-Leninism'. I refused point blank and demanded a flight back home. The apparatchik left the room in a nervous state.

Over dinner that night an affable Algerian professor and a representative of Frelimo from Mozambique couldn't believe what I'd done. The Algerian said he had sold himself for $5000, the friend from Frelimo was too ashamed to name the sum he'd accepted. The next morning I was offered $10,000, which would have come in extremely handy for the magazine I was editing. I was tempted to accept and then make a purely satirical speech, but I declined. They still wouldn't let me leave. There was no flight to Europe for a week. I said I'd fly to Pakistan. They told me that was difficult too. The Vietnamese ambassador came to see me. He pleaded with me not to leave. 'The personality cult is bad here,' he said. 'Very, very bad.'

At an official reception the day before the conference began we were all introduced to GBL. Never in my life had I felt such an aversion to a political figure on the left. His bloated neck seemed to be inviting a bullet. I wished I'd been a Decembrist. The only words he addressed to me were distinctly odd: 'London, yes? "The Red Flag". They still sing it?'

They made the mistake of seating me on the plenum. I didn't applaud a single speech, but I did keep notes. The Politburo star who opened the conference – the subject was 'the task of social science to thoroughly defend the great leader Comrade Kim Il-sung's revolutionary thinking and propagate it extensively' – quoted a GBL speech. 'There is a revolutionary song which says: "Let cowards flinch and traitors sneer. We'll keep the Red Flag flying here." This expresses our unvarying determination.' I wondered who in Moscow had introduced him to the anthem of British social democracy. His appalling speech was interrupted 143 times for applause, standing ovations etc. My table in the hotel restaurant expanded each day as more and more desperadoes came to joke about our situation. Our codename for GBL was Peterson.

The reason for the absurdly narcissistic cult was obvious. Who the hell was Kim Il-sung? Where did he come from? Had he ever operated as a guerrilla leader? There had been other well-known Korean Communists, including a female general. Kim Il-sung killed some of them. Others had fled to China during the Japanese occupation and fought alongside Mao's partisans. Many veterans of the Long March were Koreans. It is possible that Kim Il-sung operated as a guerrilla in China and then fled to Russia. We don't know for sure. What we do know is that the Red Army freed the country in 1945 and the Chinese saved it during the Korean War. But these facts were never mentioned in DPRK propaganda. 'Juche', an aggressive form of self-reliance, was the word coined to designate this xenophobia. When I asked the interpreter on my first trip whether he had read any Marx or Engels or Lenin, he looked puzzled. 'No,' he told me. 'Everything is interpreted by Comrade Kim Il-sung.' He wasn't sure whether any of the classic texts were available in libraries.

At one stage it appeared that the United States was going to buy out the North Koreans. Clinton despatched Madeleine Albright to Pyongyang in 2000 to do a deal – loadsamoney for the Kims, denuclearisation of sorts followed by a soft reunification with the South – but it didn't go through. Bush had no interest at all in contact. Why? I got an answer of sorts after a public debate on the Iraq war in Berlin in 2003. My opponent was Ruth Wedgwood from Yale, an adviser to Donald Rumsfeld. Over lunch I asked her about their plans for North Korea. She was cogent. 'You haven't seen the glint in the eyes of the South Korean military,' she said. 'They're desperate to get hold of the North's nuclear arsenal. That's unacceptable.' Why? 'Because if a unified Korea becomes a nuclear power, it will be impossible to stop Japan from becoming one too and if you have China, Japan and a unified Korea as nuclear states, it shifts the relationship of forces against us.' Obama seems to agree with this way of thinking. His problem is China. The Chinese once appeared indifferent to Korea's fate. That's no longer the case. The areas near the border with China are experiencing a boom and Chinese TV programmes are heaven compared to Kimmist output. How long will Beijing allow this absurd opera to continue?

26 January 2012

Mother One,
Mother Two
Jeremy Harding

To think back at all is to fall quickly, almost instinctively, on two names – Colin, the name of my adoptive father, and Maureen, the name of my adoptive mother – and on the significant word 'adopted', which has the weight of a name. Appended to this little trio of terms, like an intake of breath at the end of a short announcement, is the nameless presence of the 'birth mother', as she's mostly called by adoption experts: the first mother, that's to say, also the eternal mother-in-waiting. But you wouldn't – I wouldn't – really want to say 'my mother' about either of these mothers, even though I do. Then there's adoption. 'My adoption'? It sounds like an affliction, or a misfortune, though it was far from being either.

I seem to see Maureen, Mother Two, walking up a set of steps onto a raised wooden deck in front of a shingled house with double doors leading into a boxy living room. The blonde hair is well arranged, the eyebrows have been tended, making them dark and thin. She's humming 'I'd risk everything for one kiss, everything . . .' But the memory isn't accurate. That song was written much later, after we'd moved out of the house I'm thinking of. Mother Two seems resolute, indifferent to almost everything but the double doorway and the tune I can't put my finger on.

For long periods of my childhood, I grew up with the fact of water. I was raised by a river. 'Thick' is a good word for the way water seemed to me when I was young and still seems now: sustaining, brown, benign – or white, decisive, invigorating, rushing over a weir, churning from the back of a boat. Having been adopted, I was spared the binding notion of blood, with all its passion and fatalism. I simply took the platitude and stood it on its head. I am no longer sure what to think, except that my recent interest in origins is a perversity on my part, like going back over a dispute that was settled years ago.

Doubly perverse because of my debt to water. I owe nothing to blood, but I owe a great deal to the eccentric couple who adopted me in London and then carted me off to a world of slippery landing-stages, locks and leaking boats, flooded gardens and impassable roads; more than I owe to my lost progenitors: the absent father and the enigmatic Mother One, who conceived and bore me, and for one reason or another decided to leave it at that. And wouldn't the wise course be to do the same – to leave it at that? There's an unsettling sense that the urge to know more about Mother One is disloyal, not just to Colin and Maureen, but to the life I lived with them and the course that life went on to take. Not that I'm above disloyalty.

In the photo of my christening, Maureen has a hairband studded with pearls. The baby is sullen and inscrutable: pointless to wonder where it thought it was. It is wrapped in a long shawl and at first sight preparing to levitate, though on closer inspection the opposite seems true: it has plummeted through thin air and Maureen, having broken its fall at the last moment, now has it in her arms as though it had been there all along. Colin, who is wearing a bowler hat and leather gloves and earning £1200 a year on the London Stock Exchange, looks as if he'd just got away with an ingenious robbery.

Secrecy was paramount. As far as Colin's parents knew, Maureen had given birth to the bright new member of the family in a London clinic. This make-believe must have been hard to keep up, not least since Colin and Maureen had the use of a flat below Colin's parents for several months of her slimline pregnancy.

For Maureen especially, the adoption was a source of other, steeper fantasies, which she divulged in fits and starts. Much of what she said was unreliable, I see now. She liked to tell vivid and abrupt tales about her own past. But the elementary versions of the adoption story – the ones she began telling her little boy when he was about five – weren't in the least deceitful. And perhaps her stories improved as they acquired more detail, in subsequent retellings. Or maybe they got blowsier, like Maureen herself, and altogether less reliable. While she spent her time embroidering the daydream of an earlier, more splendid existence, I was happy enough in the pursuit of adventure on and around the extraordinary structure where we spent several summers: a dilapidated houseboat brought out of the water and set down about twenty yards from the bank.

I can't put a year to it, though I imagine it now as an early evening in September. Maureen sat me down in the main room of the houseboat and explained that the word for a child with no parents was 'orphan'. She was an orphan herself, she told me, and had been brought up by her grandmother. She said nothing about her parents dying, and I understood only that she'd been unable to stay with these people, whoever they were.

Did I know, she went on, that I was a bit like her – a bit like an orphan?

No.

But I wasn't really an orphan; I was like an orphan. (Possibly a little amphibious creature, a young boy might have thought, part dwarf, part dolphin.) When I was born, Maureen explained, I was extremely small and it was around that time, or that size, in my life that Colin had paid a visit to the hospital. Afterwards, the three of us had lived happily. A double happiness that was somehow threefold:

Colin and Maureen were happy that he had gone to the hospital; and I was happy, surely, as a result of his doing so.

Maureen used the word 'adopted' – I imagine her saying, 'You're what I call adopted' – and asked me to say it with her. I don't think she mentioned anything about another mother in this, the first telling. Not long after our conversation, Colin appeared at the far end of the garden, having walked the ten minutes from the village railway station. He stepped through a diminutive wrought-iron gateway nearly overrun by brambles and known as 'the main gate'. Quite possibly I thought he had been to the hospital again.

Yet nothing that Maureen had said seemed odd. She was my mother, and a generous mother, and descriptions of the kind she gave came easily – naturally, you'd say – in those days. They spoke eloquently, urgently, of the world as she saw it, and to a child, the way a mother sees a thing is mostly how it is. I recall being intrigued by our talk, slightly restless I suppose. And in that memory, which is only partly to be trusted, the evening sun shines through the back window of the main room; the flat roof of the houseboat – the piratical quarter-deck in the games I played – is beckoning.

She must have told her tale with delicacy. It was persuasive and straightforward and led me to conclude that all children were simply dispensed from a hospital. (I recall tiffs at school, before I'd reached the age of six, about how babies arrived in families: I was sure the tummy story was playground obscurantism.) Then, some time afterwards, at an inopportune moment when the weather was fine and there was a lot going on outside, parents sat their children down, described the comings and goings from hospital and coached them in the mastery of a new word: 'adopted'.

I continued to wonder in a cursory way whether Colin had plans to bring home more children, and at the next telling, perhaps a few months later, when Maureen introduced the character of the little girl in London who'd given me up, my thoughts prowled across the water and established a tenuous link with the unfamiliar world in which I imagined her. But Maureen's own potted autobiography was in many ways the star turn of these little talks and it gripped me. Her grandmother had taken her to Egypt (where was that? Was it in London?); pyramids (what were they?) towered above the desert (but where was that?). There was a stone animal, the 'sphinx', which I took for a long time to be a pair of something, such as slippers or scissors. Time had elapsed. Slowly? Quickly? I can't say. At some point, Maureen and her grandmother had returned to England to live in a big house – but how big? Bigger than the houseboat or our flat in London? Bigger than both of them put together. Maureen's grandmother had a horse-drawn carriage, driven by a coachman. Maureen used to ride in it, and the dalmatians kept by the old lady – 'Dalmatians?' 'Spotted dogs' – would trot behind.

Had I been older, I'd have thought of Maureen as an eligible young lady in an early 19th-century novel, pale and presentable, with witty conversation and a range of accomplishments. But her story took place some time in the 1920s, about a hundred years too late. Now and then, or was it once, she went skittering over snow and ice in a cold place called Chamonix, definitely near London.

Yet in the unfolding of this family origin myth, with its puzzles and enigmas, my own provenance and Maureen's background were endowed with a fantastic, deceptive clarity. Adoption was the way all children came into their families. Very likely their mothers had all been to Egypt and surged up long gravel driveways in a jingling coach and four with dalmatians bringing up the rear.

I have no doubt that when I was marched off with Maureen to see *Oliver!* on the stage, I recognised a little of my absent mother – Mother One – in the character of Nancy. She was one of Maureen's favourite stage characters – I'm not sure she'd read the novel

– and *Oliver!* was one of her favourite shows. It was tender and harsh, and it was tender precisely because it was harsh, or was it the other way about? At the beating heart of the thing were a would-be mother in the form of Nancy and an orphaned child.

Only one heroine had mattered more to Maureen than Nancy. We'd been to see *My Fair Lady* during its first run in the West End, with the London cast, before I was sent away to school. That would have been 1958 or 1959. Maureen had promptly fallen in love with Eliza Doolittle. I remembered a lot about the show, and particularly Eliza's brassiness, her startling aversion to nonsense. I couldn't have said any of it this way at the time, and the class fable – or is it a fable about essential human qualities? – was lost on me. But I grasped quite quickly how Colin and Maureen loved a cheeky Cockney. And how they fell about when Stanley Holloway sang 'Get Me to the Church on Time'. Once they'd bought the soundtrack of the show, it became the theme music of our weekends, especially on Sunday mornings, an hour or so after breakfast, when Maureen would acquire her first target of the day, cruising the length of the living-room – 'I could have spread my wings and done a thousand things' – then banking suddenly in the direction of the drinks cabinet to obliterate a gin and tonic.

When I was 13 or so, my sister Jill – Maureen's daughter by her earlier marriage to Colin's predecessor, the personable Graham – announced that our mother's horse-and-carriage story was rubbish. In those days, I didn't give the information any thought. Now, though, I wondered if it wasn't linked in some way to her romance with the idea of the poor working girl, which seemed to shed a glimmer of light on her character, or at any rate on her story, though I couldn't yet say what it clarified. Eliza's songs, both before and after Higgins's breakthrough, were forever on her lips. When she wasn't singing them out loud, you might catch her whispering them, as though rehearsing some sweet flattery. So while all the songs seemed, in their different ways, to hint obscurely at my absent Mother One, they must have spoken to Maureen about someone far closer to home. And at some stage I must have wondered, as I was wondering now, whether that someone wasn't herself. I must also have harboured a suspicion that the marriages to Colin and Graham had brought Maureen a long way from her own origins. As the dissimulated adoptee, I might not have been the only member of our threesome who'd come up in the world.

You couldn't tell with Colin whether he was a covetous person given to ostentatious acts of generosity, or whether he had a core of generosity that was slowly overwhelmed, confining him to intermittent gestures of good will and prodigality. Either way, he was an excellent host and, very much to his credit in my eyes, a person who preferred to count the costs later rather than sooner. And so, in the middle of the 1960s, he indulged Maureen in a way that he never did again. Her dream was to become a flower-girl herself, only posher than Eliza in the first instance: more, in fact, like the original Liza, in the afterword to *Pygmalion*, who's left Professor Higgins's establishment, married Freddy Eynsford-Hill and opened a flower shop.

Maureen was already well prepared. She had begun working for a florist in South Kensington after I'd been away at school for four or five years and she'd gone on to run a stall in Rutland Mews East. It was a success. Colin raised a loan and they rented premises off the Brompton Road.

Maureen's talent for arranging flowers was now obvious, dramatic even, and she was soon being patronised by London celebrities, whose names were a constant struggle for her. 'You know, darling, the actor!' she'd say of Michael Caine. 'The curly-haired one who kills all the nignogs with the hay tutus and enormous spears in that film your father likes, I call him Alfie.'

She sold arrangements to Jean Shrimpton, Alec Guinness, Tony Blackburn, and others whose names she got confused. Names of flowers, too, were a struggle, even though she knew exactly what she had in mind: myosotis, chrysanthemum and anemone would come out sounding like rare distempers in farm animals. 'Pansies' was always said with an involuntary smile, even when she was referring to the flower itself. Or she might remark of a gay client: 'He's what I call a pansy.' And then: 'I love pansies, they have a wonderful sense of humour.'

There was a glamour about the cramped shop that made Maureen glamorous too, even when she worked herself into a state of exhaustion, and as I thought of that time now, my teenage self seemed to be aligned with the little boy who'd prefigured him, both of them deeply fond of this person their mother. The brusque set of her face eased up, she wore less clogging foundation; the peekaboo eyes got bigger and took more in; her hours were often very long, and in the four months or so that I'd be home from school, I found her mostly cheerful. She was good with the customers and good at the back of the shop, cutting and dressing, primping the fussier commissions, going by instinct on the simpler, more elegant arrangements, standing ankle-deep in stems or shuffling through green, powdery windfalls of floral foam.

There was normally a bottle of something near the kettle – gin or, around Christmas time, champagne, which the clients liked to give her. But upstairs, after hours, the mood was gloomy. Colin wasn't enjoying the new state of affairs; he complained of the mess; he'd rather Maureen was available to cook a meal at night; he felt she had no head for business. All this he made perfectly clear. She soldiered on regardless.

Twice a week at five in the morning she'd have to be on the way to the market at Covent Garden to buy in stock. These trips were the high point of her week and when I was around I used to go with her. In the flower market, she seemed younger and funnier than I'd thought she could be, shy but oddly at home with the traders, confused about money, though sure of what she wanted to buy. For their part, they appeared to worship her. They fetched and carried for her with a mixture of deference and cheek – the caricature of the Cockney working man that she and Colin used to delight in – so that I saw her in quite another light than the narrow, unkind glare of family life. They called her 'Mrs H.' or 'Maureen'. And she called them by their first names. She knew every one of them straight off, unlike the names of her celebrity customers.

The last time I recall driving back with her to Knightsbridge at seven a.m. in sparse traffic with an open box of white carnations on my lap and the tips of some loose gladioli prodding me in the ear, she was singing 'Wouldn't It Be Loverly?' It's the famous song that Eliza Doolittle sings while she darts about the barrows in Covent Garden at the beginning of My Fair Lady. A witty gloss on aspiration. But in which direction – up or down – was Mother Two hoping to go by then?

My father – not Colin, but Mother One's lover – entered the picture via Maureen, at a time when the lesser tellings, or embellishments of the adoption story were in order. I'd guess I was 13 or 14. I'm not sure how the conversation went.

'Your father,' Maureen seems to be saying in her amiable, speculative way, 'was a waiter, I think, or a what's-its-name, you know, a steward, on a . . . what I call a Scandinavian ship.' 'What I call' was one of Maureen's most punctual expressions. It gave her a good deal of licence. She might use it while naming a perfectly familiar object, in which case it seemed to endow her with distinction and consign the object in question to everlasting banality ('It's what I call a lawnmower'). Or she might use it when she felt that what she had to say was true but difficult ('He's what I call a layabout'). Or she might flourish it like a white flag: I have a rough idea what I mean and you'd do well to follow my drift, because if you want to set me straight, I may have trouble following yours.

Scandinavia was a case of the white flag that didn't quite mean surrender.

'He might have been Norwegian, or you know. A Belgian. Or what's the other one up there.'

In any case Scandinavia appealed to me.

I have no carbon-dating system for events and conversations in our family, but some time in the late 1960s, I guess, Maureen let it be known that 'the little girl' who'd given birth to me was in fact 'a little Irish girl', and that she'd been serving on a counter when she fell pregnant in 1951. She seemed to think the shop was a branch of Woolworth's. There were plenty in Britain by then.

Maureen and I had been regular visitors to our local Woolworth's in the early 1960s, where dreary cover versions of chart hits were available on the Embassy budget label. Maureen herself was so spendthrift and exuberant on these outings, so pleased to saunter round the counters, that she might simply have assigned our little Irish girl to Woolworth's on a festive, one-world impulse: everyone could be happy in Woolworth's – shop girls, customers and little boys. Which cast doubt on her announcement, I thought. Still, it would do to be going on with.

Then she gave out the name of the girl: Marjorie Welch or Welsh, or possibly Margaret, or wait, it could have been Mary. Something Irish in any case. Somebody Welch beginning with M.

She repeated the story about a Scandinavian father, a waiter on merchant ships, whom I now cast in a less glamorous light. No longer a Viking, and only just a seafarer: a person whose main distinction, aside from leaving Mother One in some distress, was to manage a tray of cocktail sausages in gale-force weather.

A year or two later, there was a more important disclosure. I was having supper with Colin and Maureen at one of Colin's shabby, expensive clubs in central London, when Maureen asked me, out of nowhere, if I'd felt 'awkward' about being an adopted child. I was taken aback by the question, and Colin, who preferred not to talk about our family's peculiarities, was visibly ruffled.

'Come on, darling, these are lunatic questions,' he said. 'Our son has come to see us, which is unusual enough, and I've brought you to the club for dinner. Let him relax for heaven's sake.'

'No,' I put in, resolutely. 'I'm glad I was adopted.'

'That's good, darling,' Maureen said, 'because I adore you really, you and the doggies of course, you are the only thing I ever, I mean in my entire life, really ever ever.'

Colin tapped the wine bottle and raised a knowing eyebrow.

'No,' Maureen protested, 'no, I won't have that, Colin. I'm not sloshed, not in the . . .' And then: 'That little Irish girl, you know, darling, what's-her-name, little Moira Welch, she had other children. After you, I mean. And she came to us . . . well, not her . . . but we were' – short pause – 'approached I call it, more than once, and I was asked if we wanted to adopt more babies, if you see what I mean. And those little babies, you see, they were your sisters. Your father thinks I'm tight.'

'My sisters.'

'Oh I wish I'd said something,' said Maureen with the Dalmatian plantation fantasy she'd lifted from Disney and Dodie Smith creeping unmistakably over her, as she imagined a litter of amenable puppies rolling at her feet.

I was charmed and aghast. Colin lit a cigar and blew the smoke past Maureen's ear.

'This is nonsense,' he said.

'Why didn't you adopt them?' I found the question impossible to stifle, even though it must have sounded sharp, or peevish. Something was said about the cost of educating children, and then, on the subject of when these approaches were made, Maureen grew vague. Perhaps when I was four or five years old – or was it earlier? Colin said nothing and as quickly as it had blown up, like a squall over the half-eaten cutlets, the matter was dropped.

Leaving the club, I helped Maureen into her coat and brushed the dandruff from the shoulders of Colin's suit before she could make a vengeful, attentive fuss about it and perhaps fall over in the process. I was always struck, when I performed these rituals of departure, how small both Colin and Maureen were. It must have got harder, as the years went by, to keep the origins of their little boy secret. How does a pair of miniature horses pretend to the rest of the menage that the giraffe in their corner is the straightforward outcome of a good day's rutting?

Maybe the sisters were tall as well.

As a small boy, I'd tended to take Maureen's affection and run with it. The ease of the taking and the fluency of the movement were proof, I supposed, of Maureen's kindness as a mother: she was good with small children in the way she was good with flowers, why not? But she was terrific, I saw now, with make-believe. Jill's assertion that the grandmother stuff was all nonsense had failed to make a proper impression on me. Now, I found, Maureen's nonsense was seriously interesting. The orphaning, the trip to Egypt, the skiing in Chamonix, all of that was in the way of a fairy tale about her past. She'd founded an emblematic home from home, a stunning house, on the heights of upward mobility, from which to survey what she'd made of herself. And paradoxically, because of that fantastic establishment, her marriage to Graham became a little more real and a little less like the fairy tale it must have seemed for the working-class girl I'd begun to believe she was.

When Maureen divorced away from extraordinary wealth and married sideways, she stuck to her story. And the further she got from her childhood, the more committed she grew to the fairy tale. Was that why it became more deeply felt in the telling?

Her switch had been a bad idea from the outset. With Graham, she had been a bridge widow, and she'd originally met Colin – in one version of the story – in the lobby of a bridge club. Colin wasn't going to abandon the bridge table for a happy marriage. But he was better-looking than Graham, more wicked and debonair, and so at first Maureen may not have noticed that her sideways move involved a downward gradient. But the more conspicuous it grew, the plainer it would have been to her that her first marriage was indeed a dream come true, which she'd thrown away for Colin's wastrel charms. At that point, I guess, she'd begun to look back on the years with Graham as a benign enchantment, part make-believe, part not.

Meanwhile, everything that had been asked of her as Graham's wife was still expected of her. The la-di-da voice had to be kept up to the mark. The drinking needed a bit of discipline even if the parties never stopped.

The returns, on the other hand, were fewer. There was nothing like the same degree of ease. Colin's cars broke down, his plans were erratic and in London his parents were too close by. His shacks in the country were chilly and damp. Even his income was liable to dry up when he had a run of bad luck at cards or in the City.

After Colin's death in 1991, Maureen went into sheltered accommodation – an attractive, expensive block of flats off Holland Park Avenue. There she'd taken to drink in a big way. She'd scarcely settled in when Jill came up to London.

Jill and Maureen were by now very much alike.

The Jill of my childhood had been a stubby girl with pigtails, a sweet, bemused sort of person. When she wasn't at boarding school or off at her father's, she'd spent her time at riding school or gymkhanas. She'd been mad about horses and later about teenage boys, especially boys with a tendency to bolt.

I knew her no better, possibly less well, than I knew our nannies, but by the time I'd grown up, things had turned out badly for Jill, and when she started coming to London to see Maureen in the first stages of her decline, she, too, was flailing at the edge of her own undoing. She'd become as slight and haggard as her mother, with the same mannerisms, the same blonde hair – though Maureen's was greyer and thinner since Colin's death – and the same way of taking pleasure to desolate extremes. Both were now known for extravagant feats of bad behaviour after a drink or two, which is how they entertained one another on Jill's visits, returning in due course to the flats in Maureen's new residence, ringing every bell on the console and subjecting the staff to what was later described as 'racial abuse'.

A few weeks after the management had issued a stern warning, I was summoned by a nurse on duty at the flats. Maureen had been missing most of the day.

'I'm afraid your sister's decided to visit again,' the nurse said over the phone. She spoke with an air of foreboding which nonetheless suggested the worst was already well underway.

Maybe I should threaten to disown Maureen and Jill, I thought as I got in the car. Possibly shout and wave my arms at them in a show of consternation. But by now there were no family ties substantial enough to revoke. Should I shout and wave my arms anyway?

Driving west along Notting Hill Gate, I thought I saw them. I stopped the car on a yellow line. No doubt about it at this range. Like a spent, delirious swimmer who's crawled up the beach to the wrong bathing hut, Jill was hammering on the glass door of a restaurant while the waiters rapidly secured it from the inside. Maureen, meanwhile, was sitting on the pavement with her shoes off, legs stretched out over the kerb, as though she were lounging on the Deauville sands. It was nine at night. The traffic was humming down to Shepherd's Bush.

After that, Maureen had been moved on. She was now two establishments further afield, well out of London and well out of range. We'd last spoken in the middle of the night, when she was still allowed to keep a dog, a neurotic miniature like every dog she'd owned. She'd called me to say that she'd packed a suitcase for him – I knew immediately she meant the dog – but she couldn't recall the way to his school. 'He's a sweet chap but he can't sit here with me all day, not now the holidays are over. Is that unreasonable of me?'

'Are you sure you're not thinking of Jeremy?' I asked.

'Yes, of course. D'you take me for a fool?'

'No, but this is . . . You're on the phone to Jeremy now.'

'Don't be ridiculous. Who?'

'You've muddled me up with your dog,' I went on, 'and it's gone two in the morning.'

'I'm so sorry.' She sounded mortified. 'I had no idea it was so late. Now just remind me who this is again, and I'll have one of the staff here ring you back.'

The following morning she called again. Was I in a position to cover the cost of the dog's education? 'Just this term anyhow, until we're sorted out and we've talked to the bank.'

'Consider it covered,' I said.

'Oh thank you, darling,' she said with a sigh of relief. 'He's such a lucky little chap.'

My brother Peter – Maureen's son by her marriage to Graham – told me the news of her death over the phone. At the crematorium in Leatherhead, near Peter's house, the River Mole had burst its banks. The cloud had lifted after several days of heavy rain. It was a cold, bright autumn day. Floodwater sparkled on the lawns below the ceremonial building, built in the style of a supermarket, and there were shiny slicks either side of the cloister, where you half expected to find a cash machine in the wall. Looking across the water, I remembered Maureen, struggling with the dank existence to which life with Colin had swept her off, a life of misty Thames-side billets – the life I'd loved and she hadn't – the power cuts and winter flooding that submerged the lawns for weeks at a stretch so that the only access was by boat across the drowned rose beds. I remembered the ritual lighting of paraffin stoves to dry out the dank rooms; and then I wondered in a vague sort of way whether all this damp around the crematorium would make it hard to get a good blaze going under our mother.

Peter had transferred some old 8mm footage onto a videotape, which he ran at the brief, jovial send-off after the funeral. In the old reels, Maureen looked charming and funny, with a range of hats and pretty dresses, period pieces in their own right, and in most scenes, she was somewhere quite smart: a private club in Maidenhead, a golf tournament in another redoubt of the home counties, or a big provincial wedding, with a marquee. Under the various hats a ripple of fair hair, a flash of a smile, but the pale blue eyes always a bit elusive. And here she is again at a family event, maybe a christening, with Graham and Colin – Husband One and Husband Two – standing motionless as people did in those days when they realised a movie camera was pointed their way.

Peter gave me a handful of oddments before I left, in a John Lewis bag with white and green stripes, folded over and taped down. There were some photos, he said, and some papers he thought I'd find interesting.

He used Maureen's old formula: 'The photos,' he said, 'have what I call sentimental value.'

31 March 2005

Treason
V.G. Kiernan

I WENT TO Cambridge, to read history, in 1931, and stayed seven
years. My undergraduate time was passed in premises – stair-
case I, no 2 – on the ground floor of the Whewell's Court annexe
of Trinity College. Close by were two incongruous neighbours:
A.E. Housman, anchored by misanthropy to this out-of-the-way
spot, and James Klugmann, the chief Communist student organ-
iser, and later a life-long Party worker. I.2 was not an ideal
residence. When a gust of wind blew, the small fire, over which
toast could be made with the help of a long fork and much
patience, threw out billowing clouds of smoke, enough sometimes
to drive me out into the court gasping for breath. During vaca-
tions mice nibbled at the backs of my books. Most of the thoughts
of years in that cramped room have vanished, as they no doubt
deserved to. Traces of sundry things have survived a half-century,
the best of them books. Early in my second year I was reading
for the first time Boswell's *Hebrides*, a cherished companion ever
since; it was a tea-time luxury, accompanied by one daily cigarette,
a limit I was not wise enough to keep to for long, and I can still
see the electric blue of the October sky as dusk gathered. Later
on I moved to a nobler abode, in Great Court, on the top floor of
a staircase beside the main gate. Here I was surrounded by the
'mighty dead', and could listen on summer nights to the fountain's

murmur, and on spring days walk out, when work stuck fast, and look at the daffodils by the riverside.

In those days the deportment of senior Cambridge was oppressively genteel and ritualistic. Sciences flourished, as some had always done; history was in a stagnant condition, and at Trinity in particular was heavily overlaid by conservatism and clericalism. There was in general a stifling atmosphere of closed windows, drawn blinds, expiring candles, sleepwalking; outside, a mounting tumult of history in the making, instead of history laid to rest in neat graveyard rows of dusty tomes. With amenities such as the Backs, Wordsworth's *Prelude*, and a second-hand bicycle on which to explore the placid countryside, I was reasonably content, attended lectures as by law obliged, and took their stale fare for granted, like the weather. I became a socialist, then a Communist, before graduating to Marxism, the historical materialism that has been my Ariadne's thread ever since. Slow conversion may last longer than sudden enlightenment; and convictions, as Nietzsche said, are the backbone of life.

We had no time then to assimilate Marxist theory more than very roughly; it was only beginning to take root in England, though it had one remarkable expounder at Cambridge in Maurice Dobb, to whom a section is devoted in Professor H.J. Kaye's recent study of British Marxist historians. We felt, all the same, that it could lift us to a plane far above the Cambridge academic level. We were quite right, as the rapid advance of Marxist ideas and influence since then has demonstrated. Our main concerns, however, were practical ones, popularising socialism and the USSR, fraternising with hunger-marchers, denouncing fascism and the National Government, warning of the approach of war. We belonged to the era of the Third International, genuinely international at least in spirit, when the Cause stood high above any national or parochial claims. Some of us have lived to see multinational capitalism, instead of international socialism, in control of most of the world: but at the time we had not the shadow of a doubt that capitalism was nearing its end. It was both too abominable, and too inept and suicidally divided, to last much longer. Socialism would take its place, and mankind be transformed not much less quickly.

At such a time, punctilios of 'loyalty' to things of the dying past seemed as archaic as the minutiae of drawing-room manners. And it was about the defenders of the old order that a strong smell of treason hung. We saw pillars of British society trooping to Nuremberg to hobnob with Nazi gangsters; we saw the 'National' government sabotaging the Spanish Republic's struggle, from class prejudice, and to benefit investors like Rio Tinto, blind to the obvious prospect of the Mediterranean being turned into a fascist lake and the lifelines of empire cut. From Spain the vibrations of civil war spread over Europe. The frenzied enthusiasm of the French Right for Franco was the overture to its eager surrender to Hitler in 1940. Amid that tumult the sense of an absolute divide between 'whatsoever things are good' and everything Tory was easy to acquire, and with some of us has remained unshakable. Our watchword was Voltaire's: *Ecrasez l'infâme.*

Feelings like these were to carry a small number of our generation, from Cambridge and elsewhere, into acts of 'treason', in the lawyer's meaning, not the only or best one. Those acts, amounting in sum to very little, have been sedulously embroidered and exaggerated, and the public has been continually reminded of them. For good measure, politics and sex have been mixed up, as if radicalism went hand in hand with homosexuality. In fact, an innocent could live in left-wing Cambridge without ever suspecting that such a thing existed, outside of Classical literature. The aim of all this pseudo-patriotic hubbub is to distract attention from the distempers of our ancien régime, keep people from thinking about the nuclear war they may well be drifting towards, and make them fancy that without zealous leaders to fend off a legion of spies and subversives, all would be lost. It also helps to nourish the illusion of Britain as a great power, with priceless secrets to be stolen. Writing books about secret-stealers is an easier way than most of earning a living; it benefits from the vogue of spy films and novelettes, symptom of an uneasy society in need of the reassurance of happy endings. 'Truth is sometimes stranger than fiction,' as Mrs Thatcher said when telling the House one of her whoppers. It can certainly be made to look stranger and more fearsome.

Guy Burgess was one of those – James Klugmann and John Cornford were the chief – who helped to induct me into the Party. We belonged to the same college, and hence to the same 'cell'. I remember Burgess as a rather plump, fresh-faced youth, of guileless, almost cherubic expression. I heard him spoken of as the most popular man in the college, but he must have suffered from tensions; he smoked cigarettes all day, and had somehow imbibed a notion that the body expels nicotine very easily. He told me once a story that had evidently made a deep impression on him – of a Hungarian refugee who had been given shelter at his home, a formerly ardent political worker reduced to a wreck by beatings on the soles of the feet. I came on Burgess one day in his room sitting at a small table, a glass of spirits in front of him, glumly trying to put together a talk for a cell meeting that evening; he confessed that when he had to give any sort of formal talk he felt foolish. I never saw him after our exit from Cambridge. He did what he felt it right for him to do; I honour his memory.

Individuals who saw something of the machinations of government from the inside must have seen much to disgust them. If details of whatever secrets they gave away are still being hushed up, it must be because they were secrets discreditable to their superiors. We are always hearing nowadays of 'sensitive papers'. Paper is not sensitive, but those who write on it often have good cause to be, and prefer to blush unread. Anthony Blunt was quoted in his *Times* obituary (28 March 1983) as saying that he acted during the war 'from a conviction that we were not doing enough to help a hard pressed ally'. It is a political if not mathematical certainty that the same men who were adamant against collective security before 1939 were hard at work after 1941 to ensure that the conflict would end with Russia bled nearly to death, as exhausted as Germany. They were treacherously imperilling the whole Allied war effort and the chances of victory. When another Cambridge man, Leo Long, made his public recantation in November 1981, it appeared that what he had taken part in doing was to give Moscow more British information about German troop movements than the British Government chose to give it. Why did he feel obliged to sound so shamefaced? As he said, the information could do no harm to Britain.

If it is the case, as alleged early in 1982, that Maclean was trying at the end to influence Britain away from support of the American intervention in Korea, he was doing something very praiseworthy. Sir John Pratt, dismissed from the Foreign Office for opposing the Korean War, stumped the country, in spite of his age, and denounced it in fiery terms. I was his chairman at a big meeting in Edinburgh when he referred to his campaign as one of invective against the Government: 'invective', he said very truly, belonged to an old, honourable tradition that ought to be revived. It is indeed a mark of political decadence that there has been so little of it against Mrs Thatcher's regime: none since the war has more deserved it.

Treason has never been easy to define precisely, a fact illustrated by the long series of Tudor laws about it. It is an accusation easy to bandy about, but one that can be levelled in different directions. Antony in Shakespeare's play succeeds by his demagogy in turning popular feeling against the conspirators, and sets the crowd shouting: 'They were traitors!' They had plotted against a usurping dictator; Caesar had plotted against the Republic. In recent years Rome has been canonising batches of Catholics whom Queen Elizabeth's judges sentenced as traitors. Two centuries ago British conservatives were abusing Yankee rebels in the same strain. During the French Revolutionary wars Tory Britain had open arms for all French reactionaries who were plotting against their own country, and welcomed them as allies against it. All the modern empires regarded resistance as treasonable, and employed multitudes of native collaborators, who in the eyes of nationalists were betraying their own people, like black policemen in South Africa today. A Russian who abandons his native land and settles in a hostile country is always credited with the most laudable motives, like the archetypal author of I chose freedom.

In 1982 when there were American outcries about information leakage for fifteen years from Cheltenham to the Russians, the Guardian made the comment that this flood appeared to have done no perceptible harm. Life seems to jog along just the same whether the Official Secrets mystification is being eavesdropped or not. Much the same can be said of the whole spy scare, kept going for reasons mostly remote from the ostensible one. Searching for spies and traitors to explain why things are as they are is always a search for excuses. 'We are betrayed by what is false within': not Mrs Thatcher's 'enemy within' – miners, for instance, who object to being thrown out of work and have to be ridden down by police storm-troopers with horse and hound – but the falsity engrained in the entire fabric of capitalist society. The real anti-patriots are those who deepen and worsen it, for their own benefit. They are far more of a danger to Britain than any givers-away or sellers of 'sensitive papers', chiefly concealing no more than official trumpery and balderdash.

Morally, the 'treason' of the Thirties cannot for a moment be compared with the morass of crooked dealing, profit-gorging, deception, looting of national resources and indifference to national welfare, that make up the world of Thatcherism. The latest bright Tory idea is to let agriculture follow industry into decay, and turn loose a barbarous horde of 'developers' over what is left of the countryside. One way or another, the country is being drained of vitality, while constantly assured that all is well, because National Security (or Official Secrecy – to Mrs Thatcher the two terms are synonymous) is being vigilantly preserved, and no soldiers with snow on their boots are marching along Whitehall. So far as our unemployed and old people, at any rate, are concerned, they must be feeling like the famished labourer in the Anti-Corn Law cartoon: 'I be protected, and I be starving.'

Garaudy, the French Marxist and former Communist, wrote of his and my generation, with our eyes on Hitler, Franco, McCarthy: 'We were fighting absolute evil: how, then, could we not feel that our cause was the cause of absolute good?' Painful experience showed that the second of these beliefs was in part illusion. But our ideals and aims were valid, and mean as much now as they did then. If we have not been invariably right, our opponents have been almost infallibly wrong, in anything where public morality or human progress is concerned. After a decade or two of uneasy recovery following the war, economy and society are sinking into another quagmire. None of our fundamental problems have been solved, and on present lines never will be. In Rome, in times of emergency, a 'final decree' of the Senate gave plenary power to the consuls to save the state. In Britain now, a government once elected, even by a minority of the electorate, can feel free to claim plenary power to do whatever it likes, and without telling anyone what it is really doing. It is to Britain's credit that the majority of voters have always been against Thatcherism: but we have been learning that a minority government can do the country immense harm, moral and material, much of it beyond repair. The system of representation that allows this is indefensible, the case for a change has become unanswerable. The alternative is going to be a dictatorship of the rich.

25 June 1987

The Lady in the Van
Alan Bennett

'I RAN INTO a snake this afternoon,' Miss Shepherd said. 'It was coming up Parkway. It was a long, grey snake, a boa constrictor possibly, it looked poisonous. It was keeping close to the wall and seemed to know its way. I've a feeling it may have been heading for the van.' I was relieved that on this occasion she didn't demand that I ring the police, as she regularly did if anything out of the ordinary occurred. Perhaps this was too out of the ordinary (though it turned out the pet shop in Parkway had been broken into the previous night, so she may have seen a snake). She brought her mug over and I made her a drink which she took back to the van. 'I thought I'd better tell you,' she said, 'just to be on the safe side. I've had some close shaves with snakes.'

This encounter with the putative boa constrictor was in the summer of 1971 when Miss Shepherd and her van had for some months been at a permanent halt opposite my house in Camden Town. I had first come across her a few years previously, stood by her van, stalled as usual, near the convent at the top of the street. The convent (which was to have a subsequent career as the Japanese School) was a gaunt reformatory-like building that housed a dwindling garrison of aged nuns and was notable for a striking crucifix attached to the wall overlooking the traffic lights. There was something about the position of Christ, pressing himself against the grim pebbledash beneath the barred windows of the convent, that called up visions of the Stalag and the searchlight and which had caused us to dub him 'The Christ of Colditz'. Miss Shepherd, not looking un-crucified herself, was standing by her vehicle in an attitude with which I was to become very familiar, left arm extended with the palm flat against the side of the van indicating ownership, the right arm summoning anyone who was fool enough to take notice of her, on this occasion me. Nearly six foot, she was a commanding figure and would have been more so had she not been kitted out in greasy raincoat, orange skirt, Ben Hogan golfing cap and carpet slippers. She would be going on sixty at this time.

She must have prevailed on me to push the van as far as Albany Street, though I recall nothing of the exchange. What I do remember was being overtaken by two policemen in a panda car as I trundled the van across Gloucester Bridge; I thought that, as the van was certainly holding up the traffic, they might have lent a hand. They were wiser than I knew. The other feature of this first run-in with Miss Shepherd was her driving technique. Scarcely had I put my shoulder to the back of the van, an old Bedford, than a long arm was stretched elegantly out of the driver's window to indicate in textbook fashion that she (or rather I) was moving off. A few yards further on, as we were about to turn into Albany Street, the arm emerged again, twirling elaborately in the air to indicate that we were branching left, the movement done with such boneless grace that this section of the Highway Code might have been choreographed by Petipa with Ulanova at the wheel. Her 'I am coming to a halt' was less poised, as she had plainly not expected me to give up pushing and shouted angrily back that it was the other end of Albany Street she wanted, a mile further on. But I had had enough by this time and left her there with no thanks for my trouble. Far from it. She even climbed out of the van and came running after me, shouting that I had no business abandoning her, so that passers-by looked at me as if I had done some injury to this pathetic scarecrow. 'Some people!' I suppose I thought, feeling foolish that I'd been taken for a ride (or taken her for one) and cross that I'd fared worse than if I'd never lifted a finger, these mixed feelings to be the invariable aftermath of any transaction involving Miss Shepherd. One seldom was able to do her a good turn without some thoughts of strangulation.

It must have been a year or so after this, and so some time in the late 1960s, that the van first appeared in Gloucester Crescent. In those days the street was still a bit of a mixture. Its large semi-detached villas had originally been built to house the Victorian middle class, then it had gone down in the world, and though it had never entirely decayed, many of the villas degenerated into rooming-houses and so were among the earliest candidates for what is now called 'gentrification', but which was then called 'knocking through'. Young professional couples, many of them in journalism or television, bought up the houses, converted them and (an invariable feature of such conversions) knocked the basement rooms together to form a large kitchen-dining-room. In the mid-1960s I wrote a BBC TV series, *Life in NW1*, based on one such family, the Stringalongs, whom Mark Boxer then took over to people a cartoon strip in the *Listener*, and who kept cropping up in his drawings for the rest of his life. What made the social set-up funny was the disparity between the style in which the new arrivals found themselves able to live and their progressive opinions: guilt, put simply, which today's gentrifiers are said famously not to feel (or 'not to have a problem about'). We did have a problem, though I'm not sure we were any better for it. There was a gap between our social position and our social obligations. It was in this gap that Miss Shepherd (in her van) was able to live.

October 1969
When she is not in the van Miss S. spends much of her day sitting on the pavement in Parkway, where she has a pitch outside Williams

343

and Glyn's Bank. She sells tracts, entitled 'True View: Mattering Things', which she writes herself though this isn't something she will admit. 'I sell them but so far as the authorship is concerned, I'll say they are anonymous and that's as far as I'm prepared to go.' She generally chalks the gist of the current pamphlet on the pavement, though with no attempt at artistry. 'St Francis FLUNG money from him' is today's message and prospective customers have to step over it to get into the bank. She also makes a few coppers selling pencils. 'A gentleman came the other day and said that the pencil he had bought from me was the best pencil on the market at the present time. It lasted him three months. He'll be back for another one shortly.' D., one of the more conventional neighbours (and not a Knocker-Through), stops me and says: 'Tell me, is she a *genuine* eccentric?'

April 1970
Today we moved the old lady's van. An obstruction order had been put under the windscreen wiper, stating that it was stationed outside No 63 and is a danger to public health. This order, Miss S. insists, is a statutory order: 'And statutory means standing, in this case standing outside No 63, so if the van is moved on, the order will be invalid.' Nobody ventures to argue with this but she can't decide whether her next pitch should be outside No 61 or further on. Eventually she decides there is 'a nice space' outside 62 and plumps for that. Nick Tomalin and I heave away at the back of the van but while she is gracefully indicating that she is moving off (for all of the 15 feet) the van doesn't budge. 'Have you let the handbrake off?' Nick Tomalin asks. There is a pause. 'I'm just in the process of taking it off.' As we are poised for the move, another Camden Town eccentric materialises, a tall elderly figure in long overcoat and Homburg hat, with a distinguished grey moustache and in his buttonhole a flag for the Primrose League. He takes off a grubby canary glove and leans a

shaking hand against the rear of the van (OLU 246), and when we have moved it forward the few statutory feet, he puts on his glove again, saying: 'If you should need me I'm just round the corner' (i.e. in Arlington House, the working men's hostel). I ask Miss S. how long she has had the van. 'Since 1965,' she says, 'though don't spread that around. I got it to put my things in. I came down from St Albans in it and plan to go back there eventually. I'm just pedalling water at the moment. I've always been in the transport line. Chiefly delivery and chauffeuring. You know,' she says mysteriously, 'renovated army vehicles. And I've got good topography. I always have had. I knew Kensington in the black-out.'

This van (there were to be three others in the course of the next twenty years) was originally brown but by the time it had reached the Crescent it had been given a coat of yellow. Miss S. was fond of yellow ('It's the papal colour') and was never content to leave her vehicles long in their original trim. Sooner or later she could be seen moving slowly round her immobile home, thoughtfully touching up the rust from a tiny tin of primrose paint, looking in her long dress and sun hat much as Vanessa Bell would have looked had she gone in for painting Bedford vans. Miss S. never appreciated the difference between car enamel and ordinary gloss paint and even this she never bothered to mix. The result was that all her vehicles ended up looking as if they had been given a coat of badly-made custard or plastered with scrambled egg. Still, there were few occasions on which one saw Miss Shepherd genuinely happy and one of them was when she was putting paint on. A few years before she died she went in for a Reliant Robin (to put more of her things in). It was actually yellow to start with, but that didn't save it from an additional coat which she applied as Monet might have done, standing back to judge the effect of each brush-stroke. The Reliant stood outside my gate. It was towed away earlier this year, a scatter of yellow drops on the kerb all that remains to mark its final parking place.

January 1971

Charity in Gloucester Crescent takes refined forms. The publishers next door are bringing out some Classical volume and to celebrate the event last night held a Roman Dinner. This morning the au pair was to be seen knocking at the window of the van with a plate of Roman remains. But Miss S. is never easy to help. After 12 last night I saw her striding up the Crescent waving her stick and telling someone to be off. Then I heard a retreating middle-class voice say plaintively: 'But I only asked if you were all right.'

June 1971

Scarcely a day passes now without some sort of incident involving the old lady. Yesterday evening around ten a sports car swerves over to her side of the road so that the driver, rich, smart and in his twenties, can lean over and bang on the side of the van, presumably to flush out for his grinning girlfriend the old witch who lives there. I shout at him and he sounds his horn and roars off. Miss S. of course wants the police called, but I can't see the point and indeed around five this morning I wake to find two policemen at much the same game, idly shining their torches in the windows in the hope that she'll wake up and enliven a dull hour of their beat. Tonight a white car reverses dramatically up the street, screeches to a halt beside the van and a burly young man jumps out and gives the van a terrific shaking. Assuming (hoping, probably) he would have driven off by the time I get outside, I find he's still there, and ask him what the fuck he thinks he's doing. His response is quite mild. 'What's up with you then?' he asks. 'You still on the telly? You nervous? You're trembling all over.' He then calls me a fucking cunt and drives off. After all that, of course, Miss S. isn't in the van at all, so I end up as usual more furious with her than I am with the lout.

These attacks, I'm sure, disturbed my peace of mind more than they did hers. Living in the way she did every day must have brought

346

such cruelties. Some of the stallholders in the Inverness Street market used to persecute her with medieval relish – and children too, who both inflict and suffer such casual cruelties themselves. One night two drunks systematically smashed all the windows of the van, the flying glass cutting her face. Furious over any small liberty, she was only mildly disturbed by this. 'They may have had too much to drink by mistake,' she says, 'that does occur through not having eaten, possibly. I don't want a case.' She's far more interested in 'a ginger feller I saw in Parkway in company with Mr Khrushchev. Has he disappeared recently?'

But to find such sadism and intolerance so close at hand began actively to depress me and having to be on the alert for every senseless attack made it impossible to work. There came a day when after a long succession of such incidents I suggested that she spend at least the nights in a lean-to at the side of my house. Initially reluctant, as with any change, over the next two years she gradually abandoned the van for the hut.

In giving her sanctuary in my garden and landing myself with a tenancy that went on eventually for fifteen years I was never under any illusion that the impulse was purely charitable. And of course it made me furious that I had been driven to such a pass. But I wanted a quiet life as much as, and possibly more than, she did. In the garden she was at least out of harm's way.

October 1973

I have run a lead out to the lean-to and now regularly have to mend Miss S.'s electric fire which she keeps fusing by plugging too many appliances into the attachment. I sit on the steps fiddling with the fuse while she squats on her haunches in the hut. 'Aren't you cold? You could come in here. I could light a candle and then it would be a bit warmer. The toad's been in once or twice. He was in here with a slug. I think he may be in love with the slug. I tried to turn it out and it got very disturbed. I thought he was going to go for me.' She complains that there is not enough room in the shed and suggests I get her a tent which she could then use to store some of her things. 'It would only be three feet high and by rights ought to be erected in a meadow. Then there are these shatterproof greenhouses. Or something could be done with old raincoats possibly.'

March 1974
The council are introducing parking restrictions in the Crescent. Residents' bays have been provided and yellow lines drawn up the rest of the street. To begin with, the workmen are very understanding, painting the yellow line as far as the van, then beginning again on the other side so that technically it is still legally parked. However, a higher official has now stepped in and served a removal order on it, so all this week there has been a great deal of activity as Miss S. transports cargoes of plastic bags across the road, through the garden and into the hut. While professing faith in divine protection for the van, she is prudently clearing out her belongings against its possible removal. A notice she has written declaring the council's action illegal twirls idly under the windscreen wiper. 'The notice was served on a Sunday. I believe you can serve search warrants on a Sunday but nothing else, possibly. I should have the Freedom of the Land for the good articles I've sold on the economy.' She is particularly concerned about the tyres of the van which 'may be miraculous. They've only been pumped up twice since 1964. If I get another vehicle' – and Lady W. is threatening to buy her one – 'I'd like them transferred.'

The old van was towed away in April 1974 and another one provided by Lady W. ('a titled Catholic lady', as Miss S. always referred to her). Happy to run to a new (albeit old) van, Lady W. was understandably not anxious to have it parked outside her front door and eventually, and perhaps by now inevitably, the van and Miss S. ended up in my garden.

This van was roadworthy and Miss S. insisted on being the one to drive it through the gate into the garden, a manoeuvre which once again enabled her to go through her full repertoire of hand signals. Once the van was on site Miss S. applied the handbrake with such determination that like Excalibur it could never thereafter be released, rusting so firmly into place that when the van came to be moved ten years later it had to be hoisted over the wall by the council crane.

This van (and its successor, bought in 1983) now occupied a paved area between my front door and the garden gate, the bonnet of the van hard by my front step, its rear door, which Miss S. always used to get in and out of, a few feet from the gate. Callers at the house had to squeeze past the back of the van and come down the side and while they waited for my door to be opened they would be scrutinised from behind the murky windscreen by Miss Shepherd. If they were unlucky, they would find the rear door open with Miss S. dangling her large white legs over the back. The interior of the van, a midden of old clothes, plastic bags and half-eaten food, was not easy to ignore but should anyone Miss S. did not know venture to speak to her she would promptly tuck her legs back and wordlessly shut the door. For the first few years of her sojourn in the garden I would try and explain to mystified callers how this situation had arisen, but after a while I ceased to care and when I didn't mention it nor did anyone else.

At night the impression was haunting. I had run a cable out from the house to give her light and heating and through the ragged draperies that hung over the windows of the van a visitor would glimpse Miss S.'s spectral figure, often bent over in prayer or lying on her side like an effigy on a tomb, her face resting on one hand, listening to Radio 4. Did she hear any movement she would straight-away switch off the light and wait like an animal that has been disturbed until she was sure the coast was clear and she could put the light on again. She retired early and would complain if anyone called or left late at night. On one occasion Coral Browne was coming away from the house with her husband, Vincent Price, and they were talking quietly. 'Pipe down,' snapped the voice from the van, 'I'm trying to sleep.' For someone who had brought terror to millions it was an unexpected taste of his own medicine.

December 1974
Miss S. has been explaining to me why the old Bedford (the van not the music hall) ceased to go 'possibly'. She had put in some of her home-made petrol, based on a recipe for petrol substitute she read about several years ago in a newspaper. 'It was a spoonful of petrol, a gallon of water and a pinch of something you could get in every High Street. Well, I got it into my head, I don't know why, that it was bicarbonate of soda, only I think I was mistaken. It must be either sodium chloride or sodium nitrate, only I've since been told sodium chloride is salt and the man in Boots wouldn't sell me the other, saying it might cause explosions. Though I think me being an older person he knew I would be more responsible. Though not all old ladies perhaps.'

February 1975
Miss S. rings and when I open the door she makes a bee-line for the kitchen stairs. 'I'd like to see you. I've called several times. I wonder whether I can use the toilet first.' I say I think this is pushing it a bit. 'I'm not pushing it at all. I just will do the interview better if I can use the toilet first.' Afterwards she sits down in her green mac and purple headscarf, the knuckles of one large mottled hand resting on the clean scrubbed table, and explains how she has devised a method of 'getting on the wireless'. I was to ask the BBC to give me a phone-in programme ('something someone like you could get put on in a jiffy') and then she would ring me up from the house. 'Either that or I could get on *Petticoat Line*. I know a darn sight more on moral matters than most of them. I could sing my song over the telephone. It's a

lovely song, called "The End of the World".' (Which is pure *Beyond the Fringe*.) 'I won't commit myself to singing it, not at this moment, but I probably would. Some sense should be said and knowledge known. It could all be anonymous. I could be called The Lady Behind the Curtain. Or A Woman of Britain. You could take a nom-de-plume view of it.' This idea of The Woman Behind the Curtain has obviously taken her fancy and she begins to expand on it, demonstrating where the curtain could be, her side of it coincidentally taking in the television and the easy chair. She could be behind the curtain, she explains, do her periodic broadcasts and the rest of the time 'be a guest at the television and take in some civilisation. Perhaps there could be gaps filled with nice classical music. I know one: Prelude and "Liebestraum" by Liszt. I believe he was a Catholic priest. It means "love's dream", only not the sexy stuff. It's the love of God and the sanctification of labour and so on, which would recommend it to celibates like you and me, possibly.' Shocked at this tentative bracketing of our conditions, I quickly get rid of her and, though it's a bitter cold night, open the windows wide to get rid of the smell.

The Woman Behind the Curtain remained a favourite project of hers and in 1976 she wrote to Aiman (sic) Andrews: 'Now that This is Your Life is ended, having cost too much etc, I might be able to do a bit as The Lady Behind the Curtain. All you need do is put a curtain up to hide me but permit words of sense to come forth in answer to some questions. Sense is needed.' Hygiene was needed too, but possibly in an effort to persuade me about being behind the curtain she brought the subject up herself: 'I'm by nature a very clean person. I have a testimonial for a Clean Room, awarded me some years ago and my aunt, herself spotless, said I was the cleanest of my mother's children particularly in the unseen places.' I never fathomed her toilet arrangements. She only once asked me to buy her toilet rolls ('I use them to wipe my face'), but whatever happened in that department I took to be part of some complicated arrangement involving the plastic bags she used to hurl from the van every morning. When she could still manage stairs she did very occasionally use my loo but I didn't encourage it; it was here on the threshold of the toilet that my charity stopped short. Once when I was having some building work done (and was, I suppose, conscious of what the workmen were thinking), I very boldly said there was a smell of urine. 'Well, what can you expect when they're raining bricks down on me all day? And then I think there's a mouse. So that would make a cheesy smell, possibly.'

Miss S.'s daily emergence from the van was highly dramatic. Suddenly and without warning the rear door would be flung open to reveal the tattered draperies that masked the terrible interior. There was a pause, then through the veils would be hurled several bulging plastic sacks. Another pause, before slowly and with great caution one sturdy slippered leg came feeling for the floor before the other followed and one had the first sight of the day's wardrobe. Hats were always a feature: a black railwayman's hat with a long neb worn slightly on the skew so that she looked like a drunken signalman or a French guardsman of the 1880s; there was her Charlie Brown pitcher's hat; and in June 1977 an octagonal straw table mat, tied on with a chiffon scarf and a bit of cardboard for the peak. She also went in for green eyeshades. Her skirts had a telescopic appearance as they had often been lengthened many times over by the simple expedient of sewing a strip of extra cloth around the hem, though with no attempt at matching. One skirt was made by sewing several orange dusters together. When she fell foul of authority she put it down to her clothes. Once late at night the police rang me from Tunbridge Wells. They had picked her up on the station, thinking her dress was a nighty. She was indignant. 'Does it look like a nighty? You see lots of people wearing dresses like this. I don't think this style can have got to Tunbridge Wells yet.'

Miss S. seldom wore stockings and alternated between black pumps and brown carpet slippers. Her hands and feet were large and she was what my grandmother would have called 'a big-boned woman'. She was middle-class and spoke in a middle-class way, though her querulous and often resentful demeanour tended to obscure this; it wasn't a gentle or a genteel voice. Running through her vocabulary was a streak of schoolgirl slang. She wouldn't say she was tired, she was 'all done up'; petrol was 'juice' and if she wasn't keen on doing something she'd say 'I'm darned if I will.' All her conversation was impregnated with the vocabulary of her peculiar brand of Catholic fanaticism ('the dire importance of justice deeds'). It was the language of the leaflets she wrote, the 'possibly' with which she ended so many of her sentences an echo of the 'Subject to the Roman Catholic Church in her rights etc' with which she headed every leaflet.

May 1976

I have had some manure delivered for the garden and since the manure heap is not far from the van, Miss S. is concerned that people passing might think the smell is coming from there. She wants me to put a notice on the gate to the effect that the smell is the manure not her. I say no, without adding, as I could, that the manure actually smells much nicer. I am working in the garden when Miss B., the social worker, comes with a boxful of clothes. Miss S. is reluctant to open the van door as she is listening to *Any Answers*, but eventually she slides on her bottom to the door of the van and examines the clothes. She is unimpressed.

Miss S.: I only asked for one coat.
Miss B.: Well, I brought three just in case you wanted a change.
Miss S.: I haven't got room for three. Besides, I was planning to wash this coat in the near future. That makes four.
Miss B.: This is my old nursing mac.
Miss S.: I have a mac. Besides, green doesn't suit me. Have you got the stick?

353

Miss B.: No. That's being sent down. It had to be made specially.
Miss S.: Will it be long enough?
Miss B.: Yes. It's a special stick.
Miss S.: I don't want a special stick. I want an ordinary stick. Only
        longer. Does it have a rubber thing on it?

When Miss B. has gone Miss S. sits at the door of the van slowly turning over the contents of the box like a chimpanzee, sniffing them and holding them up and muttering to herself.

June 1976
I am sitting on the steps mending my bike when Miss S. emerges for her evening stroll. 'I went to Devon on Saturday,' she said. 'On this frisbee.' I suppose she means freebee, a countrywide concession to pensioners that BR ran last weekend. 'Dawlish I went to. People very nice. The man over the loudspeaker called us Ladies and Gentlemen, and so he should. There was one person shouted, only he wasn't one of us, the son of somebody I think.' And almost for the first time ever she smiled, and said how they had all been bunched up trying to get into this one carriage, a great crowd, and how she had been hoisted up. 'It would have made a film,' she said. 'I thought of you.' And she stands there in her grimy raincoat, strands of lank grey hair escaping from under her headscarf. I am thankful people had been nice to her and wonder what the carriage must have been like all that hot afternoon. She then tells me about a programme on Francis Thompson she'd heard on the wireless, how he had tried to become a priest but had felt he had failed in his vocation, and had become a tramp. Then, unusually, she told me a little of her own life, and how she tried to become a nun on two occasions, had undergone instruction as a novice but was forced to give it up on account of ill-health, and that she had felt for many years that she had failed. But that this was wrong, and it was not a

354

failure. 'If I could have had more modern clothes, longer sleep and better air, possibly, I would have made it.'

'A bit of a spree,' she called her trip to Dawlish. 'My spree.'

June 1977

On this the day of the Jubilee Miss S. has stuck a paper Union Jack in the cracked back window of the van. It is the only one in the Crescent. Yesterday she was wearing a headscarf and pinned across the front of it a blue Spontex sponge fastened at each side with a large safety pin, the sponge meant to form some kind of peak against the (very watery) sun. It looked like a favour worn by a medieval knight or a fillet to ward off evil spirits. Still, it's better than last week's effort, an Afrika Korps cap from Lawrence Corner: Miss Shepherd – Desert Fox.

September 1979

Miss S. shows me a photograph she has taken of herself in a cubicle at Waterloo. She is very low in the frame, her mouth pulled down, the photo looking as if it has been taken after death. She is very pleased with it. 'I don't take a good photograph usually. That's the only photograph I've seen looks anything like me.' She wants two copies making of it. I say that it would be easier for her to go back to Waterloo and do two more. No. That would 'take it out of her'. 'I had one taken in France once when I was 21 or 22. Had to go into the next village for it. I came out cross-eyed. I saw someone else's photo on their bus pass and she'd come out looking like a nigger. You don't want to come out like a nigger if you can help it, do you?'

June 1980

Miss S. has gone into her summer rig: a raincoat turned inside out with brown canvas panels and a large label declaring it the Emerald Weatherproof. This is topped off with a lavender chiffon scarf tied round a sun visor made from an old cornflakes packet. She asks me to do her some shopping. 'I want a small packet of Eno's, some milk and some jelly babies. The jelly babies aren't urgent. Oh and Mr Bennett. Could you get me one of those little bottles of whisky. I believe Bell's is very good. I don't drink it. I just use it to rub on.'

August 1980

I am filming and Miss S. sees me leaving early each morning and returning late. Tonight her scrawny hand comes out with a letter marked 'Please consider carefully':

> An easier way for Mr Bennett to earn could be possibly with my co-operative part. Two young men could follow me in a car, one with a camera to get a funny film like 'Old Mother Riley Joins Up' possibly. If the car stalls they could then push it. Or they could go on the buses with her at a distance. Comedy happens without trying sometimes, or at least an interesting film covering a Senior Citizen's use of the buses can occur. One day to Hounslow, another to Reading or Heathrow. The bus people ought to be pleased, but it might need their permission. Then Mr Bennett could put his feet up more and rake it in, possibly.

October 1980

Miss S. has started hankering after a caravan trailer and has just missed one she saw in the *Exchange and Mart*: 'little net curtains all round, three bunks'. 'I wouldn't use them all, except,' she says ominously, 'to put things on. Nice little windows – £275. They said it was sold only they may have thought I was just an old tramp . . . I was thinking of offering to help Mrs Thatcher with the economy. I wouldn't ask any money as I'm on social security, so it would come cheap for her. I might ask her for some perks though. Like a caravan. I would write to her but she's away. I know what's required. It's perfectly simple: justice.'

No political party quite catered to Miss S.'s views, though the National Front came close. She was passionately anti-Communist and as long ago as 1945 had written a letter to Jesus 'concerning the dreadful situation feared from the Yalta agreement'. The trouble was that her political opinions, while never moderate, were always tempered by her idiosyncratic view of the human physiognomy. Older was invariably wiser, which is fair if debatable, except that with Miss S. taller was wiser too. But height had its drawbacks and it was perhaps because she was tall herself that she believed a person's height added to their burdens, put them under some strain. Hence, though she was in sympathy with Mr Heath on everything except the Common Market, 'I do think that Mr Wilson, personally, may have seen better in regard to Europe being on the opposition bench with less salary and being older, smaller and under less strain.' She was vehemently opposed to the Common Market, the 'common' always underlined when she wrote about it on the pavement as if it were the sheer vulgarity of the economic union she particularly objected to. Never very lucid in her leaflets, she got especially confused over the EEC. 'Not long ago a soul wrote, or else was considering writing' – she cannot recall as to which and it may have been something of either – 'that she disassociated from the Common Market entry and the injustices feared concerning it, or something like that.' 'Enoch', as she invariably called Mr Powell, had got it right and she wrote him several letters telling him so, but in the absence of a wholly congenial party she founded her own, the Fidelis Party. 'It will be a party caring for Justice (and as such not needing opposition). Justice in the world today with its gigantic ignorant conduct requires the rule of a Good Dictator, possibly.'

Miss S. never regarded herself as being at the bottom of the social heap. That place was occupied by 'the desperate poor' – i.e those with no roof over their heads. She herself was 'a cut above those in dire need' and one of her responsibilities in society she saw as interceding

357

for them and for those whose plight she thought Mrs Thatcher had overlooked. Could it be brought to her attention (and she wrote Mrs T. several letters on the subject) alleviation would surely follow.

Occasionally she would write letters to other public figures. In August 1978 it was to the College of Cardinals, then busy electing a pope. 'Your Eminences. I would like to suggest humbly that an older pope might be admirable. Height can count towards knowledge too probably.' However this older (and hopefully taller) pope she was recommending might find the ceremony a bit of a trial so, ever the expert on headgear, she suggests that 'at the coronation there could be a not so heavy crown, of light plastic possibly or cardboard for instance.'

February 1981

Miss S. has flu so I am doing her shopping. I wait every morning by the side window of the van and, with the dark interior and her grimy hand holding back the tattered purple curtain, it is as if I am at the Confessional. The chief items this morning were ginger nuts ('very warming') and grape juice. 'I think this is what they must have been drinking at Cana,' she says as I hand her the bottle. 'Jesus wouldn't have wanted them rolling about drunk and this is non-alcoholic. It wouldn't do for everyone but in my opinion it's better than champagne.'

October 1981

The curtain is drawn aside this morning and Miss S. still in what I take to be her nightclothes talks of 'the discernment of spirits' that enabled her to sense an angelic presence near her when she was ill. At an earlier period, when she had her pitch outside the bank, she had sensed a similar angelic presence and now, having seen his campaign leaflet, who should this turn out to be, 'possibly', but Our Conservative Candidate Mr Pasley-Tyler. She embarks on a long disquisition on her well-worn theme of age in politics. Mrs Thatcher is too young and travels too much. Not like President Reagan. 'You wouldn't catch him making all those U-turns round Australia.'

January 1982

'Do you see he's been found, that American soldier?' This is Colonel Dozo, kidnapped by the Red Brigade and found after a shoot-out in a flat in Padua. 'Yes, he's been found,' she says triumphantly, 'and I know who found him.' Thinking it unlikely she has an acquaintance in the Italian version of the SAS, I ask whom she means. 'St Anthony of course. The patron saint of lost things. St Anthony of Padua.' 'Well,' I want to say, 'he didn't have far to look.'

May 1982

As I am leaving for Yorkshire Miss S.'s hand comes out like the Ancient Mariner's: do I know if there are any steps at Leeds Station? 'Why?' I ask warily, thinking she may be having thoughts of camping on my other doorstep. It turns out she just wants somewhere to go for a ride, so I suggest Bristol. 'Yes, I've been to Bristol. On the way back I came through Bath. That looked nice. Some beautifully parked cars.' She then recalls driving her reconditioned Army vehicles and taking them up to Derbyshire. 'I did it in the war,' she says, 'actually I overdid it in the war,' and somehow that is the thin end of the wedge that has landed her up here, yearning for travel on this May morning 40 years later.

'Land' is a word Miss S. prefers to 'country'. 'This land'. Used in this sense, it's part of the rhetoric, if not of madness at any rate of obsession. Jehovah's Witnesses talk of 'this land' and the National Front. Land is country plus destiny, country in the sight of God. Mrs Thatcher talks of 'this land'.

February 1983

A. telephones me in Yorkshire to say that the basement is under three inches of water, the boiler having burst. When told that the basement has been flooded, Miss S.'s only comment is: 'What a waste of water.'

April 1983

'I've been having bad nights,' says Miss S., 'but if I were elected I might have better nights.' She wants me to get her nomination papers so that she can stand for Parliament in the coming election. She would be the Fidelis Party candidate. The party, never very numerous, is now considerably reduced. Once she could count on five votes but now there are only two, one of whom is me, and I don't like to tell her I'm in the SDP. Still, I promise to write to the Town Hall for nomination papers. 'There's no kitty as yet,' she says, 'and I wouldn't want to do any of that meeting people. I'd be no good at that. The secretaries can do that (you get expenses). But I'd be very good at voting, better than they are, probably.'

May 1983

Miss S. asks me to witness her signature on the nomination form. 'I'm signing,' she says: 'Are you witnessing?' She has approached various nuns to be her nominees. 'One sister I know would have signed but I haven't seen her for some years and she's got rather confused in the interim. I don't know what I'll do about leaflets. It would have to be an economy job, I couldn't run to the expense. Maybe I'll just write my manifesto on the pavement, that goes round like wildfire.'

May 1983

Miss S. has received her nomination papers. 'What should I describe myself as?' she asks through the window slit. 'I thought Elderly Spinster possibly. It also says Title. Well my title is' – and she laughs one of her rare laughs – 'Mrs Shepherd. That's what some people call me out of politeness. And I don't deny it. Mother Teresa always says she's married to God. I could say I was married to the Good Shepherd, and that's what it's to do with, Parliament, looking after the flock. When I'm elected, do you think I shall have to live in Downing Street or could I run things from the van?'

I speak to her later in the day and the nomination business is beginning to get her down. 'Do you know anything about the Act of 1974? It refers to disqualifications under it. Anyway, it's all giving me a headache. I think there may be another election soon after this one, so it'll have been good preparation anyway.'

June 1984
Miss S. has been looking in *Exchange and Mart* again and has answered an advert for a white Morris Minor. 'It's the kind of car I'm used to – or I used to be used to. I feel the need to be mobile.' I raise the matter of a licence and insurance, which she always treats as tiresome formalities. 'What you don't understand is that I am insured. I am insured in heaven.' She claims that since she has been insured in heaven there has not been a scratch on the van. I point out that this is less to do with the celestial insurance than with the fact that the van is parked the whole time in my garden. She concedes that when she was on the road the van did used to get the occasional knock. 'Somebody came up behind me once and scratched the van. I wanted him to pay something, half a crown I think it was. He wouldn't.'

October 1984
Some new staircarpet fitted today. Spotting the old carpet being thrown out, Miss S. says it would be just the thing to put on the roof of the van to deaden the sound of rain. This exchange comes just as I am leaving for work, but I say that I do not want the van festooned with bits of old carpet – it looks bad enough as it is. When I come back in the evening I find half the carpet remnants slung over the roof. I ask Miss S. who has put them there as she can't have done it

herself. 'A friend,' she says mysteriously. 'A well-wisher.' Enraged, I pull down a token piece but the majority of it stays put.

April 1985
Miss S. has written to Mrs Thatcher applying for a post in 'the Ministry of Transport advisory, to do with drink and driving and that'. She also shows me the text of a letter she is proposing to send to the Argentinian Embassy on behalf of General Galtieri. 'What he doesn't understand is that Mrs Thatcher isn't the Iron Lady. It's me.'

To Someone in Charge of Argentina. 19 April 1985

Dear Sir,
I am writing to help mercy towards the poor general who led your forces in the war actually as a person of true knowledge more than might be. I was concerned with Justice, Love and, in a manner of speaking, I was in the war, as it were, shaking hands with your then leader, welcoming him in spirit (it may have been to do with love of Catholic education for Malvinas for instance) greatly meaning kindly negotiators etc . . . but I fear that he may have thought it was Mrs Thatcher welcoming him in that way and it may hence have unduly influenced him.

Therefore I beg you to have mercy on him indeed. Let him go, reinstate him, if feasible. You may read publicly this letter if you wish to explain mercy etc.
I remain.

Yours truly

A Member of the Fidelis Party
(Servants of Justice)

P.S. Others may have contributed to undue influence also.

P.P.S. Possibly without realising it.

Translate into Argentinian if you shd wish.

Sometime in 1980 Miss S. acquired a car, but before she'd managed to get more than a jaunt or two in it ('It's a real goer!') it was stolen and later found stripped and abandoned in the basement of the council flats in Maiden Lane. I went to collect what was left ('though the police may require it for evidence, possibly') and found that even in the short time she'd had the Mini she'd managed to stuff it with the usual quota of plastic bags, kitchen rolls and old blankets, all plentifully doused in talcum powder. When she got a Reliant Robin in 1984 it was much the same, a second wardrobe as much as a second car. Miss Shepherd could afford to splash out on these vehicles because being parked in the garden meant that she had a permanent address, and so qualified for full social security and its various allowances. Since her only outgoings were on food, she was able to put by something and had an account in the Halifax and quite a few savings certificates. Indeed I heard people passing say, 'You know she's a millionaire,' the inference being no one in their right mind would let her live there if she weren't.

Her Reliant saw more action than the Mini and she would tootle off in it on a Sunday morning, park on Primrose Hill ('The air is better') and even got as far as Hounslow. More often than not, though, she was happy (and I think she was happy then) just to sit in the Reliant and rev the engine. However, since she generally chose to do this first thing on Sunday morning, it didn't endear her to the neighbours. Besides, what she described as 'a lifetime with motors' had failed to teach her that revving a car does not charge the battery, so that when it regularly ran down I had to take it out and recharge it, knowing full well this would just mean more revving. ('No,' she insisted, 'I may be going to Cornwall next week, possibly.') This recharging of the battery wasn't really the issue: I was just ashamed to be seen delving under the bonnet of such a joke car.

March 1987

The nuns up the road, or as Miss S. always refers to them 'the sisters', have taken to doing some of her shopping. One of them leaves a bag on the back step of the van this morning. There are the inevitable ginger nuts and several packets of sanitary towels. I can see these would be difficult articles for her to ask me to get, though to ask a nun to get them would seem quite hard for her too. They form some part of her elaborate toilet arrangements and are occasionally to be seen laid drying across the soup-encrusted electric ring. As the postman says this morning, 'the smell sometimes knocks you back a bit.'

May 1987

Miss S. wants to spread a blanket over the roof (in addition to the bit of carpet) in order to deaden the sound of the rain. I point out that within a few weeks it will be dank and disgusting. 'No,' she says. 'Weather-beaten.'

She has put a Conservative poster in the side window of the van. The only person who can see it is me.

This morning she was sitting at the open door of the van and as I edge by she chucks out an empty packet of Ariel. The blanket hanging over the pushchair is covered in washing powder. 'Have you spilt it?' I inquire. 'No,' she says crossly, irritated at having to explain the obvious. 'That's washing powder. When it rains the blanket will get washed.' As I work at my table now I can see her bending over the pushchair, picking at bits of soap flakes and redistributing them over the blanket. No rain is at the moment forecast.

June 1987
Miss S. had persuaded the social services to allocate her a wheelchair, though what she'd really set her heart on was the electric version.

Miss S.: That boy over the road has one, why not me?
Me: He can't walk.
Miss S.: How does he know? He hasn't tried.
Me: Miss Shepherd, he has spina bifida.
Miss S.: Well, I was round-shouldered as a child. That may not be serious now but it was quite serious then. I've gone through two wars, an infant in the first and not on full rations, in the ambulances in the second, besides being failed by the ATS. Why should old people be disregarded?

Thwarted in her ambition for a powered chair Miss S. compensated by acquiring (I never found out where from) a second wheelchair ('in case the other conks out, possibly'). The full inventory of her wheeled vehicles now read: one van; one Reliant Robin; two wheelchairs; one folding wheely; one folding (two-seater) wheely. Now and again I would thin out the wheelies by smuggling one onto a skip. She would put down this disappearance to children (never a favourite) and the number would shortly be made up by yet another wheely from Reg's junk stall. Miss S. never mastered the technique of self-propulsion in the wheelchair because she refused to use the inner handwheel ('I can't be doing with all that silliness'). Instead, she preferred to punt herself along with two walking sticks, looking in the process rather like a skier on the flat. Eventually I had to remove the handwheel ('The extra weight affects my health').

July 1987
Miss S. (bright green visor, purple skirt, brown cardigan, turquoise fluorescent ankle socks) punts her way out through the gate in

the wheelchair in a complicated manoeuvre which would be much simplified did she just push the chair out, as well she can. A passer-by takes pity on her and she is whisked down to the market. Except not quite whisked, because the journey is made more difficult than need be by Miss S.'s refusal to take her feet off the ground, so the Good Samaritan finds himself pushing a wheelchair continually slurred and braked by these large trailing carpet-slippered feet. Her legs are so thin now the feet are as slack and flat as those of a camel.

Still, there will be one moment to relish on this, as on all these journeys. When she has been pushed back from the market she will tell (and it is tell, there is never any thanks) whoever is pushing the chair to leave her opposite the gate but on the crown of the road. Then, when she thinks no one is looking, she lifts her feet, pushes herself off and freewheels the few yards down to the gate. The look on her face is one of pure pleasure.

October 1987

I have been filming abroad. 'When you were in Yugoslavia,' asks Miss S., 'did you come across the Virgin Mary?' 'No,' I say, 'I don't think so.' 'Oh, well, she's appearing there. She's been appearing there every day for several years.' It's as if I've missed the major tourist attraction.

January 1988

I ask Miss S. if it was her birthday yesterday. She agrees guardedly. 'So you're 77.' 'Yes. How did you know?' 'I saw it once when you filled out the census form.' I give her a bottle of whisky, explaining that it's just to rub on. 'Oh. Thank you.' Pause. 'Mr Bennett. Don't tell anybody.' 'About the whisky?' 'No. About my birthday.' Pause. 'Mr Bennett.' 'Yes?' 'About the whisky either.'

March 1988

'I've been doing a bit of spring cleaning,' says Miss S., kneeling in front of a Kienholz-like tableau of filth and decay. Says she has been discussing the possibility of a bungalow with the social worker to which she would be prepared to contribute 'a few hundred or so'. It's possible that the bungalow might be made of asbestos, 'but I could wear a mask. I wouldn't mind that and of course it would be much better from the fire point of view.' Hands in mittens made from old socks. A sanitary towel drying over the ring and a glossy leaflet from the Halifax offering 'fabulous investment opportunities'.

April 1988

Miss S. asks me to get Tom M. to take a photograph of her for her new bus pass. 'That would make a comedy, you know. Sitting on a bus and your bus pass out of date. You could make a fortune out of that with very little work involved, possibly. I was a born tragedian,' she says, 'or a comedian possibly. One or the other anyway. But I didn't realise it at the time. Big feet.' She pushes out her red unstockinged ankles. 'Big hands.' The fingers stained brown. 'Tall. People trip over me. That's comedy. I wish they didn't, of course. I'd like it easier but there it is. I'm not suggesting you do it,' she says hastily, feeling perhaps she's come too near self-revelation, 'only it might make people laugh.' All of this is said with a straight face and no hint of a smile, sitting in the wheelchair with her hands pressed between her knees and her baseball cap on.

May 1988

Miss S. sits in her wheelchair in the road, paint pot in hand, dabbing at the bodywork of the Reliant which she will shortly enter, start and rev for a contented half-hour before switching off and paddling down the road in her wheelchair. She has been nattering at Tom M. to mend the clutch, but there are conditions: it mustn't be on Sunday, which is the feast of St Peter and St Paul and a day of obligation. Nor can it be the following Sunday apparently, through the Feast of the Assumption falling on the Monday and being transferred back to the previous day.

Amid all the chaos of her life and now, I think, more or less incontinent she trips with fanatical precision through this liturgical minefield.

September 1988

Miss S. has started thinking about a flat again, though not the one the council offered her a few years ago. This time she has her eye on something much closer to home. My home. We had been talking in the hall and I left her sitting on the step while I came back to work. This is often what happens, me sitting at my table, wanting to get on, Miss S. sitting outside rambling. This time she goes on talking about the flat, soliloquising almost, but knowing that I can hear: 'It need only be a little flat, even a room possibly. Of course, I can't manage stairs, so it would have to be on the ground floor. Though I'd pay to have a lift put in.' (Louder.) 'And the lift wouldn't be wasted. They'd have it for their old age. And they'll have to be thinking about their old age quite soon.' The tone of it is somehow familiar from years ago. Then I realise it's like one of the meant-to-be-overheard soliloquies of Richmal Crompton's William.

Her outfit this morning: orange skirt, made out of three or four large dusters; a striped blue satin jacket; a green headscarf, blue eyeshield topped off by a khaki peaked cap with a skull-and-crossbones badge and Rambo across the peak.

February 1989

Miss S.'s religion is an odd mixture of traditional faith and a belief in the power of positive thinking. This morning, as ever, the Reliant battery is running low and she asks me to fix it. The usual argument takes place:

Me: Well, of course it's run down. It will run down unless you run the car. Revving up doesn't charge it. The wheels have to go round.

Miss S.: Stop talking like that. This car is not the same. There are miracles. There is faith. Negative thoughts don't help. (*She presses the starter again and it coughs weakly.*) There, you see. The devil's heard you. You shouldn't say negative things.

The interior of the van now indescribable.

March 1989

Miss S. sits in the wheelchair trying to open the neck of the gate with her walking stick. She tries it with one end, then reverses the stick and tries with the other. Sitting at my table, trying to work, I watch her idly, much as one would watch an ant trying to get round some obstacle. Now she bangs on the gate to attract the attention of a passer-by. Now she is wailing. Banging and wailing. I go out. She stops wailing, and explains she has her washing to do. As I manoeuvre her through the gate, I ask her if she's fit to go. Yes, only she will need help. I explain that I can't push her there. (Why can't I?) No, she doesn't want that. Would I just push her as far as the corner? I do so. Would I just push her a bit further? I explain that I can't take her to the launderette. (And anyway there is no launderette any more so which launderette is she going to?) Eventually feeling like Fletcher Christian (only not Christian) abandoning Captain Bligh, I leave her in the wheelchair outside Mary H.'s. Someone will come along. I would be more ashamed if I did not feel, even when she is poorly, that she knows exactly what's she's about.

March 1989

There is a thin layer of talcum powder around the back door of the van and odd bits of screwed-up tissues smeared with what may or may not be shit, though there is no doubt about the main item of litter which is a stained incontinence pad. My method of retrieving these items would not be unfamiliar at Sellafield. I don rubber gloves, put each hand inside a plastic bag as an additional protection, then, having swept the faecal artefacts together, gingerly pick them up and put them in the bin. 'Those aren't all my rubbish,' comes a voice from the van. 'Some of them blow in under the gate.'

April 1989

Miss S. has asked me to telephone the social services and I tell her that a social worker will be calling. 'What time?' 'I don't know. But you're not going to be out. You haven't been out for a week.' 'I might be. Miracles do happen. Besides, she may not be able to talk to me. I may not be at the door end of the van. I might be at the other end.' 'So she can talk to you there.' 'And what if I'm in the middle?'

Miss C. thinks her heart is failing. She calls her Mary. I find this strange, though it is of course her name.

April 1989

A staple of Miss S.'s shopping list these days is sherbet lemons. I have a stock of them in the house but she insists I invest in yet more so that a perpetual supply of sherbet lemons may never be in doubt. 'I'm on them now. I don't want to have to go off them.' I ask her if she would like a cup of coffee.

'Well, I wouldn't want you to go to all that trouble. I'll just have half a cup.'

Towards the end of her life Miss S. was befriended by an ex-nurse who lived locally. She put me in touch with a day centre who agreed to take Miss Shepherd in, give her a bath and a medical examination

and even a bed in a single room where she could stay if she wanted:
In retrospect I see I should have done something on the same lines
years before, except that it was only when age and illness had weak-
ened Miss Shepherd that she would accept such help. Even now it
was not easy.

27 April 1989
A red ambulance calls to take Miss S. to the day centre. Miss B.
talks to her for a while in the van, gradually coaxing her out and
into the wheelchair, shit streaks over her swollen feet, a piece of
toilet roll clinging to one scaly ankle. 'And if I don't like it,' she
keeps asking, 'can I come back?' I reassure her, but looking at the
inside of the van and trying to cope with the stench, I find it hard
to see how she can go on living here much longer. Once she sees
the room they are offering her, the bath, the clean sheets, I can't
imagine her wanting to come back. And indeed she makes more
fuss than usual about locking the van door, which suggests she
accepts that she may not be returning. I note how, with none of my
distaste, the ambulance driver bends over her as he puts her on the
hoist, his careful rearrangement of her greasy clothing, pulling her
skirt down over her knees in the interest of modesty. The chair goes
on the hoist and slowly she rises and comes into view above the
level of the garden wall and is wheeled into the ambulance. There
is a certain distinction about her as she leaves, a Dorothy Hodgkin
of vagabonds, a derelict Nobel Prize-winner, the heavy folds of her
grimy face set in a kind of resigned satisfaction. She may even be
enjoying herself.

When she has gone I walk round the van noting the occasions
of our old battles – the carpet tiles she managed to smuggle onto
the roof, the blanket strapped on to muffle the sound of the rain, the
black bags under the van stuffed with her old clothes – sites of skir-
mishes all of which I'd lost. Now I imagine her bathed and bandaged

and cleanly clothed and starting a new life. I even see myself visiting and taking flowers.

This fantasy rapidly fades when around 2.30 Miss S. reappears, washed and in clean clothes, it's true, and with a long pair of white hospital socks over her shrunken legs, but obviously very pleased to be back. She has a telephone number where her new friends can be contacted and she gives it to me. 'They can be reached,' she says, 'any time, even over the holiday. They're on a long-distance bleep.'

As I am leaving for the theatre, she bangs on the door of the van with her stick. I open the door. She is lying wrapped in clean white sheets on a quilt laid over all the accumulated filth and rubbish of the van. She is still worrying that I will have her taken to hospital. I tell her there's no question of it and that she can stay as long as she wants. I close the door, but there is another bang and I reassure her again. Once more I close the door but she bangs again. 'Mr Bennett.' I have to strain to hear. 'I'm sorry the van's in such a state. I haven't been able to do any spring cleaning.'

28 April 1989

I am working at my table when I see Miss B. arrive with a pile of clean clothes for Miss Shepherd which must have been washed for her at the day centre yesterday. Miss B. knocks at the door of the van, then opens it, looks inside and – something nobody has ever done before – gets in. It's only a moment before she comes out and I know what has happened before she rings the bell. We go back to the van where Miss Shepherd is dead, lying on her left side, flesh cold, face gaunt, the neck stretched out as if for the block and a bee buzzing round her body.

It is a beautiful day with the garden glittering in the sunshine, strong shadows by the nettles and bluebells out under the wall, and I remember how in her occasional moments of contemplation she would sit in the wheelchair and gaze at the garden. I am filled with remorse for my harsh conduct towards her, though I know at the same time that it was not harsh. But still I never quite believed or chose to believe she was as ill as she was and I regret too all the questions I never asked her. Not that she would have answered them. I have a strong impulse to stand at the gate and tell anyone who passes.

Miss B. meanwhile goes off and returns with a nice doctor from St Pancras who seems scarcely out of her teens. She gets into the van, takes the pulse in Miss S.'s outstretched neck, checks her with a stethoscope and, to save an autopsy, certifies death as from heart failure. Then comes the priest to bless her before she is taken to the funeral parlour and he, too, gets into the van, the third person to do so this morning and all of them without distaste or ado in what to me seem three small acts of heroism. Stooping over the body, his bright white hair brushing the top of the van, the priest murmurs an inaudible prayer and makes a cross on Miss S.'s hands and head. Then they all go off and I come inside to wait for the undertakers.

I have been sitting at my table for ten minutes before I realise that the undertakers have been here all the time, and that death nowadays comes (or goes) in a grey Ford transit van that is standing outside the gate. There are three undertakers, two young and burly, the third older and more experienced, a sergeant as it were and two corporals. They bring out a rough grey-painted coffin, like a prop a conjuror might use, and making no comment on the surely extraordinary circumstances in which they find it, put a sheet of white plastic bin-liner over the body and manhandle it into their magic box, where it falls with a bit of a thud. Across the road, office workers stroll down from the Piano Factory for their lunch, but nobody stops or even looks much, and the Asian woman who has to wait while the box is carried over the pavement and put in the (other) van doesn't give it a backward glance.

Later I go round to the undertakers to arrange the funeral, and the manager apologises for their response when I had originally phoned. A woman had answered, saying: 'What exactly is it you want?' Not thinking callers rang undertakers with a great variety of requests, I was nonplussed. Then she said briskly: 'Do you want someone taking away?' The undertaker explains that her seemingly unhelpful manner was because she thought my call wasn't genuine. 'We get so many hoaxes these days. I've often gone to collect a corpse only to have it open the door.'

9 May 1989

Miss Shepherd's funeral is at our Lady of Hal, the Catholic church round the corner. The service has been slotted into the ten o'clock Mass so that, in addition to a contingent of neighbours, the congregation includes what I take to be regulars: the fat little man in thick glasses and trainers who hobbles along to the church every day from Arlington House; several nuns, among them the 99-year-old sister who was in charge when Miss S. was briefly a novice; a woman in a green straw hat like an upturned plant pot who eats toffees throughout; and another lady who plays the harmonium in tan slacks and a tea-cosy wig. The server, a middle-aged man with white hair, doesn't wear a surplice, just ordinary clothes with an open-necked shirt, and but for knowing all the sacred drill, might have been roped in from the group on the corner outside The Good Mixer. The priest is a young Irish boy with a big red peasant face and sandy hair and he, too, stripped of his cream-coloured cassock, could be wielding a pneumatic drill in the roadworks outside. I keep thinking about these characters during the terrible service and it reinforces what I have always known: that I could never be a Catholic because I'm such a snob and that the biggest sacrifice Newman made when he turned his back on the C of E was the social one.

Yet kindness abounds. In front of us is a thin old man who knows the service backwards, and seeing we have no prayer-books, he lays down his own on top of his copy of the *Sun*, goes back up the aisle to fetch us some and hands them round, all the time saying the responses without faltering. The first hymn is Newman's 'Lead Kindly Light' which I try and sing, while making no attempt at the second hymn, which is 'Kum Ba Ya'. The priest turns out to have a good strong voice, though its tone is more suited to 'Kum Ba Ya' than Newman and J.B. Dykes. The service itself is wet and wandering, even more so than the current Anglican equivalent, though occasionally one catches in the watered-down language a distant echo of 1662. Now, though, arrives the bit I dread, the celebration of fellowship, which always reminded me of the warm-up Ned Sherrin insisted on inflicting on the studio audience before *Not So Much a Programme*, when everyone had to shake hands with their neighbour. But again the nice man who fetched us the prayer-books shames me when he turns round without any fuss or embarrassment and smilingly shakes my hand. Then it is the Mass proper, the priest distributing the wafers to the 99-year-old nun and the lady with the plant pot on her head, as Miss S. lies in her coffin at his elbow. Finally there is another hymn, this one by the (to me) unknown hymnodist Kevin Norton, who's obviously reworked it from his unsuccessful entry for the Eurovision Song Contest; and with the young priest acting as lead singer and the congregation a rather subdued backing group, Miss Shepherd is carried out.

The neighbours, who are not quite mourners, wait on the pavement outside as the coffin is hoisted onto the hearse. 'A cut above her previous vehicle,' remarks Colin H.; and comedy persists when the car accompanying the hearse to the cemetery refuses to start. It's a familiar scene and one which I've played many times, with Miss S. waiting inside her vehicle as well-wishers lift the bonnet, fetch leads and give it a jump start. Except this time she's dead.

Only A. and I and Clare, the ex-nurse who lately befriended Miss S., accompany the body, swept over Hampstead Heath at a less than funereal pace, down Bishop's Avenue and up to the St Pancras Cemetery, green and lush this warm sunny day. We drive beyond the scattered woods to the furthest edge where stand long lines of new gravestones, mostly in black polished granite. Appropriately, in view of her lifelong love of the car, Miss S. is being buried within sight and sound of the North Circular Road, one carriageway the other side of the hedge with juggernauts drowning the words of the priest as he commits the body to the earth. He gives us each a go with his little plastic bottle of holy water, we throw some soil into the grave, and then everybody leaves me to whatever solitary thoughts I might have, which are not many, before we are driven back to Camden Town, life reasserted when the undertaker drops us handily outside Sainsbury's.

In the interval between Miss Shepherd's death and her funeral ten days later I found out more about her life than I had in twenty years. She had indeed driven ambulances during the war and was either blown up or narrowly escaped death when a bomb exploded nearby. I'm not sure that her eccentricity can be put down to this any more than to the legend, mentioned by one of the nuns, that it was the death of her fiancé in this incident that 'tipped her over'. It would be comforting to think that it is love, or the death of it, that unbalances the mind, but I think her early attempts to become a nun and her repeated failures ('too argumentative,' one of the sisters said) point to a personality that must already have been quite awkward when she was a girl. After the war she spent some time in mental hospitals but regularly absconded, finally remaining at large long enough to establish her competence to live unsupervised.

The turning-point in her life came when through no fault of hers a motorcyclist crashed into the side of her van. If her other vans were any guide, this one too would only have been insured in heaven so it's not surprising she left the scene of the accident ('skedaddled', she would have said) without giving her name or address. The motorcyclist subsequently died so that, while blameless in the accident, by leaving the scene of it she had committed a criminal offence. The police mounted a search for her. Having already changed her first name when she became a novice, now under very different circumstances she changed her second and, calling herself Shepherd, made her way back to Camden Town and the vicinity of the convent where she had taken her vows. And though in the years to come she had little to do with the nuns or they with her, she was never to stray far from the convent for the rest of her life.

All this I learned in the ten days between her death and her funeral. It was as if she had been a character in Dickens whose history has to be revealed and her secrets told in the general setting-to-rights before the happy ever after, though all that this amounted to was that at long last I could bring my car into the garden to stand now where the van stood all those years.

26 October 1989

Closing It Down on the Palisades
August Kleinzahler

1: September

Kettles, rain hats –
the small, unopened bottle of Angostura bitters,
its label stained and faded with the years.

The breeze is doing something in the leaves
it hasn't been,
not at this hour.
The light, as well.

Early yet for the cicadas,
their gathering rush and ebb.
Too cool,
the sun not high enough.

A cardinal darting among the shadows
in back of the yard,
only at this hour
and again at dusk.

What is it so touching
about these tiny episodes of colour
amidst the greenery and shadows,
now and at day's end,

that puts to rout all other sentiment?

2: October

The garbage truck compactor is grinding
all 24 volumes of the Encyclopaedia Britannica,
1945 edition, including Index and Atlas,
along with apple skins, bed linen, ashtrays
and all that remains of an ailing begonia.

It is raining, not yet light. The wrens
will have put off their convening on the hemlock.
The distant beach homes of Malibu
come strangely to mind, high on the cliffs
overlooking the Pacific,

and how, now and then, after a terrible storm,
the soil beneath washes away, followed
not long after by the house itself, sliding
then crashing to the rocks below, its side tables,
vanities and clocks licked at

by the gathering foam and, finally, pulled to sea.
Every Saturday they awaken me before dawn,
lights flashing, men shouting, the hydraulic whine
of the compactor as it gnashes away:
desk drawers, yearbooks, sugar bowls.

I shall miss them. I shall miss
the sound of passenger jets overhead
making their descent into Newark in rain,
before dawn, the first arrivals of the day,
with groggy visitors from Frankfurt, Bahrain.

There is hardly anything left to take –
lamps, a chair, bedspring and mattress.
The last roses still abloom out in the yard,
I can't tell you what kind, pink and white,
the tallest of them six, seven feet high.

Then, that'll be it till spring.
That'll be it till spring.

25 February 2010

Scatter My Ashes

Jenny Diski

F OR SOME TIME NOW, it's been clear to me that consciousness
of death is a kindness bestowed on us by the Great Intelligence,
so that even if all else succeeded we would always have some-
thing to worry about. This, of course, accounts for pussy cats and
lions sleeping 18 hours a day and therefore failing to invent the fax
machine. Us humans, up and anxious about death, have passed the
time thinking up civilisation as a way to distract ourselves, or at least
to let others know that we're awake, too. Unfortunately, the fax
machine having already been invented, I had to settle simply for
being up and anxious all Bank Holiday weekend, brooding darkly
and leafing restlessly through the Gazetteer of London Cemeteries.*

It began when my friend Jenny (not me in my Post-Modern mode,
but someone else entirely) made me the offer of a lifetime. She'd
bought a plot in Highgate Cemetery, she told me, which was a mere
snip at £700, especially since it accommodated three ex-people. Would
I care to share it with her? Not immediately, of course, but when the
time came. Highgate Cemetery is a very nice place, and Jenny is an
old and dear friend. I was properly honoured; no one else I've known
has ever wanted to spend eternity with me – as a rule the occasional
supper is sufficient – and I wished to express my gratitude. But at the

---

* *London Cemeteries: An Illustrated Guide and Gazetteer* by Hugh Meller (Scolar, third
edition, 352pp., £19.95, 10 March 1994, 0859679977)

same time my heart rate began to speed, and my throat to constrict: classic signs of claustrophobia and panic. I've never been any good at long-term commitment.

'Are you sure?' I asked. 'It's a bit perpetual. What about your children?'

'They can make their own arrangements,' she said darkly.

Jenny is known for going off people – even people who are not her children. She keeps a bottle of Tippex beside her address book to deal with those she's no longer on speaking terms with. I felt that apart from my reservations about making a long-term commitment, we ought to be realistic about the eternal prospects of our friendship.

'I know we get on well, but we have to think practically. Forever's, well, a very long time to be side by side.'

'Actually, one on top of the other. It's a vertical plot.'

There was a lot to think about here. Assuming that things went according to the Great Chronologist's plan, Jenny-who-isn't-me would be tucked in first, since she's twenty years older. On the other hand, I smoke several packs a day and eat salami like sweeties. There was, therefore, no guarantee that I'd get top bunk.

While I was wondering if this mattered, the Heir Apparent shuffled into the room and announced that she had something to say about all this, since, after all, she'd be in charge of arrangements. We'd already had a prior conversation about the disposal of my remains because she's a sensible girl and doesn't like to leave things to the last minute. I'd suggested cremation (so they could play 'Smoke Gets In Your Eyes' while the casket slid behind the modesty curtain) and that my ashes should be scattered over the threshold of the Hampstead branch of Nicole Farhi.

The only other really appealing possibility was a monomaniacal plan of the Victorian architect, Thomas Willson, who in 1842 designed a brick and granite sepulchral pyramid with a base area the size of Russell Square to be built on Primrose Hill. Its 94 levels (topped by an observatory) would be 'sufficiently capacious to receive five millions of the dead, where they may repose in perfect security'. The scheme foundered, but if anyone feels like reviving it, I'd be happy to make a contribution in return for a guaranteed place somewhere near the pinnacle. Failing that, I thought I would after all settle for the shared accommodation on offer in Highgate Cemetery.

'God, you're always changing your mind,' the Heir Apparent said impatiently. 'If you're buried you'll have to have a headstone. That's more of my inheritance gone, and what's it going to say on it?'

'*Jenny Diski lies here. But tells the truth over there*,' I instructed. 'Also, I'd like a dove, a winged angel, an anchor and an open book, properly carved on a nice piece of granite.'

The Heir's eyes narrowed dangerously.

'You get in for nothing if you've got a relative on site. Otherwise it's a pound a head. So there's a saving,' the other Jenny reassured her. 'And there's much more scope for drama in a proper burial. At the last funeral I went to, the grieving mistress tried to throw herself into the grave. Very satisfactory, and not a thing you can do at a cremation without making a nasty stink.'

It looked like it was decided. I wasn't to go up in smoke, but would instead fatten the worms which feed the birds which keep the London cats sleek, self-satisfied and asleep for 18 hours a day. While the other Jenny went off to spend the holiday weekend in Bradford (which gave more pause for thought about spending eternity in such eccentric company), I hunkered down with my Gazetteer to apprise myself of the interment possibilities.

It was not so much the fact of death as the quantity of it that struck me. In 1906 the Angel of Death dropped in on houses in London at the rate of once every six minutes. Oddly, London's population has returned to roughly what it was at the beginning of the century, though I suppose that the death rate (Bottomley notwithstanding) must have fallen. I added to my collection of useless but disturbing thoughts the fact that currently the total land used for burial in London is three thousand acres. Anyone with GCSE maths (3000 acres ÷ six-foot plot × three bodies deep) could work out how many dead are lying around London. I don't have GCSE maths, so I didn't try, but, according to the Gazetteer, Highgate has 51,000 plots containing 166,000 bodies. Do the rest of the arithmetic for yourselves. And if you're very keen, how many people in total have died since Homo got to its feet? More than everyone alive today? I only wonder because I like large numbers.

I was troubled by the idea of so many people dying as we wake and sleep and go about our business. It's an astonishing feat of human lack of imagination to be able to ignore all those souls up and down our streets, fluttering off minute by minute, all around us. I remembered an incident in the early Seventies (when else) during a community festival in Camden Square's central patch of railed-off greenery. Perhaps it was midsummer, or Easter, or maybe it was just one of those pseudo-spontaneous street parties that were supposed to weld us all together, before we knew the Eighties were coming. Anyway, we had a great bonfire, a lamb roasting on a spit, rock 'n' roll megawatting through monster speakers and the decidedly mixed inhabitants of the square – the teenage villains, prepubescent truants and lawless toddlers of our Free School plus the recent incoming gentry whose houses they regularly broke into. The robbers and the robbed mingled riotously to celebrate the spirit of their community.

Suddenly, someone was standing out on the street, shouting through the railings. 'There's a woman dying at number 65!' he bellowed at us revellers over and over again, and finally made himself heard. 'Hasn't she got the right to die in peace?'

There was a bit of a lull, long enough for any-man's-death-diminishes-me sort of thoughts to start rolling around in my head, before a bearded and bejeaned community hero spoke up for the collective will. He was sorry about the woman, he told her son or husband or friend, but there were a couple of hundred people out here, also belonging to this square, and we were celebrating life. Man! The very shade of Jeremy Bentham hovered over Camden Square for a second, and then a roar of affirmation went up. The Utilitarians won the day, The Stones were turned up again to ear-splitting level, and John Donne slunk back with the soon-to-be-bereaved protester to get on with private dying behind closed doors. Logical, of course, but for all that, the lamb tasted raw and rotten to me.

It's possible I take death too seriously. It's always seemed a momentous business, coming, as it generally does, after a lifetime's consideration, unlike, for example, birth, which happens (to the new-born, if not the parents) before one has a chance to consider it, so far as I can tell. For a long time I supposed it only happened to very serious and substantial people, but then my father died when I was 17 and I was amazed to discover that something as weighty as death could be done by someone so dedicated to evading life's trickier realities. I confess I was, and still am, impressed that he could have done something so committed as to die.

The Gazetteer, however, kept all such metaphysical thoughts up in the air where they belong, and my feet on the ground. It quotes from the *Builder* in 1879: 'The principles of proportion and of harmony of grace and form which are required by a well-dressed woman in her costume are equally applicable when she comes to choose a tombstone for her husband.' Though not as much fun, I should think, as burying a husband, thoughts about one's own tomb are just as sartorial. What if Armani and Calvin Klein diversified into the undertaking and stone-dressing business? I could fancy an eternity of decomposition under a layered beige, beautifully cut headstone. But could my cheapskate descendant be trusted not to shop around and dump me in the Monsoon cemetery for dead hippies?

Planning the style of one's burial is also a rather cunning way to avoid thinking about its prerequisite, I discovered. The Gazetteer has no mention of people dying or the manner of their death, and in an investigative wander around West Hampstead Cemetery (I thought I'd better wait for Jenny's return from sunny Bradford before visiting my prospective plot) there were very few indications of how the interred got there. I suppose it doesn't matter unless something extra special carried them off. I'm rather partial to the idea of being *translated*, myself, but mostly the dear departed, sorely missed, tended to fall asleep or pass away.

Except for Tony. *Tony* was carved in six-inch lettering on a slab of black marble and under it was inscribed: *I Had a Lover's Quarrel with the World 1947–1987*. I was moved. Forty-year-old Tony. One of my lot. Postwar Tony, agitated by peace and prosperity, his youth a haze of misremembered sex and drugs and rock and roll, as overfull of romantic aspirations as he was of existential despair, threw in his towel after doing the best he could to compose a resonant if pretty yukky farewell to life. Sadly, when I got home, I found it was a quote from Robert Frost. Even so, Tony didn't just pass away and wanted to be remembered for not doing so. Perhaps he died of disappointment at not even being able to think up an epitaph of his own. Mostly, disappointment of one kind or another is what my generation died young of. If it's any consolation to them, those of us who remain find ourselves with the practicalities of not having died young to attend to.

There is, apparently, a cemetery in Buenos Aires which is a veritable city of the dead, with named avenues lined with scaled-down architected homes for the late-lamented. Relatives come and housekeep on Sundays, dusting, polishing and replacing lace doilies while chatting to neighbouring survivors over the fence. This set me brooding about my one-up-one-down resting place in Highgate. What about a mausoleum, I began to wonder. It could be fitted with a wood-burning stove and comfy chairs. I'd leave funds so that a bottle of Scotch and packs of cards would be available in perpetuity, so friends and well-wishers could drop by on gloomy Sundays for a game of poker. The Heir Apparent was not keen on this idea. Quite apart from the drain on her inheritance ('To hell with the expense,' I cried. 'You're so selfish,' she hissed), there was the matter of the earth's resources to consider. She pointed severely to an article on natural death.

'There is some other kind?' I queried.

It turns out there's no legal reason not to bury your dead in the back garden. I was delighted.

'Darling, you can have me around always. Sod Highgate. You can just dig me a nice big hole and pop me under the yucca.'

She explained this wasn't a good idea because it would very likely lower the value of the house when she came to sell it, and she certainly wasn't going to dig me up and take me with her every time she moved.

I called the Natural Death Centre and a Mr Albery explained that their idea is to use European Union set-aside land to inter bodies and create lovely nature reserves full of you and me, while the farmers get paid for not growing anything useful on it. Instead of gravestones, they'll have trees. I could have a plaque if I wanted it, though he didn't sound enthusiastic. No need for embalming. All those chemicals are just to stop what's going to happen anyway from happening for a while. It seems it's perfectly all right to keep an unembalmed body at home for up to three days, and frankly who wants one around longer? And forget about coffins. Mr Albery advises the use of a simple sheet. By now the Heir was smiling broadly; it was all beginning to look like a pretty thrifty exercise.

However, it turned out that for £85 a specially woven natural woollen shroud can be purchased, which has a plank along the middle (to stop that nasty wobbling corpse effect) and four ropes at each corner for lowering it into the grave. A bargain, I thought, though the Heir muttered that one of our old sheets would do perfectly well. Still, I have a terrible dislike of the cold, especially when it gets into the bones. There was something comforting about the prospect of a woollen shroud, and I think she would have relented if just then I hadn't remembered that I have no desire in this life or after it to conserve resources, that I am and always have been an urban dweller and I didn't see why a detail like death should mean I have to end up in some draughty, disorganised, naturally set-aside bit of rustic. What I fancied was a proper old-fashioned pollution-filled London cemetery to rest my wearied bones, and if I couldn't have it, along with an expensively carved headstone and a very long and elaborate funeral, with hymns and popular hits of the Sixties sung, a certain amount of dancing, and my deeds recounted for the edification of all, then the Heir could whistle for her inheritance and I'd leave everything to the Natural Death Centre including my clothes. That did it. A proper interment at Highgate is assured.

23 June 1994

Contributors

Tariq Ali, novelist and historian, is a long-standing editor at *New Left Review*.

Julian Barnes has published eleven novels including *The Sense of an Ending*, which won the Booker Prize in 2011.

Alan Bennett is the author of *Writing Home*, *Forty Years On*, *The Madness of King George*, and much besides.

Terry Castle teaches at Stanford. Her books include *The Female Thermometer: Eighteenth-Century Culture and the Invention of the Uncanny* and *Boss Ladies, Watch Out: Essays on Women, Sex and Writing*.

Jenny Diski is the author of ten novels and two works of non-fiction, *Skating to Antarctica* and *What I Don't Know About Animals*.

Anne Enright's novels include *The Gathering*, which won the Booker Prize in 2007.

Sheila Fitzpatrick is a historian of the Soviet Union and the author of two books of memoir: *My Father's Daughter* and *A Spy in the Archives*.

Wynne Godley was director of the Department of Applied Economics at Cambridge and a fellow of King's College.

Jeremy Harding is a contributing editor at the LRB. His memoir, *Mother Country*, was published in 2006.

Tony Harrison's *Collected Poems* came out in 2007.

R.W. Johnson, an emeritus fellow of Magdalen College, Oxford, walks without crutches on a computerised prosthesis.

John Henry Jones edited William Empson's posthumous *Faustus and the Censor*.

Joe Kenyon was born in 1915 and started work in the mines as a teenager.

Frank Kermode was Lord Northcliffe Professor of Modern English Literature at University College London and King Edward VII Professor of English Literature at Cambridge. His books include *Romantic Image*, *The Sense of an Ending* and *Shakespeare's Language*. He wrote more than two hundred pieces for the LRB.

V.G. Kiernan, a professor of history at Edinburgh, was the author of nearly twenty books – among them, *The Duel in European History*, *The Lords of Human Kind* and *Colonial Empires and Armies 1815–1960*.

August Kleinzahler has published numerous books of poetry and two volumes of prose, *Cutty, One Rock: Low Characters and Strange Places, Gently Explained* and *Music: I–LXIV*. He lives in San Francisco.

Hilary Mantel won her first Booker Prize for *Wolf Hall* in 2009 and her second for *Bring Up the Bodies* in 2012.

Paul Myerscough is an editor at the LRB.

Andrew O'Hagan has published four novels; *The Illuminations* will come out in 2014. He is also the author of *The Missing*, a work of non-fiction, and *The Atlantic Ocean*, a collection of essays.

Denise Riley's *Selected Poems* was published in 2000.

Lorna Sage taught English at the University of East Anglia. The week before she died, her memoir, *Bad Blood*, won the Whitbread Biography Award.

Edward Said, University Professor of English and Comparative Literature at Columbia University, was the author of *Orientalism* and *Culture and Imperialism*.

Christopher Tayler is a contributing editor at the LRB.

A.J.P. Taylor, a fellow of Magdalen College, Oxford, was the author of *The Struggle for Mastery in Europe*, among other celebrated works of history.

Keith Thomas is a fellow of All Souls College, Oxford. His books on the social and cultural history of early modern England include *Religion and the Decline of Magic*, *Man and the Natural World* and *The Ends of Life*.

Allon White's collected essays, *Carnival, Hysteria and Writing*, were published after his death in 1988 at the age of thirty-six.

Mary-Kay Wilmers is the editor of the LRB. Her book, *The Eitingons: A Twentieth-Century Story*, was published in 2009.

Emily Witt lives in New York.

Richard Wollheim was Grote Professor of the Philosophy of Mind and Logic at University College London and the author of *Art and Its Objects*, *On the Emotions* and *The Mind and Its Depths*, among other works of philosophy and psychoanalysis.